DICTIONARY

THEME-BASED

British English Collection

ENGLISH ARABIC

The most useful words
To expand your lexicon and sharpen
your language skills

9000 words

Theme-based dictionary British English-Egyptian Arabic - 9000 words

By Andrey Taranov

T&P Books vocabularies are intended for helping you learn, memorize and review foreign words. The dictionary is divided into themes, covering all major spheres of everyday activities, business, science, culture, etc.

The process of learning words using T&P Books' theme-based dictionaries gives you the following advantages:

- Correctly grouped source information predetermines success at subsequent stages of word memorization
- Availability of words derived from the same root allowing memorization of word units (rather than separate words)
- Small units of words facilitate the process of establishing associative links needed for consolidation of vocabulary
- Level of language knowledge can be estimated by the number of learned words

T&P Books Publishing
www.tpbooks.com

This book is also available in E-book formats.
Please visit www.tpbooks.com or the major online bookstores.

EGYPTIAN ARABIC THEME-BASED DICTIONARY
British English collection

T&P Books vocabularies are intended to help you learn, memorize, and review foreign words. The vocabulary contains over 9000 commonly used words arranged thematically.

- Vocabulary contains the most commonly used words
- Recommended as an addition to any language course
- Meets the needs of beginners and advanced learners of foreign languages
- Convenient for daily use, revision sessions, and self-testing activities
- Allows you to assess your vocabulary

Special features of the vocabulary

- Words are organized according to their meaning, not alphabetically
- Words are presented in three columns to facilitate the reviewing and self-testing processes
- Words in groups are divided into small blocks to facilitate the learning process
- The vocabulary offers a convenient and simple transcription of each foreign word

The vocabulary has 256 topics including:

Basic Concepts, Numbers, Colors, Months, Seasons, Units of Measurement, Clothing & Accessories, Food & Nutrition, Restaurant, Family Members, Relatives, Character, Feelings, Emotions, Diseases, City, Town, Sightseeing, Shopping, Money, House, Home, Office, Working in the Office, Import & Export, Marketing, Job Search, Sports, Education, Computer, Internet, Tools, Nature, Countries, Nationalities and more ...

TABLE OF CONTENTS

PRONUNCIATION GUIDE

T&P phonetic alphabet	Egyptian Arabic example	English example
[a]	[ṭaffa] طفّى	shorter than in 'ask'
[ā]	[eχtār] إختار	calf, palm
[e]	[setta] ستّة	elm, medal
[i]	[minā'] ميناء	shorter than in 'feet'
[ī]	[ebrīl] إبريل	feet, meter
[o]	[oɣosṭos] أغسطس	pod, John
[ō]	[ḥalazōn] حلزون	fall, bomb
[u]	[kalkutta] كلكتا	book
[ū]	[gamūs] جاموس	fuel, tuna
[b]	[bedāya] بداية	baby, book
[d]	[sa'āda] سعادة	day, doctor
[ḍ]	[waḍ'] وضع	[d] pharyngeal
[ʒ]	[arʒantīn] الأرجنتين	forge, pleasure
[ẓ]	[ẓahar] ظهر	[z] pharyngeal
[f]	[χafīf] خفيف	face, food
[g]	[bahga] بهجة	game, gold
[h]	[ettegāh] إتّجاه	home, have
[ḥ]	[ḥabb] حبّ	[h] pharyngeal
[y]	[dahaby] ذهبي	yes, New York
[k]	[korsy] كرسي	clock, kiss
[l]	[lammaḥ] لمّح	lace, people
[m]	[marṣad] مرصد	magic, milk
[n]	[ganūb] جنوب	sang, thing
[p]	[kaputʃino] كابتشينو	pencil, private
[q]	[wasaq] وثق	king, club
[r]	[roḥe] روح	rice, radio
[s]	[soχreya] سخرية	city, boss
[ṣ]	[me'ṣam] معصم	[s] pharyngeal
[ʃ]	['aʃā'] عشاء	machine, shark
[t]	[tanūb] تنوب	tourist, trip
[ṭ]	[χarīṭa] خريطة	[t] pharyngeal
[θ]	[mamūθ] ماموث	month, tooth
[v]	[vietnām] فيتنام	very, river
[w]	[wadda'] ودّع	vase, winter
[χ]	[baχīl] بخيل	as in Scots 'loch'

T&P phonetic alphabet	Egyptian Arabic example	English example
[ɣ]	**[etɣadda] إتغدّى**	between [g] and [h]
[z]	**[me'za] معزة**	zebra, please
['] (ayn)	**[sab'a] سبعة**	voiced pharyngeal fricative
['] (hamza)	**[sa'al] سأل**	glottal stop

ABBREVIATIONS used in the dictionary

Egyptian Arabic abbreviations

du	-	plural noun (double)
f	-	feminine noun
m	-	masculine noun
pl	-	plural

English abbreviations

ab.	-	about
adj	-	adjective
adv	-	adverb
anim.	-	animate
as adj	-	attributive noun used as adjective
e.g.	-	for example
etc.	-	et cetera
fam.	-	familiar
fem.	-	feminine
form.	-	formal
inanim.	-	inanimate
masc.	-	masculine
math	-	mathematics
mil.	-	military
n	-	noun
pl	-	plural
pron.	-	pronoun
sb	-	somebody
sing.	-	singular
sth	-	something
v aux	-	auxiliary verb
vi	-	intransitive verb
vi, vt	-	intransitive, transitive verb
vt	-	transitive verb

BASIC CONCEPTS

Basic concepts. Part 1

1. Pronouns

I, me	ana	أنا
you (masc.)	enta	أنت
you (fem.)	enty	أنت
he	howwa	هوّ
she	hiya	هيّ
we	eḥna	إحنا
you (to a group)	antom	أنتم
they	hamm	همّ

2. Greetings. Salutations. Farewells

Hello! (form.)	assalamu ʿalaykum!	السلام عليكم!
Good morning!	ṣabāḥ el χeyr!	صباح الخير!
Good afternoon!	neharak saʿīd!	نهارك سعيد!
Good evening!	masāʾ el χeyr!	مساء الخير!
to say hello	sallem	سلّم
Hi! (hello)	ahlan!	أهلاً!
greeting (n)	salām (m)	سلام
to greet (vt)	sallem ʿala	سلّم على
How are you?	ezzayek?	ازّيّك؟
What's new?	aχbārak eyh?	أخبارك ايه؟
Bye-Bye! Goodbye!	maʿ el salāma!	مع السلامة!
See you soon!	aʃūfak orayeb!	أشوفك قريب!
Farewell!	maʿ el salāma!	مع السلامة!
to say goodbye	waddaʿ	ودّع
Cheers!	bay bay!	باي باي!
Thank you! Cheers!	ʃokran!	شكراً!
Thank you very much!	ʃokran geddan!	شكراً جداً!
My pleasure!	el ʿafw	العفو
Don't mention it!	la ʃokr ʿala wāgeb	لا شكر على واجب
It was nothing	el ʿafw	العفو
Excuse me! (fam.)	ʿan eznak!	عن إذنك!
Excuse me! (form.)	baʿd ezn ḥadretak!	بعد إذن حضرتك!
to excuse (forgive)	ʿazar	عذر
to apologize (vi)	eʿtazar	أعتذر

My apologies	ana 'āsef	أنا آسف
I'm sorry!	ana 'āsef!	أنا آسف!
to forgive (vt)	ʿafa	عفا
please (adv)	men faḍlak	من فضلك
Don't forget!	ma tensāʃ!	ما تنساش!
Certainly!	ṭabʿan!	طبعاً!
Of course not!	la' ṭabʿan!	لأ طبعاً!
Okay! (I agree)	ettafa'na!	إتّفقنا!
That's enough!	kefāya!	كفاية!

3. How to address

mister, sir	ya ostāz	يا أستاذ
madam	ya madām	يا مدام
miss	ya 'ānesa	يا آنسة
young man	ya ostāz	يا أستاذ
young man (little boy)	yabny	يا ابني
miss (little girl)	ya benty	يا بنتي

4. Cardinal numbers. Part 1

0 zero	ṣefr	صفر
1 one	wāḥed	واحد
1 one (fem.)	waḥda	واحدة
2 two	etneyn	إتنين
3 three	talāta	ثلاثة
4 four	arbaʿa	أربعة
5 five	χamsa	خمسة
6 six	setta	ستّة
7 seven	sabʿa	سبعة
8 eight	tamanya	ثمانية
9 nine	tesʿa	تسعة
10 ten	ʿaʃara	عشرة
11 eleven	ḥedāʃar	حداشر
12 twelve	etnāʃar	إتناشر
13 thirteen	talattāʃar	تلاتّاشر
14 fourteen	arbaʿtāʃer	أربعتاشر
15 fifteen	χamastāʃer	خمستاشر
16 sixteen	settāʃar	ستّاشر
17 seventeen	sabaʿtāʃar	سبعتاشر
18 eighteen	tamantāʃar	تمنتاشر
19 nineteen	tesʿatāʃar	تسعتاشر
20 twenty	ʿeʃrīn	عشرين
21 twenty-one	wāḥed we ʿeʃrīn	واحد وعشرين
22 twenty-two	etneyn we ʿeʃrīn	إتنين وعشرين
23 twenty-three	talāta we ʿeʃrīn	ثلاثة وعشرين
30 thirty	talatīn	ثلاثين

31 thirty-one	wāḥed we talatīn	واحد وتلاتين
32 thirty-two	etneyn we talatīn	إتنين وتلاتين
33 thirty-three	talāta we talatīn	ثلاثة وثلاثين
40 forty	arbeʿīn	أربعين
41 forty-one	wāḥed we arbeʿīn	واحد وأربعين
42 forty-two	etneyn we arbeʿīn	إتنين وأربعين
43 forty-three	talāta we arbeʿīn	ثلاثة وأربعين
50 fifty	χamsīn	خمسين
51 fifty-one	wāḥed we χamsīn	واحد وخمسين
52 fifty-two	etneyn we χamsīn	إتنين وخمسين
53 fifty-three	talāta we χamsīn	ثلاثة وخمسين
60 sixty	settīn	ستّين
61 sixty-one	wāḥed we settīn	واحد وستّين
62 sixty-two	etneyn we settīn	إتنين وستّين
63 sixty-three	talāta we settīn	ثلاثة وستّين
70 seventy	sabʿīn	سبعين
71 seventy-one	wāḥed we sabʿīn	واحد وسبعين
72 seventy-two	etneyn we sabʿīn	إتنين وسبعين
73 seventy-three	talāta we sabʿīn	ثلاثة وسبعين
80 eighty	tamanīn	ثمانين
81 eighty-one	wāḥed we tamanīn	واحد وتمانين
82 eighty-two	etneyn we tamanīn	إتنين وتمانين
83 eighty-three	talāta we tamanīn	ثلاثة وثمانين
90 ninety	tesʿīn	تسعين
91 ninety-one	wāḥed we tesʿīn	واحد وتسعين
92 ninety-two	etneyn we tesʿīn	إتنين وتسعين
93 ninety-three	talāta we tesʿīn	ثلاثة وتسعين

5. Cardinal numbers. Part 2

100 one hundred	miya	ميّة
200 two hundred	meteyn	ميتين
300 three hundred	toltomiya	تلتميّة
400 four hundred	robʿomiya	ربعميّة
500 five hundred	χomsomiya	خمسميّة
600 six hundred	sotomiya	ستميّة
700 seven hundred	sobʿomiya	سبعميّة
800 eight hundred	tomnomeʾa	ثمنمئة
900 nine hundred	tosʿomiya	تسعميّة
1000 one thousand	alf	ألف
2000 two thousand	alfeyn	ألفين
3000 three thousand	talat ʾālāf	ثلاث آلاف
10000 ten thousand	ʿaʃaret ʾālāf	عشرة آلاف
one hundred thousand	mīt alf	ميت ألف
million	millyon (m)	مليون
billion	millyār (m)	مليار

6. Ordinal numbers

first (adj)	awwel	أوّل
second (adj)	tāny	ثاني
third (adj)	tālet	ثالث
fourth (adj)	rābeʿ	رابع
fifth (adj)	χāmes	خامس
sixth (adj)	sādes	سادس
seventh (adj)	sābeʿ	سابع
eighth (adj)	tāmen	ثامن
ninth (adj)	tāseʿ	تاسع
tenth (adj)	ʿāʃer	عاشر

7. Numbers. Fractions

fraction	kasr (m)	كسر
one half	noṣṣ	نصّ
one third	telt	ثلث
one quarter	robʿ	ربع
one eighth	tomn	تمن
one tenth	ʿoʃr	عشر
two thirds	teleyn	تلتين
three quarters	talātet arbāʿ	ثلاثة أرباع

8. Numbers. Basic operations

subtraction	ṭarḥ (m)	طرح
to subtract (vi, vt)	ṭaraḥ	طرح
division	ʾesma (f)	قسمة
to divide (vt)	ʾasam	قسم
addition	gamʿ (m)	جمع
to add up (vt)	gamaʿ	جمع
to add (vi)	gamaʿ	جمع
multiplication	ḍarb (m)	ضرب
to multiply (vt)	ḍarab	ضرب

9. Numbers. Miscellaneous

digit, figure	raqam (m)	رقم
number	ʿadad (m)	عدد
numeral	ʿadady (m)	عددي
minus sign	nāʾeṣ (m)	ناقص
plus sign	zāʾed (m)	زائد
formula	moʿadla (f)	معادلة
calculation	ḥesāb (m)	حساب
to count (vi, vt)	ʿadd	عدّ

to count up	ḥasab	حسب
to compare (vt)	qāran	قارن
How much?	kām?	كام؟
sum, total	magmūʿ (m)	مجموع
result	natīga (f)	نتيجة
remainder	bāʾy (m)	باقي
a few (e.g., ~ years ago)	kām	كام
little (I had ~ time)	ʃewaya	شويّة
the rest	el bāʾy (m)	الباقي
one and a half	wāḥed w noṣṣ (m)	واحد ونصّ
dozen	desta (f)	دستة
in half (adv)	le noṣṣeyn	لنصّين
equally (evenly)	bel tasāwy	بالتساوى
half	noṣṣ (m)	نصّ
time (three ~s)	marra (f)	مرّة

10. The most important verbs. Part 1

to advise (vt)	naṣaḥ	نصح
to agree (say yes)	ettafaʾ	إتّفق
to answer (vi, vt)	gāwab	جاوب
to apologize (vi)	eʿtazar	إعتذر
to arrive (vi)	weṣel	وصل
to ask (~ oneself)	saʾal	سأل
to ask (~ sb to do sth)	ṭalab	طلب
to be (vi)	kān	كان
to be afraid	χāf	خاف
to be hungry	ʿāyez ʾākol	عايز آكل
to be interested in ...	ehtamm be	إهتمّ بـ
to be needed	maṭlūb	مطلوب
to be surprised	etfāgeʾ	إتفاجئ
to be thirsty	ʿāyez aʃrab	عايز أشرب
to begin (vt)	badaʾ	بدأ
to belong to ...	χaṣṣ	خصّ
to boast (vi)	tabāha	تباهى
to break (split into pieces)	kasar	كسر
to call (~ for help)	estaɣās	إستغاث
can (v aux)	ʾeder	قدر
to catch (vt)	mesek	مسك
to change (vt)	ɣayar	غيّر
to choose (select)	eχtār	إختار
to come down (the stairs)	nezel	نزل
to compare (vt)	qāran	قارن
to complain (vi, vt)	ʃaka	شكا
to confuse (mix up)	etlaχbaṭ	إتلخبط
to continue (vt)	wāṣel	واصل

to control (vt)	et-ḥakkem	إتحكّم
to cook (dinner)	ḥaḍḍar	حضّر
to cost (vt)	kallef	كلّف
to count (add up)	ʿadd	عدّ
to count on ...	eʿtamad ʿala ...	إعتمد على...
to create (vt)	ʿamal	عمل
to cry (weep)	baka	بكى

11. The most important verbs. Part 2

to deceive (vi, vt)	χadaʿ	خدع
to decorate (tree, street)	zayen	زيّن
to defend (a country, etc.)	dāfaʿ	دافع
to demand (request firmly)	ṭāleb	طالب
to dig (vt)	ḥafar	حفر
to discuss (vt)	nāʾeʃ	ناقش
to do (vt)	ʿamal	عمل
to doubt (have doubts)	ʃakk fe	شكّ في
to drop (let fall)	waʾʾaʿ	وقّع
to enter (room, house, etc.)	daχal	دخل
to exist (vi)	kān mawgūd	كان موّجود
to expect (foresee)	tanabbaʾ	تنبّأ
to explain (vt)	ʃaraḥ	شرح
to fall (vi)	weʾeʿ	وقع
to fancy (vt)	ʿagab	عجب
to find (vt)	laʾa	لقي
to finish (vt)	χallaṣ	خلّص
to fly (vi)	ṭār	طار
to follow ... (come after)	tatabbaʿ	تتبّع
to forget (vi, vt)	nesy	نسي
to forgive (vt)	ʿafa	عفا
to give (vt)	edda	إدّى
to give a hint	edda lamḥa	إدّى لمحة
to go (on foot)	meʃy	مشى
to go for a swim	sebeḥ	سبح
to go out (for dinner, etc.)	χarag	خرج
to guess (the answer)	χammen	خمّن
to have (vt)	malak	ملك
to have breakfast	feṭer	فطر
to have dinner	etʿasʃa	إتعشّى
to have lunch	etɣadda	إتغدّى
to hear (vt)	semeʿ	سمع
to help (vt)	sāʿed	ساعد
to hide (vt)	χabba	خبّأ
to hope (vi, vt)	tamanna	تمنّى
to hunt (vi, vt)	eṣṭād	اصطاد
to hurry (vi)	estaʿgel	إستعجل

12. The most important verbs. Part 3

to inform (vt)	'āl ly	قال لِي
to insist (vi, vt)	aṣarr	أصرّ
to insult (vt)	ahān	أهان
to invite (vt)	'azam	عزم
to joke (vi)	hazzar	هزّر
to keep (vt)	ḥafaẓ	حفظ
to keep silent, to hush	seket	سكت
to kill (vt)	'atal	قتل
to know (sb)	'eref	عرف
to know (sth)	'eref	عرف
to laugh (vi)	ḍeḥek	ضحك
to liberate (city, etc.)	ḥarrar	حرّر
to look for … (search)	dawwar 'ala	دوّر على
to love (sb)	ḥabb	حبّ
to make a mistake	ɣeleṭ	غلط
to manage, to run	adār	أدار
to mean (signify)	'aṣad	قصد
to mention (talk about)	zakar	ذكر
to miss (school, etc.)	ɣāb	غاب
to notice (see)	lāḥaẓ	لاحظ
to object (vi, vt)	e'tarad	إعترض
to observe (see)	rāqab	راقب
to open (vt)	fataḥ	فتح
to order (meal, etc.)	ṭalab	طلب
to order (mil.)	amar	أمر
to own (possess)	malak	ملك
to participate (vi)	ʃārek	شارك
to pay (vi, vt)	dafa'	دفع
to permit (vt)	samaḥ	سمح
to plan (vt)	xaṭṭeṭ	خطّط
to play (children)	le'eb	لعب
to pray (vi, vt)	ṣalla	صلّى
to prefer (vt)	faḍḍal	فضّل
to promise (vt)	wa'ad	وعد
to pronounce (vt)	naṭa'	نطق
to propose (vt)	'araḍ	عرض
to punish (vt)	'āqab	عاقب

13. The most important verbs. Part 4

to read (vi, vt)	'ara	قرأ
to recommend (vt)	naṣaḥ	نصح
to refuse (vi, vt)	rafaḍ	رفض
to regret (be sorry)	nedem	ندم
to rent (sth from sb)	est'gar	إستأجر

to repeat (say again)	karrar	كرّر
to reserve, to book	ḥagaz	حجز
to run (vi)	gery	جري
to save (rescue)	anqaz	أنقذ
to say (~ thank you)	'āl	قال
to scold (vt)	wabbeχ	وبّخ
to see (vt)	ʃāf	شاف
to sell (vt)	bā'	باع
to send (vt)	arsal	أرسل
to shoot (vi)	ḍarab bel nār	ضرب بالنار
to shout (vi)	ṣarraχ	صرّخ
to show (vt)	warra	ورّى
to sign (document)	waqqa'	وقّع
to sit down (vi)	'a'ad	قعد
to smile (vi)	ebtasam	إبتسم
to speak (vi, vt)	kallem	كلّم
to steal (money, etc.)	sara'	سرق
to stop (for pause, etc.)	wa''af	وقّف
to stop (please ~ calling me)	baṭṭal	بطّل
to study (vt)	daras	درس
to swim (vi)	'ām	عام
to take (vt)	aχad	أخد
to think (vi, vt)	fakkar	فكّر
to threaten (vt)	hadded	هدّد
to touch (with hands)	lamas	لمس
to translate (vt)	targem	ترجم
to trust (vt)	wasaq	وثق
to try (attempt)	ḥāwel	حاول
to turn (e.g., ~ left)	ḥād	حاد
to underestimate (vt)	estaχaff	إستخفّ
to understand (vt)	fehem	فهم
to unite (vt)	waḥḥed	وحّد
to wait (vt)	estanna	إستنّى
to want (wish, desire)	'āyez	عايز
to warn (vt)	ḥazzar	حذّر
to work (vi)	eʃtaɣal	إشتغل
to write (vt)	katab	كتب
to write down	katab	كتب

14. Colours

colour	lone (m)	لون
shade (tint)	daraget el lōn (m)	درجة اللون
hue	ṣabɣet lōn (f)	صبغة اللون
rainbow	qose qozaḥ (m)	قوس قزح
white (adj)	abyaḍ	أبيض
black (adj)	aswad	أسود

grey (adj)	romādy	رمادي
green (adj)	aχḍar	أخضر
yellow (adj)	aṣfar	أصفر
red (adj)	aḥmar	أحمر
blue (adj)	azra'	أزرق
light blue (adj)	azra' fāteḥ	أزرق فاتح
pink (adj)	wardy	وردي
orange (adj)	bortoqāly	برتقاليّ
violet (adj)	banaffsegy	بنفسجي
brown (adj)	bonny	بنّي
golden (adj)	dahaby	ذهبي
silvery (adj)	feḍḍy	فضي
beige (adj)	bɛ:ʒ	بيج
cream (adj)	'āgy	عاجيّ
turquoise (adj)	fayrūzy	فيروزي
cherry red (adj)	aḥmar karazy	أحمر كرزي
lilac (adj)	laylaky	ليّلكي
crimson (adj)	qormozy	قرمزي
light (adj)	fāteḥ	فاتح
dark (adj)	ɣāme'	غامق
bright, vivid (adj)	zāhy	زاهي
coloured (pencils)	melawwen	ملوّن
colour (e.g. ~ film)	melawwen	ملوّن
black-and-white (adj)	abyaḍ we aswad	أبيض وأسوّد
plain (one-coloured)	sāda	سادة
multicoloured (adj)	mota'added el alwān	متعددّ الألوان

15. Questions

Who?	mīn?	مين؟
What?	eyh?	ايه؟
Where? (at, in)	feyn?	فين؟
Where (to)?	feyn?	فين؟
From where?	meneyn?	منين؟
When?	emta	امتى؟
Why? (What for?)	'aʃān eyh?	عشان ايه؟
Why? (~ are you crying?)	leyh?	ليه؟
What for?	l eyh?	لـ ليه؟
How? (in what way)	ezāy?	إزاي؟
What? (What kind of …?)	eyh?	ايه؟
Which?	ayī?	أيّ؟
To whom?	le mīn?	لمين؟
About whom?	'an mīn?	عن مين؟
About what?	'an eyh?	عن ايه؟
With whom?	ma' mīn?	مع مين؟
How many? How much?	kām?	كام؟
Whose?	betā'et mīn?	بتاعت مين؟

16. Prepositions

with (accompanied by)	maʿ	مع
without	men ɣeyr	من غير
to (indicating direction)	ela	إلى
about (talking ~ ...)	ʿan	عن
before (in time)	ʾabl	قبل
in front of ...	ʾoddām	قدّام
under (beneath, below)	taḥt	تحت
above (over)	foʾe	فوق
on (atop)	ʿala	على
from (off, out of)	men	من
of (made from)	men	من
in (e.g. ~ ten minutes)	baʿd	بعد
over (across the top of)	men ʿala	من على

17. Function words. Adverbs. Part 1

Where? (at, in)	feyn?	فين؟
here (adv)	hena	هنا
there (adv)	henāk	هناك
somewhere (to be)	fe makānen ma	في مكان ما
nowhere (not in any place)	meʃ fi ayī makān	مش في أيّ مكان
by (near, beside)	ganb	جنب
by the window	ganb el ʃebbāk	جنب الشبّاك
Where (to)?	feyn?	فين؟
here (e.g. come ~!)	hena	هنا
there (e.g. to go ~)	henāk	هناك
from here (adv)	men hena	من هنا
from there (adv)	men henāk	من هناك
close (adv)	ʾarīb	قريب
far (adv)	beʿīd	بعيد
near (e.g. ~ Paris)	ʿand	عند
nearby (adv)	ʾarīb	قريب
not far (adv)	meʃ beʿīd	مش بعيد
left (adj)	el ʃemāl	الشمال
on the left	ʿalal ʃemāl	على الشمال
to the left	lel ʃemāl	للشمال
right (adj)	el yemīn	اليمين
on the right	ʿalal yemīn	على اليمين
to the right	lel yemīn	لليمين
in front (adv)	ʾoddām	قدّام
front (as adj)	amāmy	أمامي

ahead (the kids ran ~)	ela el amām	إلى الأمام
behind (adv)	wara'	وراء
from behind	men wara	من ورّا
back (towards the rear)	le wara	لورّا
middle	wasaṭ (m)	وسط
in the middle	fel wasat	في الوسط
at the side	ʻala ganb	على جنب
everywhere (adv)	fe kol makān	في كل مكان
around (in all directions)	ḥawaleyn	حوالين
from inside	men gowwah	من جوّه
somewhere (to go)	le 'ayī makān	لأي مكان
straight (directly)	ʻala ṭūl	على طول
back (e.g. come ~)	rogūʻ	رجوع
from anywhere	men ayī makān	من أيّ مكان
from somewhere	men makānen mā	من مكان ما
firstly (adv)	awwalan	أوّلاً
secondly (adv)	sāneyan	ثانياً
thirdly (adv)	sālesan	ثالثاً
suddenly (adv)	fag'a	فجأة
at first (in the beginning)	fel bedāya	في البداية
for the first time	le 'awwel marra	لأوّل مرّة
long before ...	'abl ... be modda ṭawīla	قبل... بمدة طويلة
anew (over again)	men gedīd	من جديد
for good (adv)	lel abad	للأبد
never (adv)	abadan	أبداً
again (adv)	tāny	تاني
now (at present)	delwa'ty	دلوقتي
often (adv)	ketīr	كثير
then (adv)	wa'taha	وقتها
urgently (quickly)	ʻala ṭūl	على طول
usually (adv)	ʻādatan	عادةً
by the way, ...	ʻala fekra ...	على فكرة...
possibly	momken	ممكن
probably (adv)	momken	ممكن
maybe (adv)	momken	ممكن
besides ...	bel eḍāfa ela ...	بالإضافة إلى...
that's why ...	ʻaʃān keda	عشان كده
in spite of ...	bel raɣm men ...	بالرغم من...
thanks to ...	be faḍl ...	بفضل...
what (pron.)	elly	إللي
that (conj.)	ennu	إنّه
something	ḥāga (f)	حاجة
anything (something)	ayī ḥāga (f)	أيّ حاجة
nothing	wala ḥāga	ولا حاجة
who (pron.)	elly	إللي
someone	ḥadd	حد

somebody	ḥadd	حدّ
nobody	wala ḥadd	ولا حدّ
nowhere (a voyage to ~)	meʃ le wala makān	مش لـ ولا مكان
nobody's	wala ḥadd	ولا حدّ
somebody's	le ḥadd	لحدّ
so (I'm ~ glad)	geddan	جداً
also (as well)	kamān	كمان
too (as well)	kamān	كمان

18. Function words. Adverbs. Part 2

Why?	leyh?	ليه؟
for some reason	le sabeben ma	لسبب ما
because ...	ʻaʃān ...	... عشان
for some purpose	le hadafen mā	لهدف ما
and	w	و
or	walla	ولّلا
but	bass	بسّ
for (e.g. ~ me)	ʻaʃān	عشان
too (excessively)	ketīr geddan	كتير جدّاً
only (exclusively)	bass	بسّ
exactly (adv)	bel ḍabṭ	بالضبط
about (more or less)	naḥw	نحو
approximately (adv)	naḥw	نحو
approximate (adj)	taqrīby	تقريبي
almost (adv)	taʼrīban	تقريباً
the rest	el bāʼy (m)	الباقي
each (adj)	koll	كلّ
any (no matter which)	ayī	أيّ
many, much (a lot of)	ketīr	كتير
many people	nās ketīr	ناس كتير
all (everyone)	koll el nās	كلّ الناس
in return for ...	fi moqābel ...	... في مقابل
in exchange (adv)	fe moqābel	في مقابل
by hand (made)	bel yad	باليد
hardly (negative opinion)	bel kād	بالكاد
probably (adv)	momken	ممكن
on purpose (intentionally)	bel ʼaṣd	بالقصد
by accident (adv)	bel ṣodfa	بالصدفة
very (adv)	ʼawy	قويّ
for example (adv)	masalan	مثلاً
between	beyn	بين
among	wesṭ	وسط
so much (such a lot)	ketīr	كتير
especially (adv)	χāṣṣa	خاصّة

Basic concepts. Part 2

19. Opposites

rich (adj)	ɣany	غني
poor (adj)	faʾīr	فقير
ill, sick (adj)	marīḍ	مريض
well (not sick)	salīm	سليم
big (adj)	kebīr	كبير
small (adj)	ṣaɣīr	صغير
quickly (adv)	bosorʿa	بسرعة
slowly (adv)	bo boṭʾ	ببطء
fast (adj)	sareeʿ	سريع
slow (adj)	baṭīʾ	بطيء
glad (adj)	farḥān	فرحان
sad (adj)	ḥazīn	حزين
together (adv)	maʿ baʿḍ	مع بعض
separately (adv)	le waḥdo	لوحده
aloud (to read)	beṣote ʿāly	بصوت عالي
silently (to oneself)	beṣamt	بصمت
tall (adj)	ʿāly	عالي
low (adj)	wāṭy	واطي
deep (adj)	ʿamīq	عميق
shallow (adj)	ḍaḥl	ضحل
yes	aywa	أيوه
no	laʾ	لأ
distant (in space)	beʿīd	بعيد
nearby (adj)	ʾarīb	قريب
far (adv)	beʿīd	بعيد
nearby (adv)	ʾarīb	قريب
long (adj)	ṭawīl	طويل
short (adj)	ʾaṣīr	قصير
good (kindhearted)	ṭayeb	طيّب
evil (adj)	ʃerrīr	شرير

married (adj)	metgawwez	متجوّز
single (adj)	a'zab	أعزب
to forbid (vt)	mana'	منع
to permit (vt)	samaḥ	سمح
end	nehāya (f)	نهاية
beginning	bedāya (f)	بداية
left (adj)	el ʃemāl	الشمال
right (adj)	el yemīn	اليمين
first (adj)	awwel	أوّل
last (adj)	'āχer	آخر
crime	garīma (f)	جريمة
punishment	'eqāb (m)	عقاب
to order (vt)	amar	أمر
to obey (vi, vt)	ṭā'	طاع
straight (adj)	mostaqīm	مستقيم
curved (adj)	monḥany	منحني
paradise	el ganna (f)	الجنّة
hell	el gaḥīm (f)	الجحيم
to be born	etwalad	إتولّد
to die (vi)	māt	مات
strong (adj)	'awy	قوّي
weak (adj)	ḍa'īf	ضعيف
old (adj)	'agūz	عجوز
young (adj)	ʃāb	شاب
old (adj)	'adīm	قديم
new (adj)	gedīd	جديد
hard (adj)	ṣalb	صلب
soft (adj)	ṭary	طري
warm (tepid)	dāfy	دافي
cold (adj)	bāred	بارد
fat (adj)	teχīn	تخين
thin (adj)	rofaya'	رفيّع
narrow (adj)	ḍaye'	ضيّق
wide (adj)	wāse'	واسع
good (adj)	kewayes	كويّس
bad (adj)	weḥeʃ	وحش
brave (adj)	ʃogā'	شجاع
cowardly (adj)	gabān	جبان

20. Weekdays

Monday	el etneyn (m)	الإتنين
Tuesday	el talāt (m)	التلات
Wednesday	el arbe'ā' (m)	الأربعاء
Thursday	el χamīs (m)	الخميس
Friday	el gom'a (m)	الجمعة
Saturday	el sabt (m)	السبت
Sunday	el aḥad (m)	الأحد
today (adv)	el naharda	النهارده
tomorrow (adv)	bokra	بكرة
the day after tomorrow	ba'd bokra (m)	بعد بكرة
yesterday (adv)	embāreḥ	امبارح
the day before yesterday	awwel embāreḥ	أوّل امبارح
day	yome (m)	يوم
working day	yome 'amal (m)	يوم عمل
public holiday	agāza rasmiya (f)	أجازة رسميّة
day off	yome el agāza (m)	يوم أجازة
weekend	nehāyet el osbū' (f)	نهاية الأسبوع
all day long	ṭūl el yome	طول اليوم
the next day (adv)	fel yome elly ba'dīh	في اليوم اللي بعديه
two days ago	men yomeyn	من يومين
the day before	fel yome elly 'ablo	في اليوم اللي قبله
daily (adj)	yawmy	يومي
every day (adv)	yawmiyan	يومياً
week	osbū' (m)	أسبوع
last week (adv)	el esbū' elly fāt	الأسبوع اللي فات
next week (adv)	el esbū' elly gayī	الأسبوع اللي جاي
weekly (adj)	osbū'y	أسبوعي
every week (adv)	osbū'iyan	أسبوعياً
twice a week	marreteyn fel osbū'	مرّتين في الأسبوع
every Tuesday	koll solasā'	كلّ ثلاثاء

21. Hours. Day and night

morning	ṣobḥ (m)	صبح
in the morning	fel ṣobḥ	في الصبح
noon, midday	ẓohr (m)	ظهر
in the afternoon	ba'd el ḍohr	بعد الظهر
evening	leyl (m)	ليل
in the evening	bel leyl	بالليل
night	leyl (m)	ليل
at night	bel leyl	بالليل
midnight	noṣṣ el leyl (m)	نصّ الليل
second	sanya (f)	ثانية
minute	deTa (f)	دقيقة
hour	sā'a (f)	ساعة

half an hour	noṣṣ sā'a (m)	نصّ ساعة
a quarter-hour	rob' sā'a (f)	ربع ساعة
fifteen minutes	χamastāʃer deʔa	خمستاشر دقيقة
24 hours	arba'a we 'eʃrīn sā'a	أربعة وعشرين ساعة
sunrise	ʃorū' el ʃams (m)	شروق الشمس
dawn	fagr (m)	فجر
early morning	ṣobḥ badry (m)	صبح بدري
sunset	ɣorūb el ʃams (m)	غروب الشمس
early in the morning	el ṣobḥ badry	الصبح بدري
this morning	el naharda el ṣobḥ	النهاردة الصبح
tomorrow morning	bokra el ṣobḥ	بكرة الصبح
this afternoon	el naharda ba'd el ḍohr	النهاردة بعد الظهر
in the afternoon	ba'd el ḍohr	بعد الظهر
tomorrow afternoon	bokra ba'd el ḍohr	بكرة بعد الظهر
tonight (this evening)	el naharda bel leyl	النهاردة بالليل
tomorrow night	bokra bel leyl	بكرة بالليل
at 3 o'clock sharp	es sā'a talāta bel ḍabṭ	الساعة تلاتة بالضبط
about 4 o'clock	es sā'a arba'a ta'rīban	الساعة أربعة تقريبا
by 12 o'clock	ḥatt es sā'a etnāʃar	حتى الساعة إتناشر
in 20 minutes	fe χelāl 'eʃrīn de'ee'a	في خلال عشرين دقيقة
in an hour	fe χelāl sā'a	في خلال ساعة
on time (adv)	fe maw'edo	في موعده
a quarter to ...	ella rob'	إلّا ربع
within an hour	χelāl sā'a	خلال ساعة
every 15 minutes	koll rob' sā'a	كلّ ربع ساعة
round the clock	leyl nahār	ليل نهار

22. Months. Seasons

January	yanāyer (m)	يناير
February	febrāyer (m)	فبراير
March	māres (m)	مارس
April	ebrīl (m)	إبريل
May	māyo (m)	مايو
June	yonyo (m)	يونيو
July	yolyo (m)	يوليو
August	oɣosṭos (m)	أغسطس
September	sebtamber (m)	سبتمبر
October	oktober (m)	أكتوبر
November	november (m)	نوفمبر
December	desember (m)	ديسمبر
spring	rabee' (m)	ربيع
in spring	fel rabee'	في الربيع
spring (as adj)	rabee'y	ربيعي
summer	ṣeyf (m)	صيف
in summer	fel ṣeyf	في الصيف

summer (as adj)	ṣeyfy	صيفي
autumn	χarīf (m)	خريف
in autumn	fel χarīf	في الخريف
autumn (as adj)	χarīfy	خريفي
winter	ʃetā' (m)	شتاء
in winter	fel ʃetā'	في الشتاء
winter (as adj)	ʃetwy	شتوّي
month	ʃahr (m)	شهر
this month	fel ʃahr da	في الشهر ده
next month	el ʃahr el gayī	الشهر الجايّ
last month	el ʃahr elly fāt	الشهر اللي فات
a month ago	men ʃahr	من شهر
in a month (a month later)	ba'd ʃahr	بعد شهر
in 2 months (2 months later)	ba'd ʃahreyn	بعد شهرين
the whole month	el ʃahr kollo	الشهر كلّه
all month long	ṭawāl el ʃahr	طوال الشهر
monthly (~ magazine)	ʃahry	شهري
monthly (adv)	ʃahry	شهري
every month	koll ʃahr	كلّ شهر
twice a month	marreteyn fel ʃahr	مرّتين في الشهر
year	sana (f)	سنة
this year	el sana di	السنة دي
next year	el sana el gaya	السنة الجايّة
last year	el sana elly fātet	السنة اللي فاتت
a year ago	men sana	من سنة
in a year	ba'd sana	بعد سنة
in two years	ba'd sanateyn	بعد سنتين
the whole year	el sana kollaha	السنة كلّها
all year long	ṭūl el sana	طول السنة
every year	koll sana	كلّ سنة
annual (adj)	sanawy	سنوّي
annually (adv)	koll sana	كلّ سنة
4 times a year	arba' marrāt fel sana	أربع مرات في السنة
date (e.g. today's ~)	tarīχ (m)	تاريخ
date (e.g. ~ of birth)	tarīχ (m)	تاريخ
calendar	natīga (f)	نتيجة
half a year	noṣṣ sana	نصّ سنة
six months	settet aʃ-hor (f)	ستّة أشهر
season (summer, etc.)	faṣl (m)	فصل
century	qarn (m)	قرن

23. Time. Miscellaneous

time	wa't (m)	وقت
moment	laḥza (f)	لحظة

instant (n)	laḥza (f)	لحظة
instant (adj)	laḥza	لحظة
lapse (of time)	fatra (f)	فترة
life	ḥayah (f)	حياة
eternity	abadiya (f)	أبديّة
epoch	ʿahd (m)	عهد
era	ʿaṣr (m)	عصر
cycle	dawra (f)	دورة
period	fatra (f)	فترة
term (short-~)	fatra (f)	فترة
the future	el mostaqbal (m)	المستقبل
future (as adj)	elly gayī	اللي جاي
next time	el marra el gaya	المرّة الجايّة
the past	el māḍy (m)	الماضي
past (recent)	elly fāt	اللي فات
last time	el marra elly fātet	المرّة اللي فاتت
later (adv)	baʿdeyn	بعدين
after (prep.)	baʿd	بعد
nowadays (adv)	el ayām di	الأيام دي
now (at this moment)	delwaʾty	دلوقتي
immediately (adv)	ḥālan	حالاً
soon (adv)	ʾarīb	قريب
in advance (beforehand)	moʾaddaman	مقدّماً
a long time ago	men zamān	من زمان
recently (adv)	men ʾorayeb	من قريّب
destiny	maṣīr (m)	مصير
recollections	zekra (f)	ذكرى
archives	arʃīf (m)	أرشيف
during ...	esnāʾ...	إثناء...
long, a long time (adv)	modda ṭawīla	مدّة طويلة
not long (adv)	le fatra ʾaṣīra	لفترة قصيرة
early (in the morning)	badry	بدري
late (not early)	metʾakҳer	متأخّر
forever (for good)	lel abad	للأبد
to start (begin)	badaʾ	بدأ
to postpone (vt)	aggel	أجّل
at the same time	fe nafs el waqt	في نفس الوقت
permanently (adv)	be ʃakl dāʾem	بشكل دائم
constant (noise, pain)	mostamerr	مستمرّ
temporary (adj)	moʾakkatan	مؤقتاً
sometimes (adv)	saʿāt	ساعات
rarely (adv)	nāderan	نادراً
often (adv)	ketīr	كثير

24. Lines and shapes

square	morabbaʿ (m)	مربّع
square (as adj)	morabbaʿ	مربع

circle	dayra (f)	دايرة
round (adj)	medawwar	مدور
triangle	mosallas (m)	مثلث
triangular (adj)	mosallasy el ʃakl	مثلّثي الشكل
oval	bayḍawy (m)	بيضوّي
oval (as adj)	bayḍawy	بيضوّي
rectangle	mostaṭīl (m)	مستطيل
rectangular (adj)	mostaṭīly	مستطيلي
pyramid	haram (m)	هرم
rhombus	mo'ayen (m)	معين
trapezium	ʃebh el monḥaref (m)	شبه المنحرف
cube	moka'ab (m)	مكعّب
prism	manʃūr (m)	منشور
circumference	moḥīṭ monḥany moɣlaq (m)	محيط منحنى مغلق
sphere	kora (f)	كرة
ball (solid sphere)	kora (f)	كرة
diameter	qaṭr (m)	قطر
radius	noṣṣ qaṭr (m)	نصّ قطر
perimeter (circle's ~)	moḥīṭ (m)	محيط
centre	wasaṭ (m)	وسط
horizontal (adj)	ofoqy	أفقي
vertical (adj)	'amūdy	عمودي
parallel (n)	motawāz (m)	متواز
parallel (as adj)	motawāzy	متوازي
line	χaṭṭ (m)	خطّ
stroke	ḥaraka (m)	حركة
straight line	χaṭṭ mostaqīm (m)	خطّ مستقيم
curve (curved line)	χaṭṭ monḥany (m)	خطّ منحني
thin (line, etc.)	rofaya'	رفيّع
contour (outline)	kontūr (m)	كنتور
intersection	taqāṭo' (m)	تقاطع
right angle	zawya mostaqīma (f)	زاوية مستقيمة
segment	'eṭ'a (f)	قطعة
sector (circular ~)	qaṭā' (m)	قطاع
side (of a triangle)	gāneb (m)	جانب
angle	zawya (f)	زاوية

25. Units of measurement

weight	wazn (m)	وزن
length	ṭūl (m)	طول
width	'arḍ (m)	عرض
height	ertefā' (m)	إرتفاع
depth	'omq (m)	عمق
volume	ḥagm (m)	حجم
area	mesāḥa (f)	مساحة
gram	gram (m)	جرام
milligram	milligrām (m)	ملّيغرام

kilogram	kilogrām (m)	كيلوغرام
ton	ṭenn (m)	طنّ
pound	reṭl (m)	رطل
ounce	onṣa (f)	أونصة
metre	metr (m)	متر
millimetre	millimetr (m)	ملّيمتر
centimetre	santimetr (m)	سنتيمتر
kilometre	kilometr (m)	كيلومتر
mile	mīl (m)	ميل
inch	boṣa (f)	بوصة
foot	'adam (m)	قدم
yard	yarda (f)	ياردة
square metre	metr morabba' (m)	متر مربّع
hectare	hektār (m)	هكتار
litre	litre (m)	لتر
degree	daraga (f)	درجة
volt	volt (m)	فولت
ampere	ambere (m)	أمبير
horsepower	ḥoṣān (m)	حصان
quantity	kemiya (f)	كميّة
a little bit of …	ʃewayet …	شويّة...
half	noṣṣ (m)	نصّ
dozen	desta (f)	دستة
piece (item)	waḥda (f)	وحدة
size	ḥagm (m)	حجم
scale (map ~)	me'yās (m)	مقياس
minimal (adj)	el adna	الأدنى
the smallest (adj)	el aṣɣar	الأصغر
medium (adj)	motawasseṭ	متوّسط
maximal (adj)	el aqṣa	الأقصى
the largest (adj)	el akbar	الأكبر

26. Containers

canning jar (glass ~)	barṭamān (m)	برطمان
tin, can	kanz (m)	كانز
bucket	gardal (m)	جردل
barrel	barmīl (m)	برميل
wash basin (e.g., plastic ~)	ḥoḍe lel ɣasīl (m)	حوض للغسيل
tank (100L water ~)	χazzān (m)	خزّان
hip flask	zamzamiya (f)	زمزميّة
jerrycan	ʒerken (m)	جركن
tank (e.g., tank car)	χazzān (m)	خزّان
mug	mugg (m)	ماجّ
cup (of coffee, etc.)	fengān (m)	فنجان

saucer	ṭaba' fengān (m)	طبق فنجان
glass (tumbler)	kobbāya (f)	كوبّاية
wine glass	kāsa (f)	كاسة
stock pot (soup pot)	ḥalla (f)	حلّة
bottle (~ of wine)	ezāza (f)	إزازة
neck (of the bottle, etc.)	'onq (m)	عنق
carafe (decanter)	dawra' zogāgy (m)	دوّرق زجاجي
pitcher	ebrī' (m)	إبريق
vessel (container)	we'ā' (m)	وعاء
pot (crock, stoneware ~)	aṣīṣ (m)	أصيص
vase	vāza (f)	فازة
flacon, bottle (perfume ~)	ezāza (f)	إزازة
vial, small bottle	ezāza (f)	إزازة
tube (of toothpaste)	anbūba (f)	أنبوبة
sack (bag)	kīs (m)	كيس
bag (paper ~, plastic ~)	kīs (m)	كيس
packet (of cigarettes, etc.)	'elba (f)	علبة
box (e.g. shoebox)	'elba (f)	علبة
crate	ṣandū' (m)	صندوق
basket	salla (f)	سلّة

27. Materials

material	madda (f)	مادّة
wood (n)	χaʃab (m)	خشب
wood-, wooden (adj)	χaʃaby	خشبي
glass (n)	ezāz (m)	إزاز
glass (as adj)	ezāz	إزاز
stone (n)	ḥagar (m)	حجر
stone (as adj)	ḥagary	حجري
plastic (n)	blastik (m)	بلاستيك
plastic (as adj)	men el blastik	من البلاستيك
rubber (n)	maṭṭāṭ (m)	مطّاط
rubber (as adj)	maṭṭāṭy	مطّاطي
cloth, fabric (n)	'omāʃ (m)	قماش
fabric (as adj)	men el 'omāʃ	من القماش
paper (n)	wara' (m)	ورق
paper (as adj)	wara'y	ورقي
cardboard (n)	kartōn (m)	كرتون
cardboard (as adj)	kartony	كرتوني
polyethylene	bolyetylen (m)	بولي ايثيلين
cellophane	sellofān (m)	سيلوفان

plywood	ablakāʃ (m)	أبلكاش
porcelain (n)	borsalīn (m)	بورسلين
porcelain (as adj)	men el borsalīn	من البورسلين
clay (n)	ṭīn (m)	طين
clay (as adj)	fokχāry	فخّاري
ceramic (n)	seramīk (m)	سيراميك
ceramic (as adj)	men el seramik	من السيراميك

28. Metals

metal (n)	maʿdan (m)	معدن
metal (as adj)	maʿdany	معدني
alloy (n)	sebīka (f)	سبيكة
gold (n)	dahab (m)	ذهب
gold, golden (adj)	dahaby	ذهبي
silver (n)	faḍḍa (f)	فضّة
silver (as adj)	feḍḍy	فضّي
iron (n)	ḥadīd (m)	حديد
iron-, made of iron (adj)	ḥadīdy	حديدي
steel (n)	fulāz (m)	فولاذ
steel (as adj)	folāzy	فولاذي
copper (n)	neḥās (m)	نحاس
copper (as adj)	neḥāsy	نحاسي
aluminium (n)	aluminyum (m)	الومينيوم
aluminium (as adj)	aluminyum	الومينيوم
bronze (n)	bronze (m)	برونز
bronze (as adj)	bronzy	برونزي
brass	neḥās aṣfar (m)	نحاس أصفر
nickel	nikel (m)	نيكل
platinum	blatīn (m)	بلاتين
mercury	zeʾbaq (m)	زئبق
tin	ʾaṣdīr (m)	قصدير
lead	roṣāṣ (m)	رصاص
zinc	zink (m)	زنك

HUMAN BEING

Human being. The body

29. Humans. Basic concepts

human being	ensān (m)	إنسان
man (adult male)	rāgel (m)	راجل
woman	set (f)	ست
child	ṭefl (m)	طفل
girl	bent (f)	بنت
boy	walad (m)	ولد
teenager	morāheq (m)	مراهق
old man	ʿagūz (m)	عجوز
old woman	ʿagūza (f)	عجوزة

30. Human anatomy

organism (body)	ʿoḍw (m)	عضو
heart	ʾalb (m)	قلب
blood	damm (m)	دم
artery	ʃeryān (m)	شريان
vein	ʿerʾ (m)	عرق
brain	mokχ (m)	مخ
nerve	ʿaṣab (m)	عصب
nerves	aʿṣāb (pl)	أعصاب
vertebra	faqra (f)	فقرة
spine (backbone)	ʿamūd faqry (m)	عمود فقري
stomach (organ)	meʿda (f)	معدة
intestines, bowels	amʿāʾ (pl)	أمعاء
intestine (e.g. large ~)	maʿy (m)	معى
liver	kebd (f)	كبد
kidney	kelya (f)	كلية
bone	ʿaḍm (m)	عظم
skeleton	haykal ʿazmy (m)	هيكل عظمي
rib	ḍelʿ (m)	ضلع
skull	gomgoma (f)	جمجمة
muscle	ʿaḍala (f)	عضلة
biceps	biseps (f)	بايسبس
triceps	triseps (f)	ترايسبس
tendon	watar (m)	وتر
joint	mefṣal (m)	مفصل

lungs	reʾateyn (du)	رئتين
genitals	aʿḍāʾ tanasoliya (pl)	أعضاء تناسلية
skin	boʃra (m)	بشرة

31. Head

head	raʾs (m)	رأس
face	weʃ (m)	وش
nose	manaχīr (m)	مناخير
mouth	boʾ (m)	بوء
eye	ʿeyn (f)	عين
eyes	ʿoyūn (pl)	عيون
pupil	ḥadʾa (f)	حدقة
eyebrow	ḥāgeb (m)	حاجب
eyelash	remʃ (m)	رمش
eyelid	gefn (m)	جفن
tongue	lesān (m)	لسان
tooth	senna (f)	سنّة
lips	ʃafāyef (pl)	شفايف
cheekbones	ʿaḍmet el χadd (f)	عضمة الخدّ
gum	lassa (f)	لثّة
palate	ḥanak (m)	حنك
nostrils	manaχer (pl)	مناخر
chin	daʾʾn (m)	دقن
jaw	fakk (m)	فكّ
cheek	χadd (m)	خدّ
forehead	gabha (f)	جبهة
temple	ṣedɣ (m)	صدغ
ear	wedn (f)	ودن
back of the head	ʾafa (m)	قفا
neck	raʾaba (f)	رقبة
throat	zore (m)	زور
hair	ʃaʿr (m)	شعر
hairstyle	tasrīḥa (f)	تسريحة
haircut	tasrīḥa (f)	تسريحة
wig	barūka (f)	باروكة
moustache	ʃanab (pl)	شنب
beard	leḥya (f)	لحية
to have (a beard, etc.)	ʿando	عنده
plait	ḍefīra (f)	ضفيرة
sideboards	sawālef (pl)	سوالف
red-haired (adj)	aḥmar el ʃaʿr	أحمر الشعر
grey (hair)	ʃaʿr abyaḍ	شعر أبيض
bald (adj)	aṣlaʿ	أصلع
bald patch	ṣalaʿ (m)	صلع
ponytail	deyl ḥoṣān (m)	ديل حصان
fringe	ʾoṣṣa (f)	قصّة

32. Human body

hand	yad (m)	يد
arm	derāʿ (f)	دراع
finger	ṣobāʿ (m)	صباع
toe	ṣobāʿ el ʾadam (m)	صباع القدم
thumb	ebhām (m)	إبهام
little finger	χonṣor (m)	خنصر
nail	ḍefr (m)	ضفر
fist	qabḍa (f)	قبضة
palm	kaff (f)	كفّ
wrist	meʿṣam (m)	معصم
forearm	sāʿed (m)	ساعد
elbow	kūʿ (m)	كوع
shoulder	ketf (f)	كتف
leg	regl (f)	رجل
foot	qadam (f)	قدم
knee	rokba (f)	ركبة
calf	semmāna (f)	سمّانة
hip	faχd (f)	فخد
heel	kaʿb (m)	كعب
body	gesm (m)	جسم
stomach	baṭn (m)	بطن
chest	ṣedr (m)	صدر
breast	sady (m)	ثدي
flank	ganb (m)	جنب
back	ḍahr (m)	ضهر
lower back	asfal el ḍahr (m)	أسفل الضهر
waist	wesṭ (f)	وسط
navel (belly button)	sorra (f)	سرّة
buttocks	ardāf (pl)	أرداف
bottom	debr (m)	دبر
beauty spot	ʃāma (f)	شامة
birthmark (café au lait spot)	waḥma	وحمة
tattoo	waʃm (m)	وشم
scar	nadba (f)	ندبة

Clothing & Accessories

33. Outerwear. Coats

clothes	malābes (pl)	ملابس
outerwear	malābes fo'aniya (pl)	ملابس فوقانيّة
winter clothing	malābes ʃetwiya (pl)	ملابس شتويّة
coat (overcoat)	balṭo (m)	بالطو
fur coat	balṭo farww (m)	بالطو فروّ
fur jacket	ʒaket farww (m)	جاكيت فروّ
down coat	balṭo maḥʃy rīʃ (m)	بالطو محشي ريش
jacket (e.g. leather ~)	ʒæket (m)	جاكيت
raincoat (trenchcoat, etc.)	ʒæket lel maṭar (m)	جاكيت للمطر
waterproof (adj)	wāqy men el maya	واقي من الميّة

34. Men's & women's clothing

shirt (button shirt)	'amīṣ (m)	قميص
trousers	banṭalone (f)	بنطلون
jeans	ʒeans (m)	جينز
suit jacket	ʒæket (f)	جاكت
suit	badla (f)	بدلة
dress (frock)	fostān (m)	فستان
skirt	ʒība (f)	جيبة
blouse	bloza (f)	بلوزة
knitted jacket (cardigan, etc.)	kardigan (m)	كارديجن
jacket (of a woman's suit)	ʒæket (m)	جاكيت
T-shirt	ti ʃirt (m)	تي شيرت
shorts (short trousers)	ʃort (m)	شورت
tracksuit	treneng (m)	ترينتج
bathrobe	robe el ḥammām (m)	روب حمّام
pyjamas	beʒāma (f)	بيجاما
jumper (sweater)	blover (f)	بلوفر
pullover	blover (m)	بلوفر
waistcoat	vest (m)	فيست
tailcoat	badlet sahra ṭawīla (f)	بدلة سهرة طويلة
dinner suit	badla (f)	بدلة
uniform	zayī muwaḥḥad (m)	زيّ موحّد
workwear	lebs el ʃoɣl (m)	لبس الشغل
boiler suit	overall (m)	اوفر اول
coat (e.g. doctor's smock)	balṭo (m)	بالطو

35. Clothing. Underwear

underwear	malābes dāχeliya (pl)	ملابس داخلية
pants	sirwāl dāχly rigāly (m)	سروال داخلي رجاليّ
panties	sirwāl dāχly nisā'y (m)	سروال داخلي نسائيّ
vest (singlet)	fanella (f)	فانلّا
socks	ʃarāb (m)	شراب
nightdress	'amīṣ nome (m)	قميص نوم
bra	setyāna (f)	ستيانة
knee highs (knee-high socks)	ʃarabāt ṭawīla (pl)	شرابات طويلة
tights	klone (m)	كلون
stockings (hold ups)	gawāreb (pl)	جوارب
swimsuit, bikini	mayo (m)	مايّوه

36. Headwear

hat	ṭa'iya (f)	طاقيّة
trilby hat	borneyṭa (f)	برنيطة
baseball cap	base bāl kāb (m)	بيس بول كاب
flatcap	ṭa'iya mosaṭṭaḥa (f)	طاقيّة مسطحة
beret	bereyh (m)	بيريه
hood	ɣaṭa' (f)	غطاء
panama hat	qobba'et banama (f)	قبّعة بناما
knit cap (knitted hat)	ays kāb (m)	آيس كاب
headscarf	eʃarb (m)	إيشارب
women's hat	borneyṭa (f)	برنيطة
hard hat	χawza (f)	خوذة
forage cap	kāb (m)	كاب
helmet	χawza (f)	خوذة
bowler	qobba'a (f)	قبّعة
top hat	qobba'a rasmiya (f)	قبّعة رسمية

37. Footwear

footwear	gezam (pl)	جزم
shoes (men's shoes)	gazma (f)	جزمة
shoes (women's shoes)	gazma (f)	جزمة
boots (e.g., cowboy ~)	būt (m)	بوت
carpet slippers	ʃebʃeb (m)	شبشب
trainers	kotʃy tennis (m)	كوتشي تنس
trainers	kotʃy (m)	كوتشي
sandals	ṣandal (pl)	صندل
cobbler (shoe repairer)	eskāfy (m)	إسكافي
heel	ka'b (m)	كعب

pair (of shoes)	goze (m)	جوز
lace (shoelace)	ʃerīʼṭ (m)	شريط
to lace up (vt)	rabaṭ	ربط
shoehorn	labbāsa el gazma (f)	لبّاسة الجزمة
shoe polish	warnīʃ el gazma (m)	ورنيش الجزمة

38. Textile. Fabrics

cotton (n)	ʼoṭn (m)	قطن
cotton (as adj)	ʼoṭny	قطني
flax (n)	kettān (m)	كتّان
flax (as adj)	men el kettān	من الكتّان
silk (n)	ḥarīr (m)	حرير
silk (as adj)	ḥarīry	حريري
wool (n)	ṣūf (m)	صوف
wool (as adj)	ṣūfiya	صوفية
velvet	moχmal (m)	مخمل
suede	geld mazʼabar (m)	جلد مزأبر
corduroy	ʼoṭṭn ʼaṭīfa (f)	قطن قطيفة
nylon (n)	nylon (m)	نايلون
nylon (as adj)	men el naylon	من النيلون
polyester (n)	bolyester (m)	بوليستر
polyester (as adj)	men el bolyastar	من البوليستر
leather (n)	geld (m)	جلد
leather (as adj)	men el geld	من الجلد
fur (n)	farww (m)	فروّ
fur (e.g. ~ coat)	men el farww	من الفروّ

39. Personal accessories

gloves	gwanty (m)	جوانتي
mittens	gwanty men ɣeyr aṣābeʻ (m)	جوانتي من غير أصابع
scarf (muffler)	skarf (m)	سكارف
glasses	naḍḍāra (f)	نظّارة
frame (eyeglass ~)	eṭār (m)	إطار
umbrella	ʃamsiya (f)	شمسيّة
walking stick	ʻaṣāya (f)	عصاية
hairbrush	forʃet ʃaʻr (f)	فرشة شعر
fan	marwaḥa (f)	مروّحة
tie (necktie)	karavetta (f)	كرافتة
bow tie	bebyona (m)	بيبيونة
braces	ḥammala (f)	حمّالة
handkerchief	mandīl (m)	منديل
comb	meʃṭ (m)	مشط
hair slide	dabbūs (m)	دبّوس

hairpin	bensa (m)	بنسة
buckle	bokla (f)	بكلة
belt	ḥezām (m)	حزام
shoulder strap	ḥammalet el ketf (f)	حمّالة الكتف
bag (handbag)	ʃanṭa (f)	شنطة
handbag	ʃanṭet yad (f)	شنطة يد
rucksack	ʃanṭet ḍahr (f)	شنطة ظهر

40. Clothing. Miscellaneous

fashion	mūḍa (f)	موضة
in vogue (adj)	fel moḍa	في الموضة
fashion designer	moṣammem azyā' (m)	مصمّم أزياء
collar	yā'a (f)	ياقة
pocket	geyb (m)	جيب
pocket (as adj)	geyb	جيب
sleeve	komm (m)	كمّ
hanging loop	'elāqa (f)	علّاقة
flies (on trousers)	lesān (m)	لسان
zip (fastener)	sosta (f)	سوستة
fastener	maʃbak (m)	مشبك
button	zerr (m)	زرّ
buttonhole	'arwa (f)	عروة
to come off (ab. button)	we'e'	وقع
to sew (vi, vt)	χayaṭ	خيّط
to embroider (vi, vt)	ṭarraz	طرّز
embroidery	taṭrīz (m)	تطريز
sewing needle	ebra (f)	إبرة
thread	χeyṭ (m)	خيط
seam	derz (m)	درز
to get dirty (vi)	ettwassaχ	إتّوسّخ
stain (mark, spot)	bo''a (f)	بقعة
to crease, to crumple	takarmaʃ	تكرمش
to tear, to rip (vt)	'aṭa'	قطع
clothes moth	'etta (f)	عثّة

41. Personal care. Cosmetics

toothpaste	ma'gūn asnān (m)	معجون أسنان
toothbrush	forʃet senān (f)	فرشة أسنان
to clean one's teeth	naḍḍaf el asnān	نظّف الأسنان
razor	mūs (m)	موس
shaving cream	krīm ḥelā'a (m)	كريم حلاقة
to shave (vi)	ḥala'	حلق
soap	ṣabūn (m)	صابون

shampoo	ʃambū (m)	شامبو
scissors	ma'aṣ (m)	مقص
nail file	mabrad (m)	مبرد
nail clippers	mel'aṭ (m)	ملقط
tweezers	mel'aṭ (m)	ملقط
cosmetics	mawād tagmīl (pl)	مواد تجميل
face mask	mask (m)	ماسك
manicure	monekīr (m)	مونيكير
to have a manicure	'amal monikīr	عمل مونيكير
pedicure	badikīr (m)	باديكير
make-up bag	ʃanṭet mekyāʒ (f)	شنطة مكياج
face powder	bodret weʃ (f)	بودرة وش
powder compact	'elbet bodra (f)	علبة بودرة
blusher	aḥmar χodūd (m)	أحمر خدود
perfume (bottled)	barfān (m)	بارفان
toilet water (lotion)	kolonya (f)	كولونيا
lotion	loʃion (m)	لوشن
cologne	kolonya (f)	كولونيا
eyeshadow	eyeʃadow (m)	ايّ شادو
eyeliner	koḥl (m)	كحل
mascara	maskara (f)	ماسكارا
lipstick	rūʒ (m)	روج
nail polish	monekīr (m)	مونيكير
hair spray	mosabbet el ʃa'r (m)	مثبّت الشعر
deodorant	mozīl 'ara' (m)	مزيل عرق
cream	krīm (m)	كريم
face cream	krīm lel weʃ (m)	كريم للوش
hand cream	krīm eyd (m)	كريم أيد
anti-wrinkle cream	krīm moḍād lel taga'īd (m)	كريم مضاد للتجاعيد
day cream	krīm en nahār (m)	كريم النهار
night cream	krīm el leyl (m)	كريم الليل
day (as adj)	nahāry	نهاري
night (as adj)	layly	ليّلي
tampon	tambon (m)	تانبون
toilet paper (toilet roll)	wara' twalet (m)	ورق تواليت
hair dryer	seʃwār (m)	سشوار

42. Jewellery

jewellery, jewels	mogawharāt (pl)	مجوّهرات
precious (e.g. ~ stone)	ɣāly	غالي
hallmark stamp	damɣa (f)	دمغة
ring	χātem (m)	خاتم
wedding ring	deblet el faraḥ (m)	دبلة الفرح
bracelet	eswera (m)	إسوّرة
earrings	ḥala' (m)	حلق

necklace (~ of pearls)	ʿo'd (m)	عقد
crown	tāg (m)	تاج
bead necklace	ʿo'd χaraz (m)	عقد خرز
diamond	almāz (m)	ألماز
emerald	zomorrod (m)	زمرّد
ruby	ya'ūt aḥmar (m)	ياقوت أحمر
sapphire	ya'ūt azra' (m)	ياقوت أزرق
pearl	lo'lo' (m)	لؤلؤ
amber	kahramān (m)	كهرمان

43. Watches. Clocks

watch (wristwatch)	sāʿa (f)	ساعة
dial	wag-h el sāʿa (m)	وجه الساعة
hand (clock, watch)	ʿa'rab el sāʿa (m)	عقرب الساعة
metal bracelet	ʃerīʾṭ sāʿa maʿdaniya (m)	شريط ساعة معدنية
watch strap	ʃerīʾṭ el sāʿa (m)	شريط الساعة
battery	baṭṭariya (f)	بطّاريّة
to be flat (battery)	χelṣet	خلصت
to change a battery	ɣayar el baṭṭariya	غيّر البطّاريّة
to run fast	saba'	سبق
to run slow	ta'akχar	تأخّر
wall clock	sāʿet ḥeyṭa (f)	ساعة حيطة
hourglass	sāʿa ramliya (f)	ساعة رمليّة
sundial	sāʿa ʃamsiya (f)	ساعة شمسيّة
alarm clock	monabbeh (m)	منبّه
watchmaker	saʿāty (m)	ساعاتي
to repair (vt)	ṣallaḥ	صلّح

Food. Nutricion

44. Food

meat	laḥma (f)	لحمة
chicken	ferāχ (m)	فراخ
poussin	farrūg (m)	فرّوج
duck	baṭṭa (f)	بطّة
goose	wezza (f)	وزّة
game	ṣeyd (m)	صيد
turkey	dīk rūmy (m)	ديك رومي
pork	laḥm el χanazīr (m)	لحم الخنزير
veal	laḥm el ʿegl (m)	لحم العجل
lamb	laḥm ḍāny (m)	لحم ضاني
beef	laḥm baqary (m)	لحم بقري
rabbit	laḥm arāneb (m)	لحم أرانب
sausage (bologna, etc.)	sogoʾʾ (m)	سجق
vienna sausage (frankfurter)	sogoʾʾ (m)	سجق
bacon	bakon (m)	بيكون
ham	hām(m)	هام
gammon	faχd χanzīr (m)	فخد خنزير
pâté	maʿgūn laḥm (m)	معجون لحم
liver	kebda (f)	كبدة
mince (minced meat)	hamburger (m)	هامبورجر
tongue	lesān (m)	لسان
egg	beyḍa (f)	بيضة
eggs	beyḍ (m)	بيض
egg white	bayāḍ el beyḍ (m)	بياض البيض
egg yolk	ṣafār el beyḍ (m)	صفار البيض
fish	samak (m)	سمك
seafood	sīfūd (pl)	سي فود
caviar	kaviar (m)	كافيار
crab	kaboria (m)	كابوريا
prawn	gammbary (m)	جمبري
oyster	maḥār (m)	محار
spiny lobster	estakoza (m)	استاكوزا
octopus	aχṭabūṭ (m)	أخطبوط
squid	kalmāry (m)	كالماري
sturgeon	samak el ḥafʃ (m)	سمك الحفش
salmon	salamon (m)	سلمون
halibut	samak el halbūt (m)	سمك الهلبوت
cod	samak el qadd (m)	سمك القد
mackerel	makerel (m)	ماكريل

tuna	tuna (f)	تونة
eel	ḥankalīs (m)	حنكليس
trout	salamon mera''aṭ (m)	سلمون مرقّط
sardine	sardīn (m)	سردين
pike	samak el karāky (m)	سمك الكراكي
herring	renga (f)	رنجة
bread	ʿeyʃ (m)	عيش
cheese	gebna (f)	جبنة
sugar	sokkar (m)	سكّر
salt	melḥ (m)	ملح
rice	rozz (m)	رزّ
pasta (macaroni)	makaruna (f)	مكرونة
noodles	nūdles (f)	نودلز
butter	zebda (f)	زبّدة
vegetable oil	zeyt (m)	زيت
sunflower oil	zeyt ʿabbād el ʃams (m)	زيت عبّاد الشمس
margarine	margarīn (m)	مارجرين
olives	zaytūn (m)	زيتون
olive oil	zeyt el zaytūn (m)	زيت الزيتون
milk	laban (m)	لبن
condensed milk	ḥalīb mokassaf (m)	حليب مكثّف
yogurt	zabādy (m)	زبادي
soured cream	kreyma ḥamḍa (f)	كريمة حامضة
cream (of milk)	krīma (f)	كريمة
mayonnaise	mayonnɛ:z (m)	مايونيز
buttercream	krīmet zebda (f)	كريمة زبدة
groats (barley ~, etc.)	ḥobūb ʾamḥ (pl)	حبوب قمح
flour	deʾī (m)	دقيق
tinned food	moʿallabāt (pl)	معلّبات
cornflakes	korn fleks (m)	كورن فليكس
honey	ʿasal (m)	عسل
jam	mrabba (m)	مربّى
chewing gum	lebān (m)	لبان

45. Drinks

water	meyāh (f)	مياه
drinking water	mayet ʃorb (m)	ميّة شرب
mineral water	maya maʿdaniya (f)	ميّة معدنية
still (adj)	rakeda	راكدة
carbonated (adj)	kanz	كانز
sparkling (adj)	kanz	كانز
ice	talg (m)	ثلج
with ice	bel talg	بالتلج

non-alcoholic (adj)	men ɣeyr koḥūl	من غير كحول
soft drink	maʃrūb ɣāzy (m)	مشروب غازي
refreshing drink	ḥāga saʾʿa (f)	حاجة ساقعة
lemonade	limonāta (f)	ليموناتة
spirits	maʃrūbāt koḥūliya (pl)	مشروبات كحولية
wine	χamra (f)	خمرة
white wine	nebīz abyaḍ (m)	نبيذ أبيض
red wine	nebī aḥmar (m)	نبيذ أحمر
liqueur	liqure (m)	ليكيور
champagne	ʃambania (f)	شمبانيا
vermouth	vermote (m)	فيرموت
whisky	wiski (m)	ويسكي
vodka	vodka (f)	فودكا
gin	ʒin (m)	جين
cognac	konyāk (m)	كونياك
rum	rum (m)	رم
coffee	ʾahwa (f)	قهوة
black coffee	ʾahwa sāda (f)	قهوة سادة
white coffee	ʾahwa bel ḥalīb (f)	قهوة بالحليب
cappuccino	kaputʃino (m)	كابتشينو
instant coffee	neskafe (m)	نيسكافيه
milk	laban (m)	لبن
cocktail	koktayl (m)	كوكتيل
milkshake	milk ʃejk (m)	ميلك شيك
juice	ʿaṣīr (m)	عصير
tomato juice	ʿaṣīr ṭamāṭem (m)	عصير طماطم
orange juice	ʿaṣīr bortoqāl (m)	عصير برتقال
freshly squeezed juice	ʿaṣīr freʃ (m)	عصير فريش
beer	bīra (f)	بيرة
lager	bīra χafīfa (f)	بيرة خفيفة
bitter	bīra ɣamʾa (f)	بيرة غامقة
tea	ʃāy (m)	شاي
black tea	ʃāy aḥmar (m)	شاي أحمر
green tea	ʃāy aχḍar (m)	شاي أخضر

46. Vegetables

vegetables	χoḍār (pl)	خضار
greens	χoḍrawāt waraqiya (pl)	خضروات ورقية
tomato	ṭamāṭem (f)	طماطم
cucumber	χeyār (m)	خيار
carrot	gazar (m)	جزر
potato	baṭāṭes (f)	بطاطس
onion	baṣal (m)	بصل
garlic	tūm (m)	ثوم

cabbage	koronb (m)	كرنب
cauliflower	'arnabīṭ (m)	قرنبيط
Brussels sprouts	koronb broksel (m)	كرنب بروكسل
broccoli	brokkoli (m)	بركولي
beetroot	bangar (m)	بنجر
aubergine	bātengān (m)	باذنجان
courgette	kōsa (f)	كوسة
pumpkin	qar' 'asaly (m)	قرع عسلي
turnip	left (m)	لفت
parsley	ba'dūnes (m)	بقدونس
dill	ʃabat (m)	شبت
lettuce	χass (m)	خسّ
celery	karfas (m)	كرفس
asparagus	helione (m)	هليون
spinach	sabāneχ (m)	سبانخ
pea	besella (f)	بسلّة
beans	fūl (m)	فول
maize	dora (f)	ذرة
kidney bean	faṣolya (f)	فاصوليا
sweet paper	felfel (m)	فلفل
radish	fegl (m)	فجل
artichoke	χarʃūf (m)	خرشوف

47. Fruits. Nuts

fruit	faχa (f)	فاكهة
apple	toffāḥa (f)	تفّاحة
pear	komettra (f)	كمّثرى
lemon	lymūn (m)	ليمون
orange	bortoqāl (m)	برتقال
strawberry (garden ~)	farawla (f)	فراولة
tangerine	yosfy (m)	يوسفي
plum	bar'ū' (m)	برقوق
peach	χawχa (f)	خوخة
apricot	meʃmeʃ (f)	مشمش
raspberry	tūt el 'alī' el aḥmar (m)	توت العليق الأحمر
pineapple	ananās (m)	أناناس
banana	moze (m)	موز
watermelon	baṭṭīχ (m)	بطّيخ
grape	'enab (m)	عنب
cherry	karaz (m)	كرز
melon	ʃammām (f)	شمّام
grapefruit	grabe frūt (m)	جريب فروت
avocado	avokado (f)	افوكاتو
papaya	babāya (m)	ببايا
mango	manga (m)	مانجة
pomegranate	rommān (m)	رمان

redcurrant	keʃmeʃ aḥmar (m)	كشمش أحمر
blackcurrant	keʃmeʃ aswad (m)	كشمش أسود
gooseberry	ʻenab el saʻlab (m)	عنب الثعلب
bilberry	ʻenab al aḥrāg (m)	عنب الأحراج
blackberry	tūt aswad (m)	توت أسود
raisin	zebīb (m)	زبيب
fig	tīn (m)	تين
date	tamr (m)	تمر
peanut	fūl sudāny (m)	فول سوداني
almond	loze (m)	لوز
walnut	ʻeyn gamal (f)	عين الجمل
hazelnut	bondoʼ (m)	بندق
coconut	goze el hend (m)	جوز هند
pistachios	fostoʼ (m)	فستق

48. Bread. Sweets

bakers' confectionery (pastry)	ḥalawīāt (pl)	حلويّات
bread	ʻeyʃ (m)	عيش
biscuits	baskawīt (m)	بسكويت
chocolate (n)	ʃokolāta (f)	شكولاتة
chocolate (as adj)	bel ʃokolāṭa	بالشكولاتة
candy (wrapped)	bonbony (m)	بونبوني
cake (e.g. cupcake)	keyka (f)	كيكة
cake (e.g. birthday ~)	torta (f)	تورتة
pie (e.g. apple ~)	feṭīra (f)	فطيرة
filling (for cake, pie)	ḥaʃwa (f)	حشوة
jam (whole fruit jam)	mrabba (m)	مربّى
marmalade	marmalād (f)	مرملاد
wafers	waffles (pl)	وافلز
ice-cream	ʼays krīm (m)	آيس كريم
pudding (Christmas ~)	būding (m)	بودنج

49. Cooked dishes

course, dish	wagba (f)	وجبة
cuisine	maṭbaχ (m)	مطبخ
recipe	waṣfa (f)	وصفة
portion	naṣīb (m)	نصيب
salad	solṭa (f)	سلطة
soup	ʃorba (f)	شوربة
clear soup (broth)	maraʼa (m)	مرقة
sandwich (bread)	sandawitʃ (m)	ساندويتش
fried eggs	beyḍ maʼly (m)	بيض مقلي
hamburger (beefburger)	hamburger (m)	هامبورجر

beefsteak	steak laḥm (m)	ستيك لحم
side dish	ṭaba' gāneby (m)	طبق جانبي
spaghetti	spaɣetti (m)	سباجيتي
mash	baṭāṭes mahrūsa (f)	بطاطس مهروسة
pizza	bītza (f)	بيتزا
porridge (oatmeal, etc.)	'aṣīda (f)	عصيدة
omelette	omlette (m)	اومليت
boiled (e.g. ~ beef)	maslū'	مسلوق
smoked (adj)	modakχen	مدخّن
fried (adj)	ma'ly	مقلي
dried (adj)	mogaffaf	مجفّف
frozen (adj)	mogammad	مجمّد
pickled (adj)	meχallel	مخلّل
sweet (sugary)	mesakkar	مسكّر
salty (adj)	māleḥ	مالح
cold (adj)	bāred	بارد
hot (adj)	soχn	سخن
bitter (adj)	morr	مرّ
tasty (adj)	ḥelw	حلو
to cook in boiling water	sala'	سلق
to cook (dinner)	ḥaḍḍar	حضّر
to fry (vt)	'ala	قلي
to heat up (food)	sakχan	سخّن
to salt (vt)	rasʃ malḥ	رشّ ملح
to pepper (vt)	rasʃ felfel	رشّ فلفل
to grate (vt)	baraʃ	برش
peel (n)	'eʃra (f)	قشرة
to peel (vt)	'asʃar	قشّر

50. Spices

salt	melḥ (m)	ملح
salty (adj)	māleḥ	مالح
to salt (vt)	rasʃ malḥ	رشّ ملح
black pepper	felfel aswad (m)	فلفل أسوّد
red pepper (milled ~)	felfel aḥmar (m)	فلفل أحمر
mustard	mosṭarda (m)	مسطردة
horseradish	fegl ḥār (m)	فجل حار
condiment	bahār (m)	بهار
spice	bahār (m)	بهار
sauce	ṣalṣa (f)	صلصة
vinegar	χall (m)	خلّ
anise	yansūn (m)	ينسون
basil	rīḥān (m)	ريحان
cloves	'oronfol (m)	قرنفل
ginger	zangabīl (m)	زنجبيل
coriander	kozbora (f)	كزبرة

cinnamon	'erfa (f)	قرفة
sesame	semsem (m)	سمسم
bay leaf	wara' el ɣār (m)	ورق الغار
paprika	babrika (f)	بابريكا
caraway	karawya (f)	كراوية
saffron	za'farān (m)	زعفران

51. Meals

food	akl (m)	أكل
to eat (vi, vt)	akal	أكل
breakfast	foṭūr (m)	فطور
to have breakfast	feṭer	فطر
lunch	ɣada' (m)	غداء
to have lunch	etɣadda	إتغدّى
dinner	'aʃā' (m)	عشاء
to have dinner	et'asʃa	إتعشّى
appetite	ʃahiya (f)	شهيّة
Enjoy your meal!	bel hana wel ʃefa!	!بالهنا والشفا
to open (~ a bottle)	fataḥ	فتح
to spill (liquid)	dala'	دلق
to spill out (vi)	dala'	دلق
to boil (vi)	ɣely	غلي
to boil (vt)	ɣely	غلي
boiled (~ water)	maɣly	مغلي
to chill, cool down (vt)	barrad	برّد
to chill (vi)	barrad	برّد
taste, flavour	ṭa'm (m)	طعم
aftertaste	ṭa'm ma ba'd el mazāq (m)	طعم ما بعد المذاق
to slim down (lose weight)	χass	خسّ
diet	reʒīm (m)	رجيم
vitamin	vitamīn (m)	فيتامين
calorie	so'ra ḥarāriya (f)	سعرة حراريّة
vegetarian (n)	nabāty (m)	نباتي
vegetarian (adj)	nabāty	نباتي
fats (nutrient)	dohūn (pl)	دهون
proteins	brotenāt (pl)	بروتينات
carbohydrates	naʃawīāt (pl)	نشويّات
slice (of lemon, ham)	ʃarīḥa (f)	شريحة
piece (of cake, pie)	'eṭ'a (f)	قطعة
crumb (of bread, cake, etc.)	fattāta (f)	فتاتة

52. Table setting

spoon	ma'la'a (f)	معلقة
knife	sekkīna (f)	سكّينة

fork	ʃawka (f)	شوكة
cup (e.g., coffee ~)	fengān (m)	فنجان
plate (dinner ~)	ṭaba' (m)	طبق
saucer	ṭaba' fengān (m)	طبق فنجان
serviette	mandīl wara' (m)	منديل ورق
toothpick	χallet senān (f)	خلة سنان

53. Restaurant

restaurant	maṭ'am (m)	مطعم
coffee bar	'ahwa (f), kaféih (m)	قهوة, كافيه
pub, bar	bār (m)	بار
tearoom	ṣalone ʃāy (m)	صالون شاي
waiter	garsone (m)	جرسون
waitress	garsona (f)	جرسونة
barman	bārman (m)	بارمان
menu	qā'emet el ṭa'ām (f)	قائمة طعام
wine list	qā'emet el χomūr (f)	قائمة خمور
to book a table	ḥagaz sofra	حجز سفرة
course, dish	wagba (f)	وجبة
to order (meal)	ṭalab	طلب
to make an order	ṭalab	طلب
aperitif	ʃarāb (m)	شراب
starter	moqabbelāt (pl)	مقبّلات
dessert, pudding	ḥalawīāt (pl)	حلويّات
bill	ḥesāb (m)	حساب
to pay the bill	dafa' el ḥesāb	دفع الحساب
to give change	edda el bā'y	ادّي الباقي
tip	ba'ʃīʃ (m)	بقشيش

Family, relatives and friends

54. Personal information. Forms

name (first name)	esm (m)	اسم
surname (last name)	esm el ʿaʾela (m)	اسم العائلة
date of birth	tarīχ el melād (m)	تاريخ الميلاد
place of birth	makān el melād (m)	مكان الميلاد
nationality	gensiya (f)	جنسيّة
place of residence	maqarr el eqāma (m)	مقرّ الإقامة
country	balad (m)	بلد
profession (occupation)	mehna (f)	مهنة
gender, sex	ginss (m)	جنس
height	ṭūl (m)	طول
weight	wazn (m)	وزن

55. Family members. Relatives

mother	walda (f)	والدة
father	wāled (m)	والد
son	walad (m)	ولد
daughter	bent (f)	بنت
younger daughter	el bent el saɣīra (f)	البنت الصغيرة
younger son	el ebn el saɣīr (m)	الابن الصغير
eldest daughter	el bent el kebīra (f)	البنت الكبيرة
eldest son	el ebn el kabīr (m)	الابن الكبير
brother	aχ (m)	أخ
elder brother	el aχ el kibīr (m)	الأخ الكبير
younger brother	el aχ el ṣoɣeyyir (m)	الأخ الصغير
sister	uχt (f)	أخت
elder sister	el uχt el kibīra (f)	الأخت الكبيرة
younger sister	el uχt el ṣoɣeyyira (f)	الأخت الصغيرة
cousin (masc.)	ibn ʿamm (m), ibn χāl (m)	إبن عمّ, إبن خال
cousin (fem.)	bint ʿamm (f), bint χāl (f)	بنت عم, بنت خال
mummy	mama (f)	ماما
dad, daddy	baba (m)	بابا
parents	waldeyn (du)	والدين
child	ṭefl (m)	طفل
children	aṭfāl (pl)	أطفال
grandmother	gedda (f)	جدّة
grandfather	gadd (m)	جدّ
grandson	ḥafīd (m)	حفيد

granddaughter	ḥafīda (f)	حفيدة
grandchildren	aḥfād (pl)	أحفاد
uncle	ʿamm (m), χāl (m)	عمّ, خال
aunt	ʿamma (f), χāla (f)	عمّة, خالة
nephew	ibn el aχ (m), ibn el uχt (m)	إبن الأخ, إبن الأخت
niece	bint el aχ (f), bint el uχt (f)	بنت الأخ, بنت الأخت
mother-in-law (wife's mother)	ḥamah (f)	حماة
father-in-law (husband's father)	ḥama (m)	حما
son-in-law (daughter's husband)	goze el bent (m)	جوز البنت
stepmother	merāt el abb (f)	مرات الأب
stepfather	goze el omm (m)	جوز الأم
infant	ṭefl raḍeeʿ (m)	طفل رضيع
baby (infant)	mawlūd (m)	موّلود
little boy, kid	walad ṣaɣīr (m)	ولد صغير
wife	goza (f)	جوزة
husband	goze (m)	جوز
spouse (husband)	goze (m)	جوز
spouse (wife)	goza (f)	جوزة
married (masc.)	metgawwez	متجوّز
married (fem.)	metgawweza	متجوّزة
single (unmarried)	aʿzab	أعزب
bachelor	aʿzab (m)	أعزب
divorced (masc.)	moṭallaq (m)	مطلّق
widow	armala (f)	أرملة
widower	armal (m)	أرمل
relative	ʾarīb (m)	قريب
close relative	nesīb ʾarīb (m)	نسيب قريب
distant relative	nesīb beʿīd (m)	نسيب بعيد
relatives	aqāreb (pl)	أقارب
orphan (boy or girl)	yatīm (m)	يتيم
guardian (of a minor)	walyī amr (m)	وليّ أمر
to adopt (a boy)	tabanna	تبنّى
to adopt (a girl)	tabanna	تبنّى

56. Friends. Colleagues

friend (masc.)	ṣadīq (m)	صديق
friend (fem.)	ṣadīqa (f)	صديقة
friendship	ṣadāqa (f)	صداقة
to be friends	ṣādaq	صادق
pal (masc.)	ṣāḥeb (m)	صاحب
pal (fem.)	ṣaḥba (f)	صاحبة
partner	rafīʾ (m)	رفيق
chief (boss)	raʾīs (m)	رئيس

superior (n)	el arfaʿ maqāman (m)	الأرفع مقاماً
owner, proprietor	ṣāḥib (m)	صاحب
subordinate (n)	tābeʿ (m)	تابع
colleague	zamīl (m)	زميل
acquaintance (person)	maʿrefa (m)	معرفة
fellow traveller	rafīʾ safar (m)	رفيق سفر
classmate	zamīl fel ṣaff (m)	زميل في الصفّ
neighbour (masc.)	gār (m)	جار
neighbour (fem.)	gāra (f)	جارة
neighbours	gerān (pl)	جيران

57. Man. Woman

woman	set (f)	ست
girl (young woman)	bent (f)	بنت
bride	ʿarūsa (f)	عروسة
beautiful (adj)	gamīla	جميلة
tall (adj)	ṭawīla	طويلة
slender (adj)	raʃīqa	رشيقة
short (adj)	ʾaṣīra	قصيرة
blonde (n)	ʃaʾra (f)	شقراء
brunette (n)	zāt al ʃaʿr el dāken (f)	ذات الشعر الداكن
ladies' (adj)	sayedāt	سيّدات
virgin (girl)	ʿazrāʾ (f)	عذراء
pregnant (adj)	ḥāmel	حامل
man (adult male)	rāgel (m)	راجل
blonde haired man	aʃʾar (m)	أشقر
dark haired man	zu el ʃaʿr el dāken (m)	ذو الشعر الداكن
tall (adj)	ṭawīl	طويل
short (adj)	ʾaṣīr	قصير
rude (rough)	waqeḥ	وقح
stocky (adj)	malyān	مليان
robust (adj)	matīn	متين
strong (adj)	ʾawy	قويّ
strength	ʾowwa (f)	قوّة
plump, fat (adj)	teχīn	تخين
swarthy (dark-skinned)	asmar	أسمر
slender (well-built)	raʃīq	رشيق
elegant (adj)	anīq	أنيق

58. Age

age	ʿomr (m)	عمر
youth (young age)	ʃabāb (m)	شباب

young (adj)	ʃāb	شاب
younger (adj)	aṣɣar	أصغر
older (adj)	akbar	أكبر
young man	ʃāb (m)	شاب
teenager	morāheq (m)	مراهق
guy, fellow	ʃāb (m)	شاب
old man	ʿagūz (m)	عجوز
old woman	ʿagūza (f)	عجوزة
adult (adj)	rāʃed (m)	راشد
middle-aged (adj)	fe montaṣaf el ʿomr	في منتصف العمر
elderly (adj)	ʿagūz	عجوز
old (adj)	ʿagūz	عجوز
retirement	maʿāʃ (m)	معاش
to retire (from job)	oḥīl ʿala el maʿāʃ	أحيل على المعاش
retiree, pensioner	motaqāʿed (m)	متقاعد

59. Children

child	ṭefl (m)	طفل
children	aṭfāl (pl)	أطفال
twins	tawʾam (du)	توأم
cradle	mahd (m)	مهد
rattle	χoʃχeyʃa (f)	خشخيشة
nappy	bambarz, ḥaffāḍ (m)	بامبرز, حفاض
dummy, comforter	bazzāza (f)	بزّازة
pram	ʿarabet aṭfāl (f)	عربة أطفال
nursery	rawḍet aṭfāl (f)	روضة أطفال
babysitter	dāda (f)	دادة
childhood	ṭofūla (f)	طفولة
doll	ʿarūsa (f)	عروسة
toy	leʿba (f)	لعبة
construction set (toy)	mokaʿʿabāt (pl)	مكعّبات
well-bred (adj)	moʾaddab	مؤدّب
ill-bred (adj)	ʾalīl el adab	قليل الأدب
spoilt (adj)	metdallaʿ	متدلّع
to be naughty	ʃefy	شقي
mischievous (adj)	laʿūb	لعوب
mischievousness	ezʿāg (m)	إزعاج
mischievous child	ṭefl laʿūb (m)	طفل لعوب
obedient (adj)	moṭeeʿ	مطيع
disobedient (adj)	ʿāq	عاق
docile (adj)	ʿāʾel	عاقل
clever (intelligent)	zaky	ذكي
child prodigy	ṭefl moʿgeza (m)	طفل معجزة

60. Married couples. Family life

to kiss (vt)	bās	باس
to kiss (vi)	bās	باس
family (n)	ʿeyla (f)	عيلة
family (as adj)	ʿāʾely	عائلي
couple	gozeyn (du)	جوزين
marriage (state)	gawāz (m)	جواز
hearth (home)	beyt (m)	بيت
dynasty	solāla ḥākema (f)	سلالة حاكمة
date	mawʿed (m)	موّعد
kiss	bosa (f)	بوسة
love (for sb)	ḥobb (m)	حبّ
to love (sb)	ḥabb	حبّ
beloved	ḥabīb	حبيب
tenderness	ḥanān (m)	حنان
tender (affectionate)	ḥanūn	حنون
faithfulness	el eχlāṣ (m)	الإخلاص
faithful (adj)	moχleṣ	مخلص
care (attention)	ʿenāya (f)	عناية
caring (~ father)	mohtamm	مهتمّ
newlyweds	ʿarūseyn (du)	عروسين
honeymoon	ʃahr el ʿasal (m)	شهر العسل
to get married (ab. woman)	tagawwaz	تجوّز
to get married (ab. man)	tagawwaz	تجوّز
wedding	faraḥ (m)	فرح
golden wedding	el zekra el χamsīn lel gawāz (f)	الذكرى الخمسين للجواز
anniversary	zekra sanawiya (f)	ذكرى سنوية
lover (masc.)	ḥabīb (m)	حبيب
mistress (lover)	ḥabība (f)	حبيبة
adultery	χeyāna zawgiya (f)	خيانة زوّجية
to cheat on ... (commit adultery)	χān	خان
jealous (adj)	ɣayūr	غيّور
to be jealous	ɣār	غار
divorce	ṭalāʾ (m)	طلاق
to divorce (vi)	ṭallaʾ	طلّق
to quarrel (vi)	etχāneʾ	إتخانق
to be reconciled (after an argument)	taṣālaḥ	تصالح
together (adv)	maʿ baʿḍ	مع بعض
sex	ginss (m)	جنس
happiness	saʿāda (f)	سعادة
happy (adj)	saʿīd	سعيد
misfortune (accident)	moṣība (m)	مصيبة
unhappy (adj)	taʿīs	تعيس

Character. Feelings. Emotions

61. Feelings. Emotions

feeling (emotion)	ʃoʿūr (m)	شعور
feelings	maʃāʿer (pl)	مشاعر
to feel (vt)	ʃaʿar	شعر
hunger	gūʿ (m)	جوع
to be hungry	ʿāyez ʾākol	عايز آكل
thirst	ʿaṭaʃ (m)	عطش
to be thirsty	ʿāyez aʃrab	عايز أشرب
sleepiness	neʿās (m)	نعاس
to feel sleepy	neʿes	نعس
tiredness	taʿab (m)	تعب
tired (adj)	taʿbān	تعبان
to get tired	teʿeb	تعب
mood (humour)	mazāg (m)	مزاج
boredom	malal (m)	ملل
to be bored	zeheʾ	زهق
seclusion	ʿozla (f)	عزلة
to seclude oneself	ʿazal	عزل
to worry (make anxious)	aʾlaʾ	أقلق
to be worried	ʾeleʾ	قلق
worrying (n)	ʾalaʾ (m)	قلق
anxiety	ʾalaʾ (m)	قلق
preoccupied (adj)	maʃɣūl el bāl	مشغول البال
to be nervous	etwattar	إتوّتر
to panic (vi)	etχaḍḍ	إتخضّ
hope	amal (m)	أمل
to hope (vi, vt)	tamanna	تمنّى
certainty	yaqīn (m)	يقين
certain, sure (adj)	motaʾakked	متأكّد
uncertainty	ʿadam el taʾakkod (m)	عدم التأكّد
uncertain (adj)	meʃ motaʾakked	مش متأكّد
drunk (adj)	sakrān	سكران
sober (adj)	ṣāḥy	صاحي
weak (adj)	ḍaʿīf	ضعيف
happy (adj)	saʿīd	سعيد
to scare (vt)	χawwef	خوّف
fury (madness)	ɣaḍab ʃedīd (m)	غضب شديد
rage (fury)	ɣaḍab (m)	غضب
depression	ekteʾāb (m)	إكتئاب
discomfort (unease)	ʿadam erteyāḥ (m)	عدم إرتياح

comfort	rāḥa (f)	راحة
to regret (be sorry)	nedem	ندم
regret	nadam (m)	ندم
bad luck	sūʾ ḥaẓẓ (m)	سوء حظ
sadness	ḥozn (f)	حزن
shame (remorse)	χagal (m)	خجل
gladness	faraḥ (m)	فرح
enthusiasm, zeal	ḥamās (m)	حماس
enthusiast	motaḥammes (m)	متحمّس
to show enthusiasm	taḥammas	تحمّس

62. Character. Personality

character	ʃaχṣiya (f)	شخصية
character flaw	ʿeyb (m)	عيب
mind, reason	ʿaʾl (m)	عقل
conscience	ḍamīr (m)	ضمير
habit (custom)	ʿāda (f)	عادة
ability (talent)	qodra (f)	قدرة
can (e.g. ~ swim)	ʿeref	عرف
patient (adj)	ṣabūr	صبور
impatient (adj)	ʾalīl el ṣabr	قليل الصبر
curious (inquisitive)	foḍūly	فضولي
curiosity	foḍūl (m)	فضول
modesty	tawāḍoʿ (m)	تواضع
modest (adj)	motawāḍeʿ	متواضع
immodest (adj)	meʃ motawāḍeʿ	مش متواضع
laziness	kasal (m)	كسل
lazy (adj)	kaslān	كسلان
lazy person (masc.)	kaslān (m)	كسلان
cunning (n)	makr (m)	مكر
cunning (as adj)	makkār	مكّار
distrust	ʿadam el seqa (m)	عدم الثقة
distrustful (adj)	ʃakkāk	شكّاك
generosity	karam (m)	كرم
generous (adj)	karīm	كريم
talented (adj)	mawhūb	موهوب
talent	mawheba (f)	موهبة
courageous (adj)	ʃogāʿ	شجاع
courage	ʃagāʿa (f)	شجاعة
honest (adj)	amīn	أمين
honesty	amāna (f)	أمانة
careful (cautious)	ḥazer	حذر
brave (courageous)	ʃogāʿ	شجاع
serious (adj)	gād	جاد

strict (severe, stern)	ṣārem	صارم
decisive (adj)	ḥāsem	حاسم
indecisive (adj)	motaradded	متردّد
shy, timid (adj)	χagūl	خجول
shyness, timidity	χagal (m)	خجل
confidence (trust)	seqa (f)	ثقة
to believe (trust)	wasaq	وثق
trusting (credulous)	saree' el taṣdīq	سريع التصديق
sincerely (adv)	beṣarāḥa	بصراحة
sincere (adj)	moχleṣ	مخلص
sincerity	eχlāṣ (m)	إخلاص
open (person)	ṣarīḥ	صريح
calm (adj)	hady	هادئ
frank (sincere)	ṣarīḥ	صريح
naïve (adj)	sāzeg	ساذج
absent-minded (adj)	ʃāred el fekr	شارد الفكر
funny (odd)	moḍḥek	مضحك
greed, stinginess	boχl (m)	بخل
greedy, stingy (adj)	ṭammā'	طماع
stingy (adj)	baχīl	بخيل
evil (adj)	ʃerrīr	شرير
stubborn (adj)	'anīd	عنيد
unpleasant (adj)	karīh	كريه
selfish person (masc.)	anāny (m)	أناني
selfish (adj)	anāny	أناني
coward	gabān (m)	جبان
cowardly (adj)	gabān	جبان

63. Sleep. Dreams

to sleep (vi)	nām	نام
sleep, sleeping	nome (m)	نوم
dream	ḥelm (m)	حلم
to dream (in sleep)	ḥelem	حلم
sleepy (adj)	na'sān	نعسان
bed	serīr (m)	سرير
mattress	martaba (f)	مرتبة
blanket (eiderdown)	baṭṭaniya (f)	بطّانيّة
pillow	maχadda (f)	مخدّة
sheet	melāya (f)	ملاية
insomnia	araq (m)	أرق
sleepless (adj)	bodūn nome	بدون نوم
sleeping pill	monawwem (m)	منوم
to take a sleeping pill	aχad monawwem	اخد منوّم
to feel sleepy	ne'es	نعس
to yawn (vi)	ettāweb	إتّاوب

to go to bed	rāḥ lel serīr	راح للسرير
to make up the bed	waḍḍab el serīr	وضّب السرير
to fall asleep	nām	نام
nightmare	kabūs (m)	كابوس
snore, snoring	ʃeχīr (m)	شخير
to snore (vi)	ʃakχar	شخّر
alarm clock	monabbeh (m)	منبّه
to wake (vt)	ṣaḥḥa	صحّى
to wake up	ṣeḥy	صحي
to get up (vi)	'ām	قام
to have a wash	ɣasal	غسل

64. Humour. Laughter. Gladness

humour (wit, fun)	hezār (m)	هزار
sense of humour	ḥess fokāhy (m)	حسّ فكاهي
to enjoy oneself	estamtaʿ	إستمتع
cheerful (merry)	farḥān	فرحان
merriment (gaiety)	bahga (f)	بهجة
smile	ebtesāma (f)	إبتسامة
to smile (vi)	ebtasam	إبتسم
to start laughing	bada' yeḍḥak	بدأ يضحك
to laugh (vi)	ḍeḥek	ضحك
laugh, laughter	ḍeḥka (f)	ضحكة
anecdote	ḥekāya (f)	حكاية
funny (anecdote, etc.)	moḍḥek	مضحك
funny (odd)	moḍḥek	مضحك
to joke (vi)	hazzar	هزّر
joke (verbal)	nokta (f)	نكتة
joy (emotion)	saʿāda (f)	سعادة
to rejoice (vi)	mereḥ	مرح
joyful (adj)	saʿīd	سعيد

65. Discussion, conversation. Part 1

communication	tawāṣol (m)	تواصل
to communicate	tawāṣal	تواصل
conversation	moḥadsa (f)	محادثة
dialogue	ḥewār (m)	حوار
discussion (discourse)	mona'ʃa (f)	مناقشة
dispute (debate)	χelāf (m)	خلاف
to dispute, to debate	χālef	خالف
interlocutor	muḥāwer (m)	محاوِر
topic (theme)	mawḍūʿ (m)	موضوع
point of view	weg-het naẓar (f)	وجهة نظر

opinion (point of view)	ra'yī (m)	رأي
speech (talk)	χeṭāb (m)	خطاب
discussion (of a report, etc.)	mona'ʃa (f)	مناقشة
to discuss (vt)	nā'eʃ	ناقش
talk (conversation)	ḥadīs (m)	حديث
to talk (to chat)	dardeʃ	دردش
meeting (encounter)	leqā' (m)	لقاء
to meet (vi, vt)	'ābel	قابل
proverb	masal (m)	مثل
saying	maqūla (f)	مقولة
riddle (poser)	loɣz (m)	لغز
to pose a riddle	toʃakkel loɣz	تشكّل لغز
password	kelmet el morūr (f)	كلمة مرور
secret	serr (m)	سرّ
oath (vow)	qasam (m)	قسم
to swear (an oath)	aqsam	أقسم
promise	wa'd (m)	وعد
to promise (vt)	wa'ad	وعد
advice (counsel)	naṣīḥa (f)	نصيحة
to advise (vt)	naṣaḥ	نصح
to follow one's advice	tatabba' naṣīḥa	تتبّع نصيحة
to listen to … (obey)	aṭā'	أطاع
news	aχbār (m)	أخبار
sensation (news)	ḍagga (f)	ضجّة
information (report)	ma'lumāt (pl)	معلومات
conclusion (decision)	estentāg (f)	إستنتاج
voice	ṣote (m)	صوت
compliment	madḥ (m)	مدح
kind (nice)	laṭīf	لطيف
word	kelma (f)	كلمة
phrase	'ebāra (f)	عبارة
answer	gawāb (m)	جواب
truth	ḥa'ī'a (f)	حقيقة
lie	kezb (m)	كذب
thought	fekra (f)	فكرة
idea (inspiration)	fekra (f)	فكرة
fantasy	χayāl (m)	خيال

66. Discussion, conversation. Part 2

respected (adj)	moḥtaram	محترم
to respect (vt)	eḥtaram	إحترم
respect	eḥterām (m)	إحترام
Dear … (letter)	'azīzy …	عزيزي...
to introduce (sb to sb)	'arraf	عرّف
to make acquaintance	ta'arraf	تعرّف

intention	niya (f)	نيّة
to intend (have in mind)	nawa	نوى
wish	omniya (f)	أمنية
to wish (~ good luck)	tamanna	تمنّى
surprise (astonishment)	mofag'a (f)	مفاجأة
to surprise (amaze)	fāga'	فاجئ
to be surprised	etfāge'	إتفاجئ
to give (vt)	edda	أدّى
to take (get hold of)	aχad	أخد
to give back	radd	ردّ
to return (give back)	ragga'	رجّع
to apologize (vi)	e'tazar	إعتذر
apology	e'tezār (m)	إعتذار
to forgive (vt)	'afa	عفا
to talk (speak)	etkallem	إتكلّم
to listen (vi)	seme'	سمع
to hear out	seme'	سمع
to understand (vt)	fehem	فهم
to show (to display)	'araḍ	عرض
to look at ...	baṣṣ	بصّ
to call (yell for sb)	nāda	نادى
to distract (disturb)	ʃaɣal	شغل
to disturb (vt)	az'ag	أزعج
to pass (to hand sth)	sallem	سلّم
demand (request)	ṭalab (m)	طلب
to request (ask)	ṭalab	طلب
demand (firm request)	maṭlab (m)	مطلب
to demand (request firmly)	ṭāleb	طالب
to tease (call names)	ɣāẓ	غاظ
to mock (make fun of)	saχar	سخر
mockery, derision	soχreya (f)	سخرية
nickname	esm el ʃohra (m)	اسم الشهرة
insinuation	talmīḥ (m)	تلميح
to insinuate (imply)	lammaḥ	لمّح
to mean (vt)	'aṣad	قصد
description	waṣf (m)	وصف
to describe (vt)	waṣaf	وصف
praise (compliments)	madḥ (m)	مدح
to praise (vt)	madaḥ	مدح
disappointment	χeybet amal (f)	خيبة أمل
to disappoint (vt)	χayab	خيّب
to be disappointed	χābet 'āmalo	خابت آماله
supposition	efterāḍ (m)	إفتراض
to suppose (assume)	eftaraḍ	إفترض
warning (caution)	taḥzīr (m)	تحذير
to warn (vt)	ḥazzar	حذّر

67. Discussion, conversation. Part 3

to talk into (convince)	aqnaʿ	أقنع
to calm down (vt)	ṭam'an	طمأن
silence (~ is golden)	sokūt (m)	سكوت
to be silent (not speaking)	seket	سكت
to whisper (vi, vt)	hamas	همس
whisper	hamsa (f)	همسة
frankly, sincerely (adv)	beṣarāḥa	بصراحة
in my opinion …	fi ra'yi …	… في رأيي
detail (of the story)	tafṣīl (m)	تفصيل
detailed (adj)	mofaṣṣal	مفصّل
in detail (adv)	bel tafṣīl	بالتفصيل
hint, clue	talmīḥ (m)	تلميح
to give a hint	edda lamḥa	أدى لمحة
look (glance)	naẓra (f)	نظرة
to have a look	alqa nazra	ألقى نظرة
fixed (look)	sābet	ثابت
to blink (vi)	ramaʃ	رمش
to wink (vi)	ɣamaz	غمز
to nod (in assent)	haz rāso	هزّ رأسه
sigh	tanhīda (f)	تنهيدة
to sigh (vi)	tanahhad	تنهّد
to shudder (vi)	ertaʿaʃ	ارتعش
gesture	eʃāret yad (f)	إشارة يد
to touch (one's arm, etc.)	lamas	لمس
to seize (e.g., ~ by the arm)	mesek	مسك
to tap (on the shoulder)	ḥazz	حزّ
Look out!	χally bālak!	خللي بالك!
Really?	feʿlan	فعلاً؟
Are you sure?	enta mota'akked?	أنت متأكّد؟
Good luck!	bel tawfī'!	بالتوفيق!
I see!	wāḍeḥ!	واضح!
What a pity!	ya χesāra!	يا خسارة!

68. Agreement. Refusal

consent	mowaf'a (f)	موافقة
to consent (vi)	wāfe'	وافق
approval	'obūl (m)	قبول
to approve (vt)	'abal	قبل
refusal	rafḍ (m)	رفض
to refuse (vi, vt)	rafaḍ	رفض
Great!	ʿaẓīm!	عظيم!
All right!	tamām!	تمام!

Okay! (I agree)	ettafa'na!	إتّفقنا!
forbidden (adj)	mamnū'	ممنوع
it's forbidden	mamnū'	ممنوع
it's impossible	mostaḥīl	مستحيل
incorrect (adj)	ɣeleṭ	غلط
to reject (~ a demand)	rafaḍ	رفض
to support (cause, idea)	ayed	أيّد
to accept (~ an apology)	'abal	قبل
to confirm (vt)	akkad	أكّد
confirmation	ta'kīd (m)	تأكيد
permission	samāḥ (m)	سماح
to permit (vt)	samaḥ	سمح
decision	qarār (m)	قرار
to say nothing (hold one's tongue)	ṣamt	صمت
condition (term)	ʃarṭ (m)	شرط
excuse (pretext)	'ozr (m)	عذر
praise (compliments)	madḥ (m)	مدح
to praise (vt)	madaḥ	مدح

69. Success. Good luck. Failure

success	nagāḥ (m)	نجاح
successfully (adv)	be nagāḥ	بنجاح
successful (adj)	nāgeḥ	ناجح
luck (good luck)	ḥazz (m)	حظّ
Good luck!	bel tawfī'!	بالتوفيق!
lucky (e.g. ~ day)	maḥẓūẓ	محظوظ
lucky (fortunate)	maḥẓūẓ	محظوظ
failure	faʃal (m)	فشل
misfortune	sū' el ḥazz (m)	سوء الحظّ
bad luck	sū' el ḥazz (m)	سوء الحظّ
unsuccessful (adj)	ɣayr nāgeḥ	غير ناجح
catastrophe	karsa (f)	كارثة
pride	faχr (m)	فخر
proud (adj)	faχūr	فخور
to be proud	eftaχar	إفتخر
winner	fā'ez (m)	فائز
to win (vi)	fāz	فاز
to lose (not win)	χeser	خسر
try	moḥawla (f)	محاولة
to try (vi)	ḥāwel	حاول
chance (opportunity)	forṣa (f)	فرصة

70. Quarrels. Negative emotions

shout (scream)	ṣarχa (f)	صرخة
to shout (vi)	ṣarraχ	صرّخ
to start to cry out	ṣarraχ	صرّخ
quarrel	χenāʾa (f)	خناقة
to quarrel (vi)	etχāneʾ	إتخانق
fight (squabble)	χenāʾa (f)	خناقة
to make a scene	taʃāgar	تشاجر
conflict	χelāf (m)	خلاف
misunderstanding	sūʾ tafāhom (m)	سوء تفاهم
insult	ehāna (f)	إهانة
to insult (vt)	ahān	أهان
insulted (adj)	mohān	مهان
resentment	esteyāʾ (m)	إستياء
to offend (vt)	ahān	أهان
to take offence	estāʾ	إستاء
indignation	saχṭ (m)	سخط
to be indignant	estāʾ	إستاء
complaint	ʃakwa (f)	شكوَى
to complain (vi, vt)	ʃaka	شكا
apology	eʿtezār (m)	إعتذار
to apologize (vi)	eʿtazar	إعتذر
to beg pardon	eʿtazar	إعتذر
criticism	naqd (m)	نقد
to criticize (vt)	naqad	نقد
accusation (charge)	ettehām (m)	إتّهام
to accuse (vt)	ettaham	إتّهم
revenge	enteqām (m)	إنتقام
to avenge (get revenge)	entaqam	إنتقم
to pay back	radd	ردّ
disdain	ezderāʾ (m)	إزدراء
to despise (vt)	eḥtaqar	إحتقر
hatred, hate	korh (f)	كره
to hate (vt)	kereh	كره
nervous (adj)	ʿaṣaby	عصبي
to be nervous	etwattar	إتوّتر
angry (mad)	ɣaḍbān	غضبان
to make angry	narfez	نرفز
humiliation	ezlāl (m)	إذلال
to humiliate (vt)	zallel	ذلّل
to humiliate oneself	tazallal	تذلّل
shock	ṣadma (f)	صدمة
to shock (vt)	ṣadam	صدم
trouble (e.g. serious ~)	moʃkela (f)	مشكلة

unpleasant (adj)	karīh	كريه
fear (dread)	χofe (m)	خوف
terrible (storm, heat)	ʃedīd	شديد
scary (e.g. ~ story)	moχīf	مخيف
horror	ro'b (m)	رعب
awful (crime, news)	baʃe'	بشع
to begin to tremble	erta'aʃ	إرتعش
to cry (weep)	baka	بكى
to start crying	bada' yebky	بدأ يبكي
tear	dama'a (f)	دمعة
fault	ɣalṭa (f)	غلطة
guilt (feeling)	zanb (m)	ذنب
dishonor (disgrace)	'ār (m)	عار
protest	eḥtegāg (m)	إحتجاج
stress	tawattor (m)	توتّر
to disturb (vt)	az'ag	أزعج
to be furious	ɣeḍeb	غضب
angry (adj)	ɣaḍbān	غضبان
to end (~ a relationship)	anha	أنهى
to swear (at sb)	ʃatam	شتم
to scare (become afraid)	χāf	خاف
to hit (strike with hand)	ḍarab	ضرب
to fight (street fight, etc.)	χāne'	خانق
to settle (a conflict)	sawwa	سوّى
discontented (adj)	meʃ rāḍy	مش راضي
furious (adj)	ɣaḍbān	غضبان
It's not good!	keda meʃ kwayes!	!كده مش كويّس
It's bad!	keda weḥeʃ!	كده وحش!

Medicine

71. Diseases

illness	maraḍ (m)	مرض
to be ill	mereḍ	مرِض
health	ṣeḥḥa (f)	صحّة
runny nose (coryza)	raʃ-ḥ fel anf (m)	رشح في الأنف
tonsillitis	eltehāb el lawzateyn (m)	إلتهاب اللوزتين
cold (illness)	zokām (m)	زكام
to catch a cold	gālo bard	جاله برد
bronchitis	eltehāb ʃoʻaby (m)	إلتهاب شعبيّ
pneumonia	eltehāb ra'awy (m)	إلتهاب رئوي
flu, influenza	influenza (f)	إنفلونزا
shortsighted (adj)	'aṣīr el naẓar	قصير النظر
longsighted (adj)	beʻīd el naẓar	بعيد النظر
strabismus (crossed eyes)	ḥawal (m)	حوَل
squint-eyed (adj)	aḥwal	أحوَل
cataract	katarakt (f)	كاتاراكت
glaucoma	glawkoma (f)	جلوكوما
stroke	sakta (f)	سكتة
heart attack	azma 'albiya (f)	أزمة قلبية
myocardial infarction	nawba 'albiya (f)	نوبة قلبية
paralysis	ʃalal (m)	شلل
to paralyse (vt)	ʃall	شلّ
allergy	ḥasasiya (f)	حساسيّة
asthma	rabw (m)	ربو
diabetes	dā' el sokkary (m)	داء السكّري
toothache	alam asnān (m)	ألم الأسنان
caries	naχr el asnān (m)	نخر الأسنان
diarrhoea	es-hāl (m)	إسهال
constipation	emsāk (m)	إمساك
stomach upset	edṭrāb el meʻda (m)	إضطراب المعدة
food poisoning	tasammom (m)	تسمم
to get food poisoning	etsammem	إتسمّم
arthritis	eltehāb el mafāṣel (m)	إلتهاب المفاصل
rickets	kosāḥ el aṭfāl (m)	كساح الأطفال
rheumatism	rheumatism (m)	روماتزم
atherosclerosis	taṣṣallob el ʃarayīn (m)	تصلّب الشرايين
gastritis	eltehāb el meʻda (m)	إلتهاب المعدة
appendicitis	eltehāb el zayda el dūdiya (m)	إلتهاب الزائدة الدودية

cholecystitis	eltehāb el marāra (m)	إلتهاب المرارة
ulcer	qorḥa (f)	قرحة
measles	maraḍ el ḥaṣba (m)	مرض الحصبة
rubella (German measles)	el ḥaṣba el almaniya (f)	الحصبة الألمانية
jaundice	yaraqān (m)	يرقان
hepatitis	eltehāb el kabed el vayrūsy (m)	إلتهاب الكبد الفيروسي
schizophrenia	fuṣām (m)	فصام
rabies (hydrophobia)	dāʾ el kalb (m)	داء الكلب
neurosis	eḍṭrāb ʿaṣaby (m)	إضطراب عصبي
concussion	ertegāg el moχ (m)	إرتجاج المخ
cancer	saraṭān (m)	سرطان
sclerosis	taṣṣallob (m)	تصلّب
multiple sclerosis	taṣṣallob motaʿadded (m)	تصلّب متعدّد
alcoholism	edmān el χamr (m)	إدمان الخمر
alcoholic (n)	modmen el χamr (m)	مدمن الخمر
syphilis	syfilis el zehry (m)	سفلس الزهري
AIDS	el eydz (m)	الايدز
tumour	waram (m)	ورم
malignant (adj)	χabīs	خبيث
benign (adj)	ḥamīd (m)	حميد
fever	ḥomma (f)	حمّى
malaria	malaria (f)	ملاريا
gangrene	ɣanɣarīna (f)	غنغرينا
seasickness	dawār el baḥr (m)	دوار البحر
epilepsy	maraḍ el ṣaraʿ (m)	مرض الصرع
epidemic	wabāʾ (m)	وباء
typhus	tyfus (m)	تيفوس
tuberculosis	maraḍ el soll (m)	مرض السلّ
cholera	kōlīra (f)	كوليرا
plague (bubonic ~)	ṭaʿūn (m)	طاعون

72. Symptoms. Treatments. Part 1

symptom	ʿaraḍ (m)	عرض
temperature	ḥarāra (f)	حرارة
high temperature (fever)	ḥomma (f)	حمّى
pulse (heartbeat)	nabḍ (m)	نبض
dizziness (vertigo)	dawχa (f)	دوخة
hot (adj)	soχn	سخن
shivering	raʿʃa (f)	رعشة
pale (e.g. ~ face)	aṣfar	أصفر
cough	koḥḥa (f)	كحّة
to cough (vi)	kaḥḥ	كحّ
to sneeze (vi)	ʿaṭas	عطس

faint	dawχa (f)	دوخة
to faint (vi)	oɣma ʿaleyh	أغمي عليه
bruise (hématome)	kadma (f)	كدمة
bump (lump)	tawarrom (m)	تورّم
to bang (bump)	etχabaṭ	إتخبط
contusion (bruise)	raḍḍa (f)	رضّة
to get a bruise	etkadam	إتكدم
to limp (vi)	ʿarag	عرج
dislocation	χalʿ (m)	خلع
to dislocate (vt)	χalaʿ	خلع
fracture	kasr (m)	كسر
to have a fracture	enkasar	إنكسر
cut (e.g. paper ~)	garḥ (m)	جرح
to cut oneself	garaḥ nafsoh	جرح نفسه
bleeding	nazīf (m)	نزيف
burn (injury)	ḥarʾ (m)	حرق
to get burned	et-ḥaraʾ	إتحرق
to prick (vt)	waχaz	وخز
to prick oneself	waχaz nafso	وخز نفسه
to injure (vt)	aṣāb	أصاب
injury	eṣāba (f)	إصابة
wound	garḥ (m)	جرح
trauma	ṣadma (f)	صدمة
to be delirious	haza	هذى
to stutter (vi)	talaʿsam	تلعثم
sunstroke	ḍarabet ʃams (f)	ضربة شمس

73. Symptoms. Treatments. Part 2

pain, ache	alam (m)	ألم
splinter (in foot, etc.)	ʃazya (f)	شظية
sweat (perspiration)	ʿerʾ (m)	عرق
to sweat (perspire)	ʿereʾ	عرق
vomiting	targeeʿ (m)	ترجيع
convulsions	taʃonnogāt (pl)	تشنّجات
pregnant (adj)	ḥāmel	حامل
to be born	etwalad	اتوّلد
delivery, labour	welāda (f)	ولادة
to deliver (~ a baby)	walad	ولد
abortion	eg-hāḍ (m)	إجهاض
breathing, respiration	tanaffos (m)	تنفّس
in-breath (inhalation)	estenʃāq (m)	إستنشاق
out-breath (exhalation)	zafīr (m)	زفير
to exhale (breathe out)	zafar	زفر
to inhale (vi)	estanʃaq	إستنشق

disabled person	moʿāq (m)	معاق
cripple	moqʿad (m)	مقعد
drug addict	modmen moχaddarāt (m)	مدمن مخدّرات
deaf (adj)	aṭraʃ	أطرش
mute (adj)	aχras	أخرس
deaf mute (adj)	aṭraʃ aχras	أطرش أخرس
mad, insane (adj)	magnūn	مجنون
madman (demented person)	magnūn (m)	مجنون
madwoman	magnūna (f)	مجنونة
to go insane	etgannen	اتجنّن
gene	ʒīn (m)	جين
immunity	manāʿa (f)	مناعة
hereditary (adj)	werāsy	وراثي
congenital (adj)	χolqy men el welāda	خلقي من الولادة
virus	virūs (m)	فيروس
microbe	mikrūb (m)	ميكروب
bacterium	garsūma (f)	جرثومة
infection	ʿadwa (f)	عدوى

74. Symptoms. Treatments. Part 3

hospital	mostaʃfa (m)	مستشفى
patient	marīḍ (m)	مريض
diagnosis	taʃχīṣ (m)	تشخيص
cure	ʃefāʾ (m)	شفاء
medical treatment	ʿelāg ṭebby (m)	علاج طبي
to get treatment	etʿāleg	اتعالج
to treat (~ a patient)	ʿālag	عالج
to nurse (look after)	marraḍ	مرّض
care (nursing ~)	ʿenāya (f)	عناية
operation, surgery	ʿamaliya grāḥiya (f)	عمليّة جراحية
to bandage (head, limb)	ḍammad	ضمّد
bandaging	taḍmīd (m)	تضميد
vaccination	talqīḥ (m)	تلقيح
to vaccinate (vt)	laqqaḥ	لقّح
injection	ḥoʾna (f)	حقنة
to give an injection	ḥaʾan ebra	حقن إبرة
attack	nawba (f)	نوبة
amputation	batr (m)	بتر
to amputate (vt)	batr	بتر
coma	γaybūba (f)	غيبوبة
to be in a coma	kān fi ḥālet γaybūba	كان في حالة غيبوبة
intensive care	el ʿenāya el morakkaza (f)	العناية المركّزة
to recover (~ from flu)	ʃefy	شفي
condition (patient's ~)	ḥāla (f)	حالة

consciousness	waʿy (m)	وعي
memory (faculty)	zākera (f)	ذاكرة
to pull out (tooth)	χalaʿ	خلع
filling	ḥaʃww (m)	حشو
to fill (a tooth)	ḥaʃa	حشا
hypnosis	el tanwīm el meɣnaṭīsy (m)	التنويم المغناطيسى
to hypnotize (vt)	nawwem	نوّم

75. Doctors

doctor	doktore (m)	دكتور
nurse	momarreḍa (f)	ممرّضة
personal doctor	doktore ʃaχṣy (m)	دكتور شخصي
dentist	doktore asnān (m)	دكتور أسنان
optician	doktore el ʿoyūn (m)	دكتور العيون
general practitioner	ṭabīb baṭna (m)	طبيب باطنة
surgeon	garrāḥ (m)	جرّاح
psychiatrist	doktore nafsāny (m)	دكتور نفساني
paediatrician	doktore aṭfāl (m)	دكتور أطفال
psychologist	aχeṣāʾy ʿelm el nafs (m)	أخصائي علم النفس
gynaecologist	doktore nesa (m)	دكتور نسا
cardiologist	doktore ʾalb (m)	دكتور قلب

76. Medicine. Drugs. Accessories

medicine, drug	dawāʾ (m)	دواء
remedy	ʿelāg (m)	علاج
to prescribe (vt)	waṣaf	وصف
prescription	waṣfa (f)	وصفة
tablet, pill	ʾorṣ (m)	قرص
ointment	marham (m)	مرهم
ampoule	ambūla (f)	أمبولة
mixture, solution	dawāʾ ʃorb (m)	دواء شراب
syrup	ʃarāb (m)	شراب
capsule	ḥabba (f)	حبّة
powder	zorūr (m)	ذرور
gauze bandage	ḍammāda ʃāʃ (f)	ضمادة شاش
cotton wool	ʾoṭn (m)	قطن
iodine	yūd (m)	يود
plaster	blaster (m)	بلاستر
eyedropper	ʾaṭṭāra (f)	قطّارة
thermometer	termometr (m)	ترمومتر
syringe	serennga (f)	سرنّجة
wheelchair	korsy motaḥarrek (m)	كرسي متحرك
crutches	ʿokkāz (m)	عكّاز

painkiller	mosakken (m)	مسكّن
laxative	molayen (m)	مليّن
spirits (ethanol)	etanol (m)	إيثانول
medicinal herbs	a'ʃāb ṭebbiya (pl)	أعشاب طبّية
herbal (~ tea)	'oʃby	عشبي

77. Smoking. Tobacco products

tobacco	tabɣ (m)	تبغ
cigarette	segāra (f)	سيجارة
cigar	segār (m)	سيجار
pipe	ɣelyone (m)	غليون
packet (of cigarettes)	'elba (f)	علبة
matches	kebrīt (m)	كبريت
matchbox	'elbet kebrīt (f)	علبة كبريت
lighter	wallā'a (f)	ولّاعة
ashtray	ṭa'ṭū'a (f)	طقطوقة
cigarette case	'elbet sagāyer (f)	علبة سجائر
cigarette holder	ḥamelet segāra (f)	حاملة سيجارة
filter (cigarette tip)	filter (m)	فلتر
to smoke (vi, vt)	dakχen	دخّن
to light a cigarette	walla' segāra	ولّع سيجارة
smoking	tadχīn (m)	تدخين
smoker	modakχen (m)	مدخّن
cigarette end	'aqab segāra (m)	عقب سيجارة
smoke, fumes	dokχān (m)	دخّان
ash	ramād (m)	رماد

HUMAN HABITAT

City

78. City. Life in the city

city, town	madīna (f)	مدينة
capital city	ʿāṣema (f)	عاصمة
village	qarya (f)	قرية
city map	xarīṭet el madinah (f)	خريطة المدينة
city centre	wesṭ el balad (m)	وسط البلد
suburb	ḍāḥeya (f)	ضاحية
suburban (adj)	el ḍawāḥy	الضواحي
outskirts	aṭrāf el madīna (pl)	أطراف المدينة
environs (suburbs)	ḍawāḥy el madīna (pl)	ضواحي المدينة
city block	ḥayī (m)	حي
residential block (area)	ḥayī sakany (m)	حي سكني
traffic	ḥaraket el morūr (f)	حركة المرور
traffic lights	eʃārāt el morūr (pl)	إشارات المرور
public transport	wasāʾel el naʾl (pl)	وسائل النقل
crossroads	taqāṭoʿ (m)	تقاطع
zebra crossing	maʿbar (m)	معبر
pedestrian subway	nafaʾ moʃāh (m)	نفق مشاه
to cross (~ the street)	ʿabar	عبر
pedestrian	māʃy (m)	ماشي
pavement	raṣīf (m)	رصيف
bridge	kobry (m)	كبري
embankment (river walk)	korneyʃ (m)	كورنيش
fountain	nafūra (f)	نافورة
allée (garden walkway)	mamʃa (m)	ممشى
park	ḥadīqa (f)	حديقة
boulevard	bolvār (m)	بولفار
square	medān (m)	ميدان
avenue (wide street)	ʃāreʿ (m)	شارع
street	ʃāreʿ (m)	شارع
side street	zoʾāʾ (m)	زقاق
dead end	ṭarīʾ masdūd (m)	طريق مسدود
house	beyt (m)	بيت
building	mabna (m)	مبنى
skyscraper	nāṭeḥet sahāb (f)	ناطحة سحاب
facade	waɣa (f)	واجهة
roof	saʾf (m)	سقف

window	ʃebbāk (m)	شبّاك
arch	qose (m)	قوس
column	ʿamūd (m)	عمود
corner	zawya (f)	زاوية
shop window	vatrīna (f)	فترينة
signboard (store sign, etc.)	yafṭa, lāfeta (f)	لافتة, يافطة
poster (e.g., playbill)	boster (m)	بوستر
advertising poster	boster eʿlān (m)	بوستر إعلان
hoarding	lawḥet eʿlanāt (f)	لوحة إعلانات
rubbish	zebāla (f)	زبالة
rubbish bin	ṣandūʾ zebāla (m)	صندوق زبالة
to litter (vi)	rama zebāla	رمى زبالة
rubbish dump	mazbala (f)	مزبلة
telephone box	koʃk telefōn (m)	كشك تليفون
lamppost	ʿamūd nūr (m)	عمود نور
bench (park ~)	korsy (m)	كرسي
police officer	ʃorṭy (m)	شرطي
police	ʃorṭa (f)	شرطة
beggar	ʃaḥḥāt (m)	شحّات
homeless (n)	motaʃarred (m)	متشرّد

79. Urban institutions

shop	maḥal (m)	محل
chemist, pharmacy	ṣaydaliya (f)	صيدليّة
optician (spectacles shop)	maḥal naḍḍārāt (m)	محل نضّارات
shopping centre	mole (m)	مول
supermarket	subermarket (m)	سوبرماركت
bakery	maχbaz (m)	مخبز
baker	χabbāz (m)	خبّاز
cake shop	ḥalawāny (m)	حلواني
grocery shop	baʾʾāla (f)	بقّالة
butcher shop	gezāra (f)	جزارة
greengrocer	dokkān χoḍār (m)	دكّان خضار
market	sūʾ (f)	سوق
coffee bar	ʾahwa (f), kaféih (m)	قهوة, كافيه
restaurant	maṭʿam (m)	مطعم
pub, bar	bār (m)	بار
pizzeria	maḥal pizza (m)	محل بيتزا
hairdresser	ṣalone ḥelāʾa (m)	صالون حلاقة
post office	maktab el barīd (m)	مكتب البريد
dry cleaners	dray klīn (m)	دراي كلين
photo studio	estudio taṣwīr (m)	إستوديو تصوير
shoe shop	maḥal gezam (m)	محل جزم
bookshop	maḥal kotob (m)	محل كتب

sports shop	maḥal mostalzamāt reyaḍiya (m)	محل مستلزمات رياضية
clothes repair shop	maḥal χeyāṭet malābes (m)	محل خياطة ملابس
formal wear hire	ta'gīr malābes rasmiya (m)	تأجير ملابس رسمية
video rental shop	maḥal ta'gīr video (m)	محل تأجير فيديو
circus	serk (m)	سيرك
zoo	ḥadīqet el ḥayawān (f)	حديقة حيوان
cinema	sinema (f)	سينما
museum	mat-ḥaf (m)	متحف
library	maktaba (f)	مكتبة
theatre	masraḥ (m)	مسرح
opera (opera house)	obra (f)	أوبرا
nightclub	malha leyly (m)	ملهى ليّلي
casino	kazino (m)	كازينو
mosque	masged (m)	مسجد
synagogue	kenīs (m)	كنيس
cathedral	katedra'iya (f)	كاتدرائية
temple	ma'bad (m)	معبد
church	kenīsa (f)	كنيسة
college	kolliya (m)	كليّة
university	gam'a (f)	جامعة
school	madrasa (f)	مدرسة
prefecture	moqaṭ'a (f)	مقاطعة
town hall	baladiya (f)	بلديّة
hotel	fondo' (m)	فندق
bank	bank (m)	بنك
embassy	safāra (f)	سفارة
travel agency	ʃerket seyāḥa (f)	شركة سياحة
information office	maktab el este'lāmāt (m)	مكتب الإستعلامات
currency exchange	ṣarrāfa (f)	صرّافة
underground, tube	metro (m)	مترو
hospital	mostaʃfa (m)	مستشفى
petrol station	maḥaṭṭet banzīn (f)	محطّة بنزين
car park	maw'ef el 'arabeyāt (m)	موقف العربيات

80. Signs

signboard (store sign, etc.)	yafṭa, lāfeta (f)	لافتة, يافطة
notice (door sign, etc.)	bayān (m)	بيان
poster	boster (m)	بوستر
direction sign	'alāmet (f)	علامة إتجاه
arrow (sign)	'alāmet eʃāra (f)	علامة إشارة
caution	taḥzīr (m)	تحذير
warning sign	lāfetat taḥzīr (f)	لافتة تحذير
to warn (vt)	ḥazzar	حذّر

rest day (weekly ~)	yome ʿoṭla (m)	يوم عطلة
timetable (schedule)	gadwal (m)	جدوّل
opening hours	aw'āt el ʿamal (pl)	أوقات العمل
WELCOME!	ahlan w sahlan!	!أهلاً وسهلا
ENTRANCE	doχūl	دخول
WAY OUT	χorūg	خروج
PUSH	edfaʿ	إدفع
PULL	es-ḥab	إسحب
OPEN	maftūḥ	مفتوح
CLOSED	moɣlaq	مغلق
WOMEN	lel sayedāt	للسيدات
MEN	lel regāl	للرجال
DISCOUNTS	χoṣomāt	خصومات
SALE	taχfeḍāt	تخفيضات
NEW!	gedīd!	!جديد
FREE	maggānan	مجّاناً
ATTENTION!	entebāh!	!إنتباه
NO VACANCIES	koll el amāken maḥgūza	كلّ الأماكن محجوزة
RESERVED	maḥgūz	محجوز
ADMINISTRATION	edāra	إدارة
STAFF ONLY	lel ʿamelīn faqaṭ	للعاملين فقط
BEWARE OF THE DOG!	eḥzar wogūd kalb	إحذر وجود الكلب
NO SMOKING	mamnūʿ el tadχīn	ممنوع التدخين
DO NOT TOUCH!	ʿadam el lams	عدم اللمس
DANGEROUS	χaṭīr	خطير
DANGER	χaṭar	خطر
HIGH VOLTAGE	tayār ʿāly	تيّار عالي
NO SWIMMING!	el sebāḥa mamnūʿa	السباحة ممنوعة
OUT OF ORDER	moʿaṭṭal	معطّل
FLAMMABLE	sareeʿ el eʃteʿāl	سريع الإشتعال
FORBIDDEN	mamnūʿ	ممنوع
NO TRESPASSING!	mamnūʿ el morūr	ممنوع المرور
WET PAINT	eḥzar ṭelāʾ ɣayr gāf	احذر طلاء غير جاف

81. Urban transport

bus, coach	buṣ (m)	باص
tram	trām (m)	ترام
trolleybus	trolly buṣ (m)	ترولي باص
route (bus ~)	χaṭṭ (m)	خطّ
number (e.g. bus ~)	raqam (m)	رقم
to go by …	rāḥ be …	... راح بـ
to get on (~ the bus)	rekeb	ركب
to get off …	nezel men	نزل من

stop (e.g. bus ~)	maw'af (m)	موّقف
next stop	el maḥaṭṭa el gaya (f)	المحطة الجايّة
terminus	'āχer maw'af (m)	آخر موقف
timetable	gadwal (m)	جدوّل
to wait (vt)	estanna	إستنّى
ticket	tazkara (f)	تذكرة
fare	ogra (f)	أجرة
cashier (ticket seller)	kaʃier (m)	كاشيير
ticket inspection	taftīʃ el tazāker (m)	تفتيش التذاكر
ticket inspector	mofatteʃ tazāker (m)	مفتّش تذاكر
to be late (for …)	met'akχer	متأخّر
to miss (~ the train, etc.)	ta'akχar	تأخّر
to be in a hurry	mesta'gel	مستعجل
taxi, cab	taksi (m)	تاكسي
taxi driver	sawwā' taksi (m)	سوّاق تاكسي
by taxi	bel taksi	بالتاكسي
taxi rank	maw'ef taksi (m)	موّقف تاكسي
to call a taxi	kallem taksi	كلّم تاكسي
to take a taxi	aχad taksi	أخد تاكسي
traffic	ḥaraket el morūr (f)	حركة المرور
traffic jam	zaḥmet el morūr (f)	زحمة المرور
rush hour	sā'et el zorwa (f)	ساعة الذروة
to park (vi)	rakan	ركن
to park (vt)	rakan	ركن
car park	maw'ef el 'arabeyāt (m)	موقف العربيات
underground, tube	metro (m)	مترو
station	maḥaṭṭa (f)	محطّة
to take the tube	aχad el metro	أخد المترو
train	qeṭār, 'aṭṭr (m)	قطار
train station	maḥaṭṭet qeṭār (f)	محطّة قطار

82. Sightseeing

monument	temsāl (m)	تمثال
fortress	'al'a (f)	قلعة
palace	'aṣr (m)	قصر
castle	'al'a (f)	قلعة
tower	borg (m)	برج
mausoleum	ḍarīḥ (m)	ضريح
architecture	handasa me'māriya (f)	هندسة معمارية
medieval (adj)	men el qorūn el wosṭa	من القرون الوسطى
ancient (adj)	'atīq	عتيق
national (adj)	waṭany	وطني
famous (monument, etc.)	maʃ-hūr	مشهور
tourist	sā'eḥ (m)	سائح
guide (person)	morʃed (m)	مرشد

excursion, sightseeing tour	gawla (f)	جولة
to show (vt)	warra	ورّى
to tell (vt)	ʾāl	قال
to find (vt)	laʾa	لقى
to get lost (lose one's way)	ḍāʿ	ضاع
map (e.g. underground ~)	χarīṭa (f)	خريطة
map (e.g. city ~)	χarīṭa (f)	خريطة
souvenir, gift	tezkār (m)	تذكار
gift shop	maḥal hadāya (m)	محل هدايا
to take pictures	ṣawwar	صوّر
to have one's picture taken	etṣawwar	إتصوّر

83. Shopping

to buy (purchase)	eʃtara	إشترى
shopping	ḥāga (f)	حاجة
to go shopping	eʃtara	إشترى
shopping	ʃobbing (m)	شوبينج
to be open (ab. shop)	maftūḥ	مفتوح
to be closed	moɣlaq	مغلق
footwear, shoes	gezam (pl)	جزم
clothes, clothing	malābes (pl)	ملابس
cosmetics	mawād tagmīl (pl)	مواد تجميل
food products	akl (m)	أكل
gift, present	hediya (f)	هديّة
shop assistant (masc.)	bayāʿ (m)	بيّاع
shop assistant (fem.)	bayāʿa (f)	بيّاعة
cash desk	ṣandūʾ el dafʿ (m)	صندوق الدفع
mirror	merāya (f)	مراية
counter (shop ~)	manḍada (f)	منضدة
fitting room	ɣorfet el ʾeyās (f)	غرفة القياس
to try on	garrab	جرّب
to fit (ab. dress, etc.)	nāseb	ناسب
to fancy (vt)	ʿagab	عجب
price	seʿr (m)	سعر
price tag	tiket el seʿr (m)	تيكت السعر
to cost (vt)	kallef	كلّف
How much?	bekām?	بكام؟
discount	χaṣm (m)	خصم
inexpensive (adj)	meʃ ɣāly	مش غالي
cheap (adj)	reχīṣ	رخيص
expensive (adj)	ɣāly	غالي
It's expensive	da ɣāly	ده غالي
hire (n)	esteʾgār (m)	إستئجار
to hire (~ a dinner jacket)	estʾgar	إستأجر

credit (trade credit)	e'temān (m)	إئتمان
on credit (adv)	bel ta'seeṭ	بالتقسيط

84. Money

money	folūs (pl)	فلوس
currency exchange	taḥwīl 'omla (m)	تحويل عملة
exchange rate	se'r el ṣarf (m)	سعر الصرف
cashpoint	makinet ṣarrāf 'āly (f)	ماكينة صرّاف آلي
coin	'erʃ (m)	قرش
dollar	dolār (m)	دولار
euro	yoro (m)	يورو
lira	lira (f)	ليرة
Deutschmark	el mark el almāny (m)	المارك الألماني
franc	frank (m)	فرنك
pound sterling	geneyh esterlīny (m)	جنيه استرليني
yen	yen (m)	ين
debt	deyn (m)	دين
debtor	modīn (m)	مدين
to lend (money)	sallef	سلّف
to borrow (vi, vt)	estalaf	إستلف
bank	bank (m)	بنك
account	ḥesāb (m)	حساب
to deposit (vt)	awda'	أودع
to deposit into the account	awda' fel ḥesāb	أوّدع في الحساب
to withdraw (vt)	saḥab men el ḥesāb	سحب من الحساب
credit card	kredit kard (f)	كريدت كارد
cash	kæʃ (m)	كاش
cheque	ʃīk (m)	شيك
to write a cheque	katab ʃīk	كتب شيك
chequebook	daftar ʃikāt (m)	دفتر شيكات
wallet	maḥfaẓa (f)	محفظة
purse	maḥfazet fakka (f)	محفظة فكّة
safe	χazzāna (f)	خزّانة
heir	wāres (m)	وارث
inheritance	werāsa (f)	وراثة
fortune (wealth)	sarwa (f)	ثروّة
lease	'a'd el egār (m)	عقد الإيجار
rent (money)	ogret el sakan (f)	أجرة السكن
to rent (sth from sb)	est'gar	إستأجر
price	se'r (m)	سعر
cost	taman (m)	ثمن
sum	mablaɣ (m)	مبلغ
to spend (vt)	ṣaraf	صرف
expenses	maṣarīf (pl)	مصاريف

to economize (vi, vt)	waffar	وفّر
economical	mowaffer	موّفر
to pay (vi, vt)	dafaʿ	دفع
payment	dafʿ (m)	دفع
change (give the ~)	el bāʾy (m)	الباقي
tax	ḍarība (f)	ضريبة
fine	ɣarāma (f)	غرامة
to fine (vt)	faraḍ ɣarāma	فرض غرامة

85. Post. Postal service

post office	maktab el barīd (m)	مكتب البريد
post (letters, etc.)	el barīd (m)	البريد
postman	sāʿy el barīd (m)	ساعي البريد
opening hours	awʾāt el ʿamal (pl)	أوقات العمل
letter	resāla (f)	رسالة
registered letter	resāla mosaggala (f)	رسالة مسجّلة
postcard	kart barīdy (m)	كرت بريدي
telegram	barqiya (f)	برقيّة
parcel	ṭard (m)	طرد
money transfer	ḥewāla māliya (f)	حوالة مالية
to receive (vt)	estalam	إستلم
to send (vt)	arsal	أرسل
sending	ersāl (m)	إرسال
address	ʿenwān (m)	عنوان
postcode	raqam el barīd (m)	رقم البريد
sender	morsel (m)	مرسل
receiver	morsel elayh (m)	مرسل إليه
name (first name)	esm (m)	اسم
surname (last name)	esm el ʿaʾela (m)	اسم العائلة
postage rate	taʿrīfa (f)	تعريفة
standard (adj)	ʿādy	عادي
economical (adj)	mowaffer	موّفر
weight	wazn (m)	وزن
to weigh (~ letters)	wazan	وزن
envelope	ẓarf (m)	ظرف
postage stamp	ṭābeʿ (m)	طابع
to stamp an envelope	alṣaq ṭābeʿ	ألصق طابع

Dwelling. House. Home

86. House. Dwelling

house	beyt (m)	بيت
at home (adv)	fel beyt	في البيت
yard	sāḥa (f)	ساحة
fence (iron ~)	sūr (m)	سور
brick (n)	ṭūb (m)	طوب
brick (as adj)	men el ṭūb	من الطوب
stone (n)	ḥagar (m)	حجر
stone (as adj)	ḥagary	حجري
concrete (n)	χarasāna (f)	خرسانة
concrete (as adj)	χarasāny	خرساني
new (new-built)	gedīd	جديد
old (adj)	ʾadīm	قديم
decrepit (house)	ʾāayel lel soqūṭ	آيل للسقوط
modern (adj)	moʿāṣer	معاصر
multistorey (adj)	motaʿadded el ṭawābeq	متعدّد الطوابق
tall (~ building)	ʿāly	عالي
floor, storey	dore (m)	دور
single-storey (adj)	zu ṭābeq wāḥed	ذو طابق واحد
ground floor	el dore el awwal (m)	الدور الأوّل
top floor	ṭābeʾ ʿolwy (m)	طابق علوي
roof	saʾf (m)	سقف
chimney	madχana (f)	مدخنة
roof tiles	qarmīd (m)	قرميد
tiled (adj)	men el qarmīd	من القرميد
loft (attic)	ʿelya (f)	علية
window	ʃebbāk (m)	شبّاك
glass	ezāz (m)	إزاز
window ledge	ḥāfet el ʃebbāk (f)	حافة الشبّاك
shutters	ʃīʃ (m)	شيش
wall	ḥeyṭa (f)	حيطة
balcony	balakona (f)	بلكونة
downpipe	masūret el taṣrīf (f)	ماسورة التصريف
upstairs (to be ~)	foʾe	فوق
to go upstairs	ṭeleʿ	طلع
to come down (the stairs)	nezel	نزل
to move (to new premises)	naʾal	نقل

87. House. Entrance. Lift

entrance	madχal (m)	مدخل
stairs (stairway)	sellem (m)	سلّم
steps	daragāt (pl)	درجات
banisters	drabzīn (m)	درابزين
lobby (hotel ~)	ṣāla (f)	صالة
postbox	ṣandū' el barīd (m)	صندوق البريد
waste bin	ṣandū' el zebāla (m)	صندوق الزبالة
refuse chute	manfaz el zebāla (m)	منفذ الزبالة
lift	asanseyr (m)	اسانسير
goods lift	asanseyr el ʃaḥn (m)	اسانسير الشحن
lift cage	kabīna (f)	كابينة
to take the lift	rekeb el asanseyr	ركب الاسانسير
flat	ʃa''a (f)	شقّة
residents (~ of a building)	sokkān (pl)	سكّان
neighbour (masc.)	gār (m)	جار
neighbour (fem.)	gāra (f)	جارة
neighbours	gerān (pl)	جيران

88. House. Electricity

electricity	kahraba' (m)	كهرباء
light bulb	lammba (f)	لمّبة
switch	meftāḥ (m)	مفتاح
fuse (plug fuse)	fuse (m)	فيوز
cable, wire (electric ~)	selk (m)	سلك
wiring	aslāk (pl)	أسلاك
electricity meter	ʿaddād (m)	عدّاد
readings	qerā'a (f)	قراءة

89. House. Doors. Locks

door	bāb (m)	باب
gate (vehicle ~)	bawwāba (f)	بوّابة
handle, doorknob	okret el bāb (f)	اوكرة الباب
to unlock (unbolt)	fataḥ	فتح
to open (vt)	fataḥ	فتح
to close (vt)	'afal	قفل
key	meftāḥ (m)	مفتاح
bunch (of keys)	rabṭa (f)	ربطة
to creak (door, etc.)	ṣarr	صر
creak	ṣarīr (m)	صرير
hinge (door ~)	mafaṣṣla (f)	مفصّلة
doormat	seggādet bāb (f)	سجّادة باب
door lock	'efl el bāb (m)	قفل الباب

keyhole	xorm el meftāḥ (m)	خرم المفتاح
crossbar (sliding bar)	terbās (m)	ترباس
door latch	terbās (m)	ترباس
padlock	'efl (m)	قفل
to ring (~ the door bell)	rann	رنّ
ringing (sound)	ranīn (m)	رنين
doorbell	garas (m)	جرس
doorbell button	zerr (m)	زر
knock (at the door)	ṭar', da'' (m)	طرق, دقّ
to knock (vi)	xabbaṭ	خبّط
code	kōd (m)	كود
combination lock	kōd (m)	كود
intercom	garas el bāb (m)	جرس الباب
number (on the door)	raqam (m)	رقم
doorplate	lawḥa (f)	لوحة
peephole	el 'eyn el seḥriya (m)	العين السحرية

90. Country house

village	qarya (f)	قرية
vegetable garden	bostān xoḍār (m)	بستان خضار
fence	sūr (m)	سور
picket fence	sūr (m)	سور
wicket gate	bawwāba far'iya (f)	بوّابة فرعيّة
granary	ʃouna (f)	شونة
cellar	serdāb (m)	سرداب
shed (garden ~)	sa'īfa (f)	سقيفة
water well	bīr (m)	بير
stove (wood-fired ~)	forn (m)	فرن
to stoke the stove	awqad el botogāz	أوقد البوتاجاز
firewood	ḥaṭab (m)	حطب
log (firewood)	'eṭ'et ḥaṭab (f)	قطعة حطب
veranda	varannda (f)	فاراندة
deck (terrace)	ʃorfa (f)	شرفة
stoop (front steps)	sellem (m)	سلّم
swing (hanging seat)	morgeyḥa (f)	مرجيحة

91. Villa. Mansion

country house	villa rīfiya (f)	فيلا ريفيّة
country-villa	villa (f)	فيلا
wing (~ of a building)	genāḥ (m)	جناح
garden	geneyna (f)	جنينة
park	ḥadīqa (f)	حديقة
conservatory (greenhouse)	dafī'a (f)	دفيئة
to look after (garden, etc.)	ehtamm	إهتمّ

swimming pool	ḥammām sebāḥa (m)	حمّام سباحة
gym (home gym)	gīm (m)	جيم
tennis court	malʿab tennis (m)	ملعب تنسّ
home theater (room)	sinema manzeliya (f)	سينما منزليّة
garage	garāʒ (m)	جراج
private property	melkiya χāṣa (f)	ملكيّة خاصّة
private land	arḍ χāṣa (m)	أرض خاصّة
warning (caution)	taḥzīr (m)	تحذير
warning sign	lāfetat taḥzīr (f)	لافتة تحذير
security	ḥerāsa (f)	حراسة
security guard	ḥāres amn (m)	حارس أمن
burglar alarm	gehāz enzār (m)	جهاز إنذار

92. Castle. Palace

castle	ʾalʿa (f)	قلعة
palace	ʾaṣr (m)	قصر
fortress	ʾalʿa (f)	قلعة
wall (round castle)	sūr (m)	سور
tower	borg (m)	برج
keep, donjon	borbg raʾīsy (m)	برج رئيسي
portcullis	bāb motaḥarrek (m)	باب متحرّك
subterranean passage	serdāb (m)	سرداب
moat	χondoq māʾy (m)	خندق مائي
chain	selsela (f)	سلسلة
arrow loop	mozɣal (m)	مزغل
magnificent (adj)	rāʾeʿ	رائع
majestic (adj)	mohīb	مهيب
impregnable (adj)	maneeʿ	منيع
medieval (adj)	men el qorūn el wosṭa	من القرون الوسطى

93. Flat

flat	ʃaʾʾa (f)	شقّة
room	oḍa (f)	أوضة
bedroom	oḍet el nome (f)	أوضة النوم
dining room	oḍet el sofra (f)	أوضة السفرة
living room	oḍet el esteqbāl (f)	أوضة الإستقبال
study (home office)	maktab (m)	مكتب
entry room	madχal (m)	مدخل
bathroom	ḥammām (m)	حمّام
water closet	ḥammām (m)	حمّام
ceiling	saʾf (m)	سقف
floor	arḍiya (f)	أرضية
corner	zawya (f)	زاوية

94. Flat. Cleaning

to clean (vi, vt)	naḍḍaf	نظّف
to put away (to stow)	ʃāl	شال
dust	ɣobār (m)	غبار
dusty (adj)	meɣabbar	مغبّر
to dust (vt)	masaḥ el ɣobār	مسح الغبار
vacuum cleaner	maknasa kahraba'iya (f)	مكنسة كهربائيّة
to vacuum (vt)	naḍḍaf be maknasa kahrabā'iya	نظّف بمكنسة كهربائيّة
to sweep (vi, vt)	kanas	كنس
sweepings	qomāma (f)	قمامة
order	nezām (m)	نظام
disorder, mess	fawḍa (m)	فوضى
mop	ʃarʃūba (f)	شرشوبة
duster	mamsaḥa (f)	ممسحة
short broom	ma'sʃa (f)	مقشّة
dustpan	lammāma (f)	لمّامة

95. Furniture. Interior

furniture	asās (m)	أثاث
table	maktab (m)	مكتب
chair	korsy (m)	كرسي
bed	serīr (m)	سرير
sofa, settee	kanaba (f)	كنبة
armchair	korsy (m)	كرسي
bookcase	χazzānet kotob (f)	خزّانة كتب
shelf	raff (m)	رفّ
wardrobe	dolāb (m)	دولاب
coat rack (wall-mounted ~)	ʃammāʿa (f)	شمّاعة
coat stand	ʃammāʿa (f)	شمّاعة
chest of drawers	dolāb adrāg (m)	دولاب أدراج
coffee table	ṭarabeyzet el 'ahwa (f)	طرابيزة القهوة
mirror	merāya (f)	مراية
carpet	seggāda (f)	سجّادة
small carpet	seggāda (f)	سجّادة
fireplace	daffāya (f)	دفّاية
candle	ʃamʿa (f)	شمعة
candlestick	ʃamʿadān (m)	شمعدان
drapes	satā'er (pl)	ستائر
wallpaper	wara' ḥā'eṭ (m)	ورق حائط
blinds (jalousie)	satā'er ofoqiya (pl)	ستائر أفقيّة
table lamp	abāʒūr (f)	اباجورة
wall lamp (sconce)	lammbet ḥā'eṭ (f)	لمّبة حائط

standard lamp	meṣbāḥ arḍy (m)	مصباح أرضي
chandelier	nagafa (f)	نجفة
leg (of a chair, table)	regl (f)	رجل
armrest	masnad (m)	مسند
back (backrest)	masnad (m)	مسند
drawer	dorg (m)	درج

96. Bedding

bedclothes	bayāḍāt el serīr (pl)	بياضات السرير
pillow	maχadda (f)	مخدّة
pillowslip	kīs el maχadda (m)	كيس المخدّة
duvet	leḥāf (m)	لحاف
sheet	melāya (f)	ملاية
bedspread	ɣaṭā' el serīr (m)	غطاء السرير

97. Kitchen

kitchen	maṭbaχ (m)	مطبخ
gas	ɣāz (m)	غاز
gas cooker	botoɣāz (m)	بوتوغاز
electric cooker	forn kaharabā'y (m)	فرن كهربائي
oven	forn (m)	فرن
microwave oven	mikroweyv (m)	ميكروويف
refrigerator	tallāga (f)	ثلاجة
freezer	freyzer (m)	فريزر
dishwasher	ɣassālet aṭbā' (f)	غسّالة أطباق
mincer	farrāmet laḥm (f)	فرّامة لحم
juicer	'aṣṣāra (f)	عصّارة
toaster	maḥmaṣet χobz (f)	محمصة خبز
mixer	χallāṭ (m)	خلّاط
coffee machine	makinet ṣon' el 'ahwa (f)	ماكينة صنع القهوة
coffee pot	ɣallāya kahraba'iya (f)	غلّاية القهوة
coffee grinder	maṭ-ḥanet 'ahwa (f)	مطحنة قهوة
kettle	ɣallāya (f)	غلّاية
teapot	barrād el ʃāy (m)	برّاد الشاي
lid	ɣaṭā' (m)	غطاء
tea strainer	maṣfāh el ʃāy (f)	مصفاة الشاي
spoon	ma'la'a (f)	معلقة
teaspoon	ma'la'et ʃāy (f)	معلقة شاي
soup spoon	ma'la'a kebīra (f)	ملعقة كبيرة
fork	ʃawka (f)	شوكة
knife	sekkīna (f)	سكّينة
tableware (dishes)	awāny (pl)	أواني
plate (dinner ~)	ṭaba' (m)	طبق

saucer	ṭaba' fengān (m)	طبق فنجان
shot glass	kāsa (f)	كاسة
glass (tumbler)	kobbāya (f)	كوبّاية
cup	fengān (m)	فنجان
sugar bowl	sokkariya (f)	سكّريّة
salt cellar	mamlaḥa (f)	مملحة
pepper pot	mobhera (f)	مبهرة
butter dish	ṭaba' zebda (m)	طبق زبدة
stock pot (soup pot)	ḥalla (f)	حلّة
frying pan (skillet)	ṭāsa (f)	طاسة
ladle	maɣrafa (f)	مغرفة
colander	maṣfāh (f)	مصفاه
tray (serving ~)	ṣeniya (f)	صينيّة
bottle	ezāza (f)	إزازة
jar (glass)	barṭamān (m)	برطمان
tin (can)	kanz (m)	كانز
bottle opener	fattāḥa (f)	فتّاحة
tin opener	fattāḥa (f)	فتّاحة
corkscrew	barrīma (f)	بريّمة
filter	filter (m)	فلتر
to filter (vt)	ṣaffa	صفّى
waste (food ~, etc.)	zebāla (f)	زبالة
waste bin (kitchen ~)	ṣandū' el zebāla (m)	صندوق الزبالة

98. Bathroom

bathroom	ḥammām (m)	حمّام
water	meyāh (f)	مياه
tap	ḥanafiya (f)	حنفيّة
hot water	maya soxna (f)	مايّة سخنة
cold water	maya barda (f)	مايّة باردة
toothpaste	ma'gūn asnān (m)	معجون أسنان
to clean one's teeth	naḍḍaf el asnān	نظّف الأسنان
toothbrush	forʃet senān (f)	فرشة أسنان
to shave (vi)	ḥala'	حلق
shaving foam	raɣwa lel ḥelā'a (f)	رغوة للحلاقة
razor	mūs (m)	موس
to wash (one's hands, etc.)	ɣasal	غسل
to have a bath	estaḥamma	إستحمّى
shower	doʃ (m)	دوش
to have a shower	axad doʃ	أخد دوش
bath	banyo (m)	بانيو
toilet (toilet bowl)	twalet (m)	تواليت
sink (washbasin)	ḥoḍe (m)	حوض
soap	ṣabūn (m)	صابون

soap dish	ṣabbāna (f)	صبّانة
sponge	līfa (f)	ليفة
shampoo	ʃambū (m)	شامبو
towel	fūṭa (f)	فوطة
bathrobe	robe el ḥammām (m)	روب حمّام
laundry (laundering)	ɣasīl (m)	غسيل
washing machine	ɣassāla (f)	غسّالة
to do the laundry	ɣasal el malābes	غسل الملابس
washing powder	mas-ḥūʾ ɣasīl (m)	مسحوق غسيل

99. Household appliances

TV, telly	televizion (m)	تليفزيون
tape recorder	gehāz tasgīl (m)	جهاز تسجيل
video	ʾāla tasgīl video (f)	آلة تسجيل فيديو
radio	gehāz radio (m)	جهاز راديو
player (CD, MP3, etc.)	blayer (m)	بليير
video projector	gehāz ʿarḍ (m)	جهاز عرض
home cinema	sinema manzeliya (f)	سينما منزليّة
DVD player	dividī blayer (m)	دي في دي بليير
amplifier	mokabbaer el ṣote (m)	مكبّر الصوت
video game console	ʾātāry (m)	أتاري
video camera	kamera video (f)	كاميرا فيديو
camera (photo)	kamera (f)	كاميرا
digital camera	kamera diʒital (f)	كاميرا ديجيتال
vacuum cleaner	maknasa kahrabaʾiya (f)	مكنسة كهربائيّة
iron (e.g. steam ~)	makwa (f)	مكواة
ironing board	lawḥet kayī (f)	لوحة كيّ
telephone	telefon (m)	تليفون
mobile phone	mobile (m)	موبايل
typewriter	ʾāla katba (f)	آلة كاتبة
sewing machine	makanet el χeyāṭa (f)	مكنة الخياطة
microphone	mikrofon (m)	ميكروفون
headphones	sammaʿāt raʾsiya (pl)	سمّاعات رأسية
remote control (TV)	remowt kontrol (m)	ريموت كنترول
CD, compact disc	sidī (m)	سي دي
cassette, tape	kasett (m)	كاسيت
vinyl record	esṭewāna mūsīqa (f)	أسطوانة موسيقى

100. Repairs. Renovation

renovations	tagdīdāt (m)	تجديدات
to renovate (vt)	gadded	جدّد
to repair, to fix (vt)	ṣallaḥ	صلّح
to put in order	nazzam	نظّم

to redo (do again)	ʿād	عاد
paint	dehān (m)	دهان
to paint (~ a wall)	dahhen	دهّن
house painter	dahhān (m)	دهّان
paintbrush	forʃet dehān (f)	فرشاة الدهان
whitewash	maḥlūl mobayeḍ (m)	محلول مبيّض
to whitewash (vt)	beyḍ	بيّض
wallpaper	waraʾ ḥāʾeṭ (m)	ورق حائط
to wallpaper (vt)	laṣaq waraʾ el ḥāʾeṭ	لصق ورق الحائط
varnish	warnīʃ (m)	ورنيش
to varnish (vt)	ṭala bel warnīʃ	طلى بالورنيش

101. Plumbing

water	meyāh (f)	مياه
hot water	maya soχna (f)	مايّة سخنة
cold water	maya barda (f)	مايّة باردة
tap	ḥanafiya (f)	حنفيّة
drop (of water)	ʾaṭra (f)	قطرة
to drip (vi)	ʾaṭṭar	قطّر
to leak (ab. pipe)	sarrab	سرّب
leak (pipe ~)	tasarrob (m)	تسرب
puddle	berka (f)	بركة
pipe	masūra (f)	ماسورة
valve (e.g., ball ~)	ṣamām (m)	صمام
to be clogged up	kān masdūd	كان مسدود
tools	adawāt (pl)	أدوات
adjustable spanner	el meftāḥ el englīzy (m)	المفتاح الإنجليزي
to unscrew (lid, filter, etc.)	fataḥ	فتح
to screw (tighten)	aḥkam el ʃadd	أحكم الشدّ
to unclog (vt)	sallek	سلّك
plumber	samkary (m)	سمكري
basement	badrome (m)	بدروم
sewerage (system)	ʃabaket el magāry (f)	شبكة المجاري

102. Fire. Conflagration

fire (accident)	ḥarīʾ (m)	حريق
flame	lahab (m)	لهب
spark	ʃarāra (f)	شرارة
smoke (from fire)	dokχān (m)	دخّان
torch (flaming stick)	ʃoʿla (f)	شعلة
campfire	nār moχayem (m)	نار مخيّم
petrol	banzīn (m)	بنزين
paraffin	kerosīn (m)	كيروسين

flammable (adj)	qābel lel eḥterāq	قابل للإحتراق
explosive (adj)	māda motafaggera	مادة متفجّرة
NO SMOKING	mamnūʿ el tadχīn	ممنوع التدخين
safety	amn (m)	أمن
danger	χaṭar (m)	خطر
dangerous (adj)	χaṭīr	خطير
to catch fire	eʃtaʿal	إشتعل
explosion	enfegār (m)	إنفجار
to set fire	aʃʿal el nār	أشعل النار
arsonist	moʃʿel ḥarīq ʿan ʿamd (m)	مشعل حريق عن عمد
arson	eḥrāq el momtalakāt (m)	إحراق الممتلكات
to blaze (vi)	awhag	أوهج
to burn (be on fire)	et-ḥaraʾ	إتحرق
to burn down	et-ḥaraʾ	إتحرق
to call the fire brigade	kallim ʾism el ḥarīʾ	كلّم قسم الحريق
firefighter, fireman	rāgel el maṭāfy (m)	راجل المطافي
fire engine	sayāret el maṭāfy (f)	سيّارة المطافي
fire brigade	ʾesm el maṭāfy (f)	قسم المطافي
fire engine ladder	sellem el maṭāfy (m)	سلّم المطافي
fire hose	χarṭūm el mayya (m)	خرطوم الميّة
fire extinguisher	ṭaffayet ḥarīʾ (f)	طفّاية حريق
helmet	χawza (f)	خوذة
siren	sarīna (f)	سرينة
to cry (for help)	ṣarraχ	صرّخ
to call for help	estaɣās	إستغاث
rescuer	monqez (m)	منقذ
to rescue (vt)	anqaz	أنقذ
to arrive (vi)	weṣel	وصل
to extinguish (vt)	ṭaffa	طفّى
water	meyāh (f)	مياه
sand	raml (m)	رمل
ruins (destruction)	ḥeṭām (pl)	حطام
to collapse (building, etc.)	enhār	إنهار
to fall down (vi)	enhār	إنهار
to cave in (ceiling, floor)	enhār	إنهار
piece of debris	ʾeṭʿet ḥeṭām (f)	قطعة حطام
ash	ramād (m)	رماد
to suffocate (die)	eθχanaʾ	إتخنق
to be killed (perish)	māt	مات

HUMAN ACTIVITIES

Job. Business. Part 1

103. Office. Working in the office

office (company ~)	maktab (m)	مكتب
office (director's ~)	maktab (m)	مكتب
reception desk	este'bāl (m)	إستقبال
secretary	sekerteyr (m)	سكرتير
director	modīr (m)	مدير
manager	modīr (m)	مدير
accountant	muḥāseb (m)	محاسب
employee	mowazzaf (m)	موظّف
furniture	asās (m)	أثاث
desk	maktab (m)	مكتب
desk chair	korsy (m)	كرسي
drawer unit	weḥdet adrāg (f)	وحدة أدراج
coat stand	ʃammā'a (f)	شمّاعة
computer	kombuter (m)	كمبيوتر
printer	ṭābe'a (f)	طابعة
fax machine	faks (m)	فاكس
photocopier	'ālet nasχ (f)	آلة نسخ
paper	wara' (m)	ورق
office supplies	adawāt maktabiya (pl)	أدوات مكتبية
mouse mat	maws bād (m)	ماوس باد
sheet of paper	wara'a (f)	ورقة
binder	malaff (m)	ملفّ
catalogue	fehras (m)	فهرس
phone directory	dalīl el telefone (m)	دليل التليفون
documentation	wasā'eq (pl)	وثائق
brochure (e.g. 12 pages ~)	naʃra (f)	نشرة
leaflet (promotional ~)	manʃūr (m)	منشور
sample	namūzag (m)	نموذج
training meeting	egtemā' tadrīb (m)	إجتماع تدريب
meeting (of managers)	egtemā' (m)	إجتماع
lunch time	fatret el ɣada' (f)	فترة الغذاء
to make a copy	ṣawwar	صوّر
to make multiple copies	ṣawwar	صوّر
to receive a fax	estalam faks	إستلم فاكس
to send a fax	ba'at faks	بعت فاكس
to call (by phone)	ettaṣal	إتّصل

to answer (vt)	gāwab	جاوب
to put through	waṣṣal	وصّل
to arrange, to set up	ḥadded	حدّد
to demonstrate (vt)	ʿaraḍ	عرض
to be absent	ɣāb	غاب
absence	ɣeyāb (m)	غياب

104. Business processes. Part 1

occupation	ʃoɣl (m)	شغل
firm	ʃerka (f)	شركة
company	ʃerka (f)	شركة
corporation	moʾassasa tegariya (f)	مؤسسة تجارية
enterprise	ʃerka (f)	شركة
agency	wekāla (f)	وكالة
agreement (contract)	ettefaqiya (f)	إتّفاقية
contract	ʿaʾd (m)	عقد
deal	ṣafqa (f)	صفقة
order (to place an ~)	ṭalab (m)	طلب
terms (of the contract)	ʃorūṭ (pl)	شروط
wholesale (adv)	bel gomla	بالجملة
wholesale (adj)	el gomla	الجملة
wholesale (n)	beyʿ bel gomla (m)	بيع بالجملة
retail (adj)	yebeeʿ bel tagzeʾa	يبيع بالتجزئة
retail (n)	maḥal yebeeʿ bel tagzeʾa (m)	محل يبيع بالتجزئة
competitor	monāfes (m)	منافس
competition	monafsa (f)	منافسة
to compete (vi)	nāfes	نافس
partner (associate)	ʃerīk (m)	شريك
partnership	ʃarāka (f)	شراكة
crisis	azma (f)	أزمة
bankruptcy	eflās (m)	إفلاس
to go bankrupt	falles	فلّس
difficulty	ṣoʿūba (f)	صعوبة
problem	moʃkela (f)	مشكلة
catastrophe	karsa (f)	كارثة
economy	eqtiṣād (m)	إقتصاد
economic (~ growth)	eqteṣādy	إقتصادي
economic recession	rokūd eqteṣādy (m)	ركود إقتصادي
goal (aim)	hadaf (m)	هدف
task	mohemma (f)	مهمّة
to trade (vi)	tāger	تاجر
network (distribution ~)	ʃabaka (f)	شبكة
inventory (stock)	el maχzūn (m)	المخزون
range (assortment)	taʃkīla (f)	تشكيلة

leader (leading company)	qā'ed (m)	قائد
large (~ company)	kebīr	كبير
monopoly	eḥtekār (m)	إحتكار
theory	naẓariya (f)	نظريّة
practice	momarsa (f)	ممارسة
experience (in my ~)	xebra (f)	خبرة
trend (tendency)	ettegāh (m)	إتّجاه
development	tanmeya (f)	تنمية

105. Business processes. Part 2

profit (foregone ~)	rebḥ (m)	ربح
profitable (~ deal)	morbeḥ	مربح
delegation (group)	wafd (m)	وفد
salary	morattab (m)	مرتّب
to correct (an error)	ṣaḥḥaḥ	صحّح
business trip	reḥlet 'amal (f)	رحلة عمل
commission	lagna (f)	لجنة
to control (vt)	et-ḥakkem	إتحكّم
conference	mo'tamar (m)	مؤتمر
licence	roxṣa (f)	رخصة
reliable (~ partner)	mawsūq	موثوق
initiative (undertaking)	mobadra (f)	مبادرة
norm (standard)	me'yār (m)	معيار
circumstance	ẓarf (m)	ظرف
duty (of an employee)	wāgeb (m)	واجب
organization (company)	monaẓẓama (f)	منظّمة
organization (process)	tanẓīm (m)	تنظيم
organized (adj)	monaẓẓam	منظّم
cancellation	elɣā' (m)	إلغاء
to cancel (call off)	alɣa	ألغى
report (official ~)	ta'rīr (m)	تقرير
patent	bara'et el exterā' (f)	براءة الإختراع
to patent (obtain patent)	saggel barā'et exterā'	سجّل براءة الإختراع
to plan (vt)	xaṭṭeṭ	خطّط
bonus (money)	'alāwa (f)	علاوة
professional (adj)	mehany	مهني
procedure	egrā' (m)	إجراء
to examine (contract, etc.)	baḥs fi	بحث في
calculation	ḥesāb (m)	حساب
reputation	som'a (f)	سمعة
risk	moxaṭra (f)	مخاطرة
to manage, to run	adār	أدار
information (report)	ma'lumāt (pl)	معلومات
property	melkiya (f)	ملكيّة

union	ettehād (m)	إتِّحاد
life insurance	ta'mīn 'alal hayah (m)	تأمين على الحياة
to insure (vt)	ammen	أمِّن
insurance	ta'mīn (m)	تأمين

auction (~ sale)	mazād (m)	مزاد
to notify (inform)	ballaɣ	بلّغ
management (process)	edāra (f)	إدارة
service (~ industry)	xadma (f)	خدمة

forum	nadwa (f)	ندوة
to function (vi)	adda wazīfa	أدّى وظيفة
stage (phase)	marhala (f)	مرحلة
legal (~ services)	qanūniya	قانونية
lawyer (legal advisor)	muhāmy (m)	محامي

106. Production. Works

plant	maṣnaʿ (m)	مصنع
factory	maṣnaʿ (m)	مصنع
workshop	warʃa (f)	ورشة
works, production site	maṣnaʿ (m)	مصنع

industry (manufacturing)	ṣenāʿa (f)	صناعة
industrial (adj)	ṣenāʿy	صناعي
heavy industry	ṣenāʿa teʾīla (f)	صناعة ثقيلة
light industry	ṣenāʿa xafīfa (f)	صناعة خفيفة

products	montagāt (pl)	منتجات
to produce (vt)	antag	أنتج
raw materials	mawād xām (pl)	مواد خام

foreman (construction ~)	raʾīs el ʿommāl (m)	رئيس العمّال
workers team (crew)	farīʾ el ʿommāl (m)	فريق العمّال
worker	ʿāmel (m)	عامل

working day	yome ʿamal (m)	يوم عمل
pause (rest break)	rāha (f)	راحة
meeting	egtemāʿ (m)	إجتماع
to discuss (vt)	nāʾeʃ	ناقش

plan	xetta (f)	خطّة
to fulfil the plan	naffez el xetta	نفّذ الخطّة
rate of output	moʿaddal el entāg (m)	معدّل الإنتاج
quality	gawda (f)	جودة
control (checking)	taftīʃ (m)	تفتيش
quality control	dabt el gawda (m)	ضبط الجودة

workplace safety	salāmet makān el ʿamal (f)	سلامة مكان العمل
discipline	endebāt (m)	إنضباط
violation (of safety rules, etc.)	moxalfa (f)	مخالفة
to violate (rules)	xālef	خالف
strike	edrāb (m)	إضراب
striker	modrab (m)	مضرب

to be on strike	aḍrab	أضرب
trade union	etteḥād el ʿomāl (m)	إتّحاد العمال
to invent (machine, etc.)	eχtaraʿ	إخترع
invention	eχterāʿ (m)	إختراع
research	baḥs (m)	بحث
to improve (make better)	ḥassen	حسّن
technology	teknoloʒia (f)	تكنولوجيا
technical drawing	rasm teqany (m)	رسم تقني
load, cargo	ʃaḥn (m)	شحن
loader (person)	ʃayāl (m)	شيّال
to load (vehicle, etc.)	ʃaḥn	شحن
loading (process)	taḥmīl (m)	تحميل
to unload (vi, vt)	farraɣ	فرّغ
unloading	tafrīɣ (m)	تفريغ
transport	wasā'el el na'l (pl)	وسائل النقل
transport company	ʃerket na'l (f)	شركة نقل
to transport (vt)	na'al	نقل
wagon	ʿarabet ʃaḥn (f)	عربة شحن
tank (e.g., oil ~)	χazzān (m)	خزّان
lorry	ʃāḥena (f)	شاحنة
machine tool	makana (f)	مكنة
mechanism	'āliya (f)	آليّة
industrial waste	moχallafāt ṣenaʿiya (pl)	مخلفات صناعية
packing (process)	taʿbe'a (f)	تعبئة
to pack (vt)	ʿabba	عبّأ

107. Contract. Agreement

contract	ʿa'd (m)	عقد
agreement	ettefā' (m)	إتّفاق
addendum	molḥa' (m)	ملحق
to sign a contract	waqqaʿ ʿala ʿa'd	وقّع على عقد
signature	tawqeeʿ (m)	توقيع
to sign (vt)	waqqaʿ	وقّع
seal (stamp)	χetm (m)	ختم
subject of the contract	mawḍūʿ el ʿa'd (m)	موضوع العقد
clause	band (m)	بند
parties (in contract)	aṭrāf (pl)	أطراف
legal address	ʿenwān qanūny (m)	عنوان قانوني
to violate the contract	χālef el ʿa'd	خالف العقد
commitment (obligation)	eltezām (m)	إلتزام
responsibility	mas'oliya (f)	مسؤوليّة
force majeure	'owwa qāhera (m)	قوّة قاهرة
dispute	χelāf (m)	خلاف
penalties	ʿoqobāt (pl)	عقوبات

108. Import & Export

import	esterād (m)	إستيراد
importer	mostawred (m)	مستوّرد
to import (vt)	estawrad	إستوّرد
import (as adj.)	wāred	وارد
export (exportation)	taṣdīr (m)	تصدير
exporter	moṣadder (m)	مصدّر
to export (vt)	ṣaddar	صدّر
export (as adj.)	sādir	صادر
goods (merchandise)	badā'e' (pl)	بضائع
consignment, lot	ʃoḥna (f)	شحنة
weight	wazn (m)	وزن
volume	ḥagm (m)	حجم
cubic metre	metr moka''ab (m)	متر مكعّب
manufacturer	el ʃerka el moṣanne'a (f)	الشركة المصنّعة
transport company	ʃerket na'l (f)	شركة نقل
container	ḥāweya (f)	حاوية
border	ḥadd (m)	حدّ
customs	gamārek (pl)	جمارك
customs duty	rasm gomroky (m)	رسم جمركي
customs officer	mowazzaf el gamārek (m)	موظّف الجمارك
smuggling	tahrīb (m)	تهريب
contraband (smuggled goods)	beḍā'a moharraba (pl)	بضاعة مهربة

109. Finances

share, stock	sahm (m)	سهم
bond (certificate)	sanad (m)	سند
promissory note	kembyāla (f)	كمبيالة
stock exchange	borṣa (f)	بورصة
stock price	se'r el sahm (m)	سعر السهم
to go down (become cheaper)	reχeṣ	رخص
to go up (become more expensive)	ʃely	غلي
share	naṣīb (m)	نصيب
controlling interest	el magmū'a el mosayṭara (f)	المجموعة المسيطرة
investment	estesmār (pl)	إستثمار
to invest (vt)	estasmar	إستثمر
percent	bel me'a - bel miya	بالمئة
interest (on investment)	fayda (f)	فائدة
profit	rebḥ (m)	ربح
profitable (adj)	morbeḥ	مربح

tax	ḍarība (f)	ضريبة
currency (foreign ~)	'omla (f)	عملة
national (adj)	waṭany	وطني
exchange (currency ~)	taḥwīl (m)	تحويل
accountant	muḥāseb (m)	محاسب
accounting	maḥasba (f)	محاسبة
bankruptcy	eflās (m)	إفلاس
collapse, ruin	enheyār (m)	إنهيار
ruin	eflās (m)	إفلاس
to be ruined (financially)	falles	فلّس
inflation	taḍakχom māly (m)	تضخّم مالي
devaluation	taχfīḍ qīmet 'omla (m)	تخفيض قيمة عملة
capital	ra's māl (m)	رأس مال
income	daχl (m)	دخل
turnover	dawret ra's el māl (f)	دورة رأس المال
resources	mawāred (pl)	موارد
monetary resources	el mawāred el naqdiya (pl)	الموارد النقديّة
overheads	nafa'āt 'āmma (pl)	نفقات عامّة
to reduce (expenses)	χaffaḍ	خفّض

110. Marketing

marketing	taswī' (m)	تسويق
market	sū' (f)	سوق
market segment	qaṭā' el sū' (m)	قطاع السوق
product	montag (m)	منتج
goods (merchandise)	baḍā'e' (pl)	بضائع
brand	mārka (f)	ماركة
trademark	marka tegāriya (f)	ماركة تجاريّة
logotype	ʃe'ār (m)	شعار
logo	ʃe'ār (m)	شعار
demand	ṭalab (m)	طلب
supply	mU'Iddāt (pl)	معدّات
need	ḥāga (f)	حاجة
consumer	mostahlek (m)	مستهلك
analysis	taḥlīl (m)	تحليل
to analyse (vt)	ḥallel	حلّل
positioning	waḍ' (m)	وضع
to position (vt)	waḍa'	وضع
price	se'r (m)	سعر
pricing policy	seyāset el as'ār (f)	سياسة الأسعار
price formation	taʃkīl el as'ār (m)	تشكيل الأسعار

111. Advertising

advertising	e'lān (m)	إعلان
to advertise (vt)	a'lan	أعلن

budget	mezaniya (f)	ميزانية
ad, advertisement	e'lān (m)	إعلان
TV advertising	e'lān fel televiziōn (m)	إعلان في التليفزيون
radio advertising	e'lān fel radio (m)	إعلان في الراديو
outdoor advertising	e'lān zahery (m)	إعلان ظاهري
mass medias	wasā'el el e'lām (pl)	وسائل الإعلام
periodical (n)	magalla dawriya (f)	مجلّة دوريّة
image (public appearance)	imyʒ (m)	إيميج
slogan	ʃe'ār (m)	شعار
motto (maxim)	ʃe'ār (m)	شعار
campaign	ḥamla (f)	حملة
advertising campaign	ḥamla e'laniya (f)	حملة إعلانيّة
target group	magmū'a mostahdafa (f)	مجموعة مستهدفة
business card	kart el 'amal (m)	كارت العمل
leaflet (promotional ~)	manʃūr (m)	منشور
brochure (e.g. 12 pages ~)	naʃra (f)	نشرة
pamphlet	kotayeb (m)	كتيّب
newsletter	naʃra eχbariya (f)	نشرة إخبارية
signboard (store sign, etc.)	yafṭa, lāfeta (f)	لافتة, يافطة
poster	boster (m)	بوستر
hoarding	lawḥet e'lanāt (f)	لوحة إعلانات

112. Banking

bank	bank (m)	بنك
branch (of a bank)	far' (m)	فرع
consultant	mowazzaf bank (m)	موظّف بنك
manager (director)	modīr (m)	مدير
bank account	ḥesāb bank (m)	حساب بنك
account number	raqam el ḥesāb (m)	رقم الحساب
current account	ḥesāb gāry (m)	حساب جاري
deposit account	ḥesāb tawfīr (m)	حساب توّفير
to open an account	fataḥ ḥesāb	فتح حساب
to close the account	'afal ḥesāb	قفل حساب
to deposit into the account	awda' fel ḥesāb	أودع في الحساب
to withdraw (vt)	saḥab men el ḥesāb	سحب من الحساب
deposit	wadee'a (f)	وديعة
to make a deposit	awda'	أودع
wire transfer	ḥewāla maṣrefiya (f)	حوالة مصرفيّة
to wire, to transfer	ḥawwel	حوّل
sum	mablaɣ (m)	مبلغ
How much?	kām?	كام؟
signature	tawqee' (m)	توقيع
to sign (vt)	waqqa'	وقّع

credit card	kredit kard (f)	كريدت كارد
code (PIN code)	kōd (m)	كود
credit card number	raqam el kredit kard (m)	رقم الكريدت كارد
cashpoint	makinet ṣarrāf ʾāly (f)	ماكينة صرّاف آلي
cheque	ʃīk (m)	شيك
to write a cheque	katab ʃīk	كتب شيك
chequebook	daftar ʃikāt (m)	دفتر شيكات
loan (bank ~)	qarḍ (m)	قرض
to apply for a loan	ʾaddem ṭalab ʿala qarḍ	قدّم طلب على قرض
to get a loan	ḥaṣal ʿala qarḍ	حصل على قرض
to give a loan	edda qarḍ	ادّى قرض
guarantee	ḍamān (m)	ضمان

113. Telephone. Phone conversation

telephone	telefon (m)	تليفون
mobile phone	mobile (m)	موبايل
answerphone	gehāz radd ʿalal mokalmāt (m)	جهاز ردّ على المكالمات
to call (by phone)	ettaṣal	إتّصل
call, ring	mokalma telefoniya (f)	مكالمة تليفونية
to dial a number	ettaṣal be raqam	إتّصل برقم
Hello!	alo!	ألو!
to ask (vt)	saʾal	سأل
to answer (vi, vt)	radd	ردّ
to hear (vt)	semeʿ	سمع
well (adv)	kewayes	كويّس
not well (adv)	meʃ kowayīs	مش كويّس
noises (interference)	taʃwīʃ (m)	تشويش
receiver	sammāʿa (f)	سمّاعة
to pick up (~ the phone)	rafaʿ el sammāʿa	رفع السمّاعة
to hang up (~ the phone)	ʾafal el sammāʿa	قفل السمّاعة
busy (engaged)	maʃɣūl	مشغول
to ring (ab. phone)	rann	رن
telephone book	dalīl el telefone (m)	دليل التليفون
local (adj)	maḥalliya	ة محلّيّة
local call	mokalma maḥalliya (f)	مكالمة محلّيّة
trunk (e.g. ~ call)	biʿīd	بعيد
trunk call	mokalma biʿīda (f)	مكالمة بعيدة المدى
international (adj)	dowly	دوّلي
international call	mokalma dowliya (f)	مكالمة دوليّة

114. Mobile telephone

mobile phone	mobile (m)	موبايل
display	ʿarḍ (m)	عرض

button	zerr (m)	زرّ
SIM card	sim kard (m)	سيم كارد
battery	baṭṭariya (f)	بطّاريّة
to be flat (battery)	χelṣet	خلصت
charger	ʃāḥen (m)	شاحن
menu	qā'ema (f)	قائمة
settings	awḍāʿ (pl)	أوضاع
tune (melody)	naɣama (f)	نغمة
to select (vt)	eχtār	إختار
calculator	'āla ḥasba (f)	آلة حاسبة
voice mail	barīd ṣawty (m)	بريد صوتي
alarm clock	monabbeh (m)	منبّه
contacts	gehāt el etteṣāl (pl)	جهات الإتّصال
SMS (text message)	resāla 'aṣīra ɛsɛmɛs (f)	sms رسالة قصيرة
subscriber	moʃtarek (m)	مشترك

115. Stationery

ballpoint pen	'alam gāf (m)	قلم جاف
fountain pen	'alam rīʃa (m)	قلم ريشة
pencil	'alam roṣāṣ (m)	قلم رصاص
highlighter	markar (m)	ماركر
felt-tip pen	'alam fulumaster (m)	قلم فلوماستر
notepad	mozakkera (f)	مذكّرة
diary	gadwal el aʿmāl (m)	جدول الأعمال
ruler	masṭara (f)	مسطرة
calculator	'āla ḥasba (f)	آلة حاسبة
rubber	astīka (f)	استيكة
drawing pin	dabbūs (m)	دبّوس
paper clip	dabbūs wara' (m)	دبّوس ورق
glue	ṣamɣ (m)	صمغ
stapler	dabbāsa (f)	دبّاسة
hole punch	χarrāma (m)	خرّامة
pencil sharpener	barrāya (f)	برّاية

116. Various kinds of documents

account (report)	ta'rīr (m)	تقرير
agreement	ettefā' (m)	إتّفاق
application form	estemāret ṭalab (m)	إستمارة طلب
authentic (adj)	aṣly	أصلي
badge (identity tag)	ʃāra (f)	شارة
business card	kart el ʿamal (m)	كارت العمل
certificate (~ of quality)	ʃahāda (f)	شهادة

cheque (e.g. draw a ~)	ʃīk (m)	شيك
bill (in restaurant)	ḥesāb (m)	حساب
constitution	dostūr (m)	دستور
contract (agreement)	ʿa'd (m)	عقد
copy	ṣūra (f)	صورة
copy (of a contract, etc.)	nosχa (f)	نسخة
customs declaration	taṣrīḥ gomroky (m)	تصريح جمركي
document	wasīqa (f)	وثيقة
driving licence	roχṣet el qeyāda (f)	رخصة قيادة
addendum	molḥa' (m)	ملحق
form	estemāra (f)	استمارة
ID card (e.g., warrant card)	beṭā'et el hawiya (f)	بطاقة الهويّة
inquiry (request)	estefsār (m)	إستفسار
invitation card	beṭā'et daʿwa (f)	بطاقة دعوة
invoice	fatūra (f)	فاتورة
law	qanūn (m)	قانون
letter (mail)	resāla (f)	رسالة
letterhead	tarwīsa (f)	ترويّسة
list (of names, etc.)	qā'ema (f)	قائمة
manuscript	maχṭūṭa (f)	مخطوطة
newsletter	naʃra eχbariya (f)	نشرة إخبارية
note (short letter)	nouta (f)	نوتة
pass (for worker, visitor)	beṭā'et morūr (f)	بطاقة مرور
passport	basbore (m)	باسبور
permit	roχṣa (f)	رخصة
curriculum vitae, CV	sīra zātiya (f)	سيرة ذاتيّة
debt note, IOU	mozakkeret deyn (f)	مذكّرة دين
receipt (for purchase)	eṣāl (m)	إيصال
till receipt	eṣāl (m)	إيصال
report (mil.)	ta'rīr (m)	تقرير
to show (ID, etc.)	'addem	قدّم
to sign (vt)	waqqaʿ	وقّع
signature	tawqeeʿ (m)	توقيع
seal (stamp)	χetm (m)	ختم
text	noṣṣ (m)	نص
ticket (for entry)	tazkara (f)	تذكرة
to cross out	ʃaṭab	شطب
to fill in (~ a form)	mala	ملأ
waybill (shipping invoice)	bolīṣet ʃaḥn (f)	بوليصة شحن
will (testament)	waṣiya (f)	وصيّة

117. Kinds of business

accounting services	χedamāt moḥasba (pl)	خدمات محاسبة
advertising	eʿlān (m)	إعلان
advertising agency	wekālet eʿlān (f)	وكالة إعلان

air-conditioners	takyīf (m)	تكييف
airline	ʃerket ṭayarān (f)	شركة طيران
alcoholic beverages	maʃrūbāt koḥūliya (pl)	مشروبات كحوليّة
antiques (antique dealers)	toḥaf (pl)	تحف
art gallery (contemporary ~)	maʻraḍ fanny (m)	معرض فنّي
audit services	χedamāt faḥṣ el ḥesābāt (pl)	خدمات فحص الحسابات
banking industry	el qeṭāʻ el maṣrefy (m)	القطاع المصرفي
beauty salon	ṣalone tagmīl (m)	صالون تجميل
bookshop	maḥal kotob (m)	محل كتب
brewery	maṣnaʻ bīra (m)	مصنع بيرة
business centre	markaz tegāry (m)	مركز تجاري
business school	kolliyet edāret el aʻmāl (f)	كليّة إدارة الأعمال
casino	kazino (m)	كازينو
chemist, pharmacy	ṣaydaliya (f)	صيدليّة
cinema	sinema (f)	سينما
construction	benāʾ (m)	بناء
consulting	esteʃāra (f)	إستشارة
dental clinic	ʻeyādet asnān (f)	عيادة أسنان
design	taṣmīm (m)	تصميم
dry cleaners	dray klīn (m)	دراي كلين
employment agency	wekālet tawẓīf (f)	وكالة توّظيف
financial services	χedamāt māliya (pl)	خدمات ماليّة
food products	akl (m)	أكل
furniture (e.g. house ~)	asās (m)	أثاث
clothing, garment	malābes (pl)	ملابس
hotel	fondoʾ (m)	فندق
ice-cream	ʾays krīm (m)	آيس كريم
industry (manufacturing)	ṣenāʻa (f)	صناعة
insurance	taʾmīn (m)	تأمين
Internet	internet (m)	إنترنت
investments (finance)	estesmarāt (pl)	إستثمارات
jeweller	ṣāʾeɣ (m)	صائغ
jewellery	mogawharāt (pl)	مجوّهرات
laundry (shop)	maɣsala (f)	مغسلة
legal adviser	χedamāt qanūniya (pl)	خدمات قانونيّة
light industry	ṣenāʻa χafīfa (f)	صناعة خفيفة
magazine	magalla (f)	مجلّة
mail order selling	beyʻ be neẓām el barīd (m)	بيع بنظام البريد
medicine	ṭebb (m)	طبّ
museum	mat-ḥaf (m)	متحف
news agency	wekāla eχbariya (f)	وكالة إخبارية
newspaper	garīda (f)	جريدة
nightclub	malha leyly (m)	ملهى ليّلي
oil (petroleum)	nafṭ (m)	نفط
courier services	χedamāt el ʃaḥn (pl)	خدمات الشحن
pharmaceutics	ṣaydala (f)	صيدلة

printing (industry)	ṭebāʿa (f)	طباعة
pub	bār (m)	بار
publishing house	dar el ṭebāʿa wel naʃr (f)	دار الطباعة والنشر
radio (~ station)	radio (m)	راديو
real estate	ʿeqarāt (pl)	عقارات
restaurant	maṭʿam (m)	مطعم
security company	ʃerket amn (f)	شركة أمن
shop	maḥal (m)	محل
sport	reyāḍa (f)	رياضة
stock exchange	borṣa (f)	بورصة
supermarket	subermarket (m)	سوبرماركت
swimming pool (public ~)	ḥammām sebāḥa (m)	حمّام سباحة
tailor shop	maḥal χeyāṭa (m)	محل خياطة
television	televizion (m)	تليفزيون
theatre	masraḥ (m)	مسرح
trade (commerce)	tegāra (f)	تجارة
transport companies	wasāʾel el naʾl (pl)	وسائل النقل
travel	safar (m)	سفر
undertakers	maktab motaʿahhed el dafn (m)	مكتب متعهّد الدفن
veterinary surgeon	doktore beṭary (m)	دكتور بيطري
warehouse	mostawdaʿ (m)	مستودع
waste collection	gamaʿ el nefayāt (m)	جمع النفايات

Job. Business. Part 2

118. Show. Exhibition

exhibition, show	maʿraḍ (m)	معرض
trade show	maʿraḍ tegāry (m)	معرض تجاري
participation	eʃterāk (m)	إشتراك
to participate (vi)	ʃārek	شارك
participant (exhibitor)	moʃtarek (m)	مشترك
director	modīr (m)	مدير
organizers' office	maktab el monaẓẓemīn (m)	مكتب المنظّمين
organizer	monazzem (m)	منظّم
to organize (vt)	nazzam	نظّم
participation form	estemāret el eʃterak (f)	إستمارة الإشتراك
to fill in (vt)	mala	ملأ
details	tafaṣīl (pl)	تفاصيل
information	esteʿlamāt (pl)	إستعلامات
price (cost, rate)	seʿr (m)	سعر
including	bema feyh	بما فيه
to include (vt)	taḍamman	تضمّن
to pay (vi, vt)	dafaʿ	دفع
registration fee	rosūm el tasgīl (pl)	رسوم التسجيل
entrance	madχal (m)	مدخل
pavilion, hall	genāḥ (m)	جناح
to register (vt)	saggel	سجّل
badge (identity tag)	ʃāra (f)	شارة
stand	koʃk (m)	كشك
to reserve, to book	ḥagaz	حجز
display case	vatrīna (f)	فترينة
spotlight	kasʃāf el nūr (m)	كشّاف النور
design	taṣmīm (m)	تصميم
to place (put, set)	ḥaṭṭ	حطّ
distributor	mowazzeʿ (m)	موزّع
supplier	mowarred (m)	مورّد
country	balad (m)	بلد
foreign (adj)	agnaby	أجنبي
product	montag (m)	منتج
association	gamʿiya (f)	جمعيّة
conference hall	qāʿet el moʾtamarāt (f)	قاعة المؤتمرات
congress	moʾtamar (m)	مؤتمر

contest (competition)	mosab'a (f)	مسابقة
visitor (attendee)	zā'er (m)	زائر
to visit (attend)	ḥaḍar	حضر
customer	zobūn (m)	زبون

119. Mass Media

newspaper	garīda (f)	جريدة
magazine	magalla (f)	مجلّة
press (printed media)	ṣaḥāfa (f)	صحافة
radio	radio (m)	راديو
radio station	maḥaṭṭet radio (f)	محطّة راديو
television	televizion (m)	تليفزيون
presenter, host	mo'addem (m)	مقدّم
newsreader	mozee' (m)	مذيع
commentator	mo'alleq (m)	معلّق
journalist	ṣaḥafy (m)	صحفي
correspondent (reporter)	morāsel (m)	مراسل
press photographer	moṣawwer ṣaḥafy (m)	مصوّر صحفي
reporter	ṣaḥafy (m)	صحفي
editor	moḥarrer (m)	محرّر
editor-in-chief	ra'īs taḥrīr (m)	رئيس تحرير
to subscribe (to …)	eʃtarak	إشترك
subscription	eʃterāk (m)	إشتراك
subscriber	moʃtarek (m)	مشترك
to read (vi, vt)	'ara	قرأ
reader	qāre' (m)	قارئ
circulation (of a newspaper)	tadāwol (m)	تداول
monthly (adj)	ʃahry	شهري
weekly (adj)	osbū'y	أسبوعي
issue (edition)	'adad (m)	عدد
new (~ issue)	gedīd	جديد
headline	'enwān (m)	عنوان
short article	maqāla saɣīra (f)	مقالة قصيرة
column (regular article)	'amūd (m)	عمود
article	maqāla (f)	مقالة
page	ṣafḥa (f)	صفحة
reportage, report	rebortāʒ (m)	ريبورتاج
event (happening)	ḥadass (m)	حدث
sensation (news)	ḍagga (f)	ضجّة
scandal	feḍīḥa (f)	فضيحة
scandalous (adj)	fāḍeḥ	فاضح
great (~ scandal)	ʃahīr	شهير
programme (e.g. cooking ~)	barnāmeg (m)	برنامج
interview	leqā' ṣaḥafy (m)	لقاء صحفي
live broadcast	ezā'a mobāʃera (f)	إذاعة مباشرة
channel	qanah (f)	قناة

120. Agriculture

agriculture	zerāʿa (f)	زراعة
peasant (masc.)	fallāḥ (m)	فلاّح
peasant (fem.)	fallāḥa (f)	فلاّحة
farmer	mozāreʿ (m)	مزارع
tractor	garrār (m)	جرّار
combine, harvester	ḥaṣṣāda (f)	حصّادة
plough	meḥrās (m)	محراث
to plough (vi, vt)	ḥaras	حرث
ploughland	ḥaql maḥrūθ (m)	حقل محروث
furrow (in field)	talem (m)	تلم
to sow (vi, vt)	bezr	بذر
seeder	bazzara (f)	بذّارة
sowing (process)	zarʿ (m)	زرع
scythe	meḥasʃ (m)	محشّ
to mow, to scythe	ḥasʃ	حشّ
spade (tool)	karīk (m)	كريك
to till (vt)	ḥaras	حرث
hoe	magrafa (f)	مجرفة
to hoe, to weed	estʾṣal nabatāt	إستأصل نباتات
weed (plant)	nabāt ṭafayly (m)	نبات طفيّلي
watering can	raʃāʃa (f)	رشّاشة
to water (plants)	saʾa	سقى
watering (act)	saʾy (m)	سقي
pitchfork	mazrāh (f)	مذراة
rake	madamma (f)	مدمّة
fertiliser	semād (m)	سماد
to fertilise (vt)	sammed	سمّد
manure (fertiliser)	semād (m)	سماد
field	ḥaql (m)	حقل
meadow	marag (m)	مرج
vegetable garden	bostān χoḍār (m)	بستان خضار
orchard (e.g. apple ~)	bostān (m)	بستان
to graze (vt)	raʿa	رعى
herdsman	rāʿy (m)	راعي
pasture	marʿa (m)	مرعى
cattle breeding	tarbeya el mawāʃy (f)	تربية المواشي
sheep farming	tarbeya aɣnām (f)	تربية أغنام
plantation	mazraʿa (f)	مزرعة
row (garden bed ~s)	ḥoḍe (m)	حوض
hothouse	dafīʾa (f)	دفيئة

drought (lack of rain)	gafāf (m)	جفاف
dry (~ summer)	gāf	جاف
grain	ḥobūb (pl)	حبوب
cereal crops	maḥaṣīl el ḥubūb (pl)	محاصيل الحبوب
to harvest, to gather	ḥaṣad	حصد
miller (person)	ṭaḥḥān (m)	طحّان
mill (e.g. gristmill)	ṭaḥūna (f)	طاحونة
to grind (grain)	ṭaḥn el ḥobūb	طحن الحبوب
flour	de'ī' (m)	دقيق
straw	'aʃ (m)	قشّ

121. Building. Building process

building site	arḍ benā' (f)	أرض بناء
to build (vt)	bana	بنى
building worker	'āmel benā' (m)	عامل بناء
project	maʃrū' (m)	مشروع
architect	mohandes me'māry (m)	مهندس معماري
worker	'āmel (m)	عامل
foundations (of a building)	asās (m)	أساس
roof	sa'f (m)	سقف
foundation pile	kawmet el asās (f)	كومة الأساس
wall	ḥeyṭa (f)	حيطة
reinforcing bars	ḥadīd taslīḥ (m)	حديد تسليح
scaffolding	sa''āla (f)	سقّالة
concrete	χarasāna (f)	خرسانة
granite	granīt (m)	جرانيت
stone	ḥagar (m)	حجر
brick	ṭūb (m)	طوب
sand	raml (m)	رمل
cement	asmant (m)	إسمنت
plaster (for walls)	ṭalā' gaṣṣ (m)	طلاء جصّ
to plaster (vt)	ṭala bel gaṣṣ	طلى بالجصّ
paint	dehān (m)	دهان
to paint (~ a wall)	dahhen	دهّن
barrel	barmīl (m)	برميل
crane	rāfe'a (f)	رافعة
to lift, to hoist (vt)	rafa'	رفع
to lower (vt)	nazzel	نزّل
bulldozer	bulldozer (m)	بولدوزر
excavator	ḥaffāra (f)	حفّارة
scoop, bucket	magrafa (f)	مجرفة
to dig (excavate)	ḥafar	حفر
hard hat	χawza (f)	خوذة

122. Science. Research. Scientists

science	ʿelm (m)	علم
scientific (adj)	ʿelmy	علمي
scientist	ʿālem (m)	عالم
theory	naẓariya (f)	نظريّة
axiom	badīhiya (f)	بديهيّة
analysis	taḥlīl (m)	تحليل
to analyse (vt)	ḥallel	حلّل
argument (strong ~)	borhān (m)	برهان
substance (matter)	madda (f)	مادّة
hypothesis	faraḍiya (f)	فرضيّة
dilemma	moʿḍela (f)	معضلة
dissertation	resāla ʿelmiya (f)	رسالة علميّة
dogma	ʿaqīda (f)	عقيدة
doctrine	mazhab (m)	مذهب
research	baḥs (m)	بحث
to research (vt)	baḥs	بحث
tests (laboratory ~)	eχtebārāt (pl)	إختبارات
laboratory	moχtabar (m)	مختبر
method	manhag (m)	منهج
molecule	gozayeʾ (m)	جزيء
monitoring	reqāba (f)	رقابة
discovery (act, event)	ekteʃāf (m)	إكتشاف
postulate	mosallama (f)	مسلّمة
principle	mabdaʾ (m)	مبدأ
forecast	tanabboʾ (m)	تنبّؤ
to forecast (vt)	tanabbaʾ	تنبّأ
synthesis	tarkīb (m)	تركيب
trend (tendency)	ettegāh (m)	إتّجاه
theorem	naẓariya (f)	نظريّة
teachings	taʿalīm (pl)	تعاليم
fact	ḥaʾīʾa (f)	حقيقة
expedition	beʿsa (f)	بعثة
experiment	tagreba (f)	تجربة
academician	akadīmy (m)	أكاديمي
bachelor (e.g. ~ of Arts)	bakaleryūs (m)	بكالوريوس
doctor (PhD)	doktore (m)	دكتور
Associate Professor	ostāz moʃārek (m)	أستاذ مشارك
Master (e.g. ~ of Arts)	maʒestīr (m)	ماجستير
professor	brofessor (m)	بروفيسور

Professions and occupations

123. Job search. Dismissal

job	‘amal (m)	عمل
staff (work force)	kawādir (pl)	كوادر
personnel	ṭāqem el ‘āmelīn (m)	طاقم العاملين
career	mehna (f)	مهنة
prospects (chances)	’āfāq (pl)	آفاق
skills (mastery)	maharāt (pl)	مهارات
selection (screening)	eχteyār (m)	إختيار
employment agency	wekālet tawẓīf (f)	وكالة توّظيف
curriculum vitae, CV	sīra zātiya (f)	سيرة ذاتيّة
job interview	mo’ablet ‘amal (f)	مقابلة عمل
vacancy	wazīfa χaleya (f)	وظيفة خالية
salary, pay	morattab (m)	مرتّب
fixed salary	rāteb sābet (m)	راتب ثابت
pay, compensation	ogra (f)	أجرة
position (job)	manṣeb (m)	منصب
duty (of an employee)	wāgeb (m)	واجب
range of duties	magmū‘a men el wāgebāt (f)	مجموعة من الواجبات
busy (I'm ~)	maʃɣūl	مشغول
to fire (dismiss)	rafad	رفد
dismissal	eqāla (m)	إقالة
unemployment	baṭāla (f)	بطالة
unemployed (n)	‘āṭel (m)	عاطل
retirement	ma‘āʃ (m)	معاش
to retire (from job)	oḥīl ‘ala el ma‘āʃ	أحيل على المعاش

124. Business people

director	modīr (m)	مدير
manager (director)	modīr (m)	مدير
boss	ra’īs (m)	رئيس
superior	motafawweq (m)	متفوّق
superiors	ro’asā’ (pl)	رؤساء
president	ra’īs (m)	رئيس
chairman	ra’īs (m)	رئيس
deputy (substitute)	nā’eb (m)	نائب
assistant	mosā‘ed (m)	مساعد

secretary	sekerteyr (m)	سكرتير
personal assistant	sekerteyr χāṣ (m)	سكرتير خاص
businessman	ragol a'māl (m)	رجل أعمال
entrepreneur	rā'ed a'māl (m)	رائد أعمال
founder	mo'asses (m)	مؤسّس
to found (vt)	asses	أسّس
founding member	mo'asses (m)	مؤسّس
partner	ʃerīk (m)	شريك
shareholder	mālek el as-hom (m)	مالك الأسهم
millionaire	millyonīr (m)	مليونير
billionaire	milliardīr (m)	ملياردير
owner, proprietor	ṣāḥeb (m)	صاحب
landowner	ṣāḥeb el arḍ (m)	صاحب الأرض
client	'amīl (m)	عميل
regular client	'amīl dā'em (m)	عميل دائم
buyer (customer)	moʃtary (m)	مشتري
visitor	zā'er (m)	زائر
professional (n)	moḥtaref (m)	محترف
expert	χabīr (m)	خبير
specialist	motaχaṣṣeṣ (m)	متخصّص
banker	ṣāḥeb maṣraf (m)	صاحب مصرف
broker	semsār (m)	سمسار
cashier	'āmel kaʃier (m)	عامل كاشيير
accountant	muḥāseb (m)	محاسب
security guard	ḥāres amn (m)	حارس أمن
investor	mostasmer (m)	مستثمر
debtor	modīn (m)	مدين
creditor	dā'en (m)	دائن
borrower	moqtareḍ (m)	مقترض
importer	mostawred (m)	مستوّرد
exporter	moṣadder (m)	مصدّر
manufacturer	el ʃerka el moṣanne'a (f)	الشركة المصنّعة
distributor	mowazze' (m)	موزّع
middleman	wasīṭ (m)	وسيط
consultant	mostaʃār (m)	مستشار
sales representative	mandūb mabi'āt (m)	مندوب مبيعات
agent	wakīl (m)	وكيل
insurance agent	wakīl el ta'mīn (m)	وكيل التأمين

125. Service professions

cook	ṭabbāχ (m)	طبّاخ
chef (kitchen chef)	el ʃeyf (m)	الشيف

baker	χabbāz (m)	خبّاز
barman	bārman (m)	بارمان
waiter	garsone (m)	جرسون
waitress	garsona (f)	جرسونة
lawyer, barrister	muḥāmy (m)	محامي
lawyer (legal expert)	muḥāmy χabīr qanūny (m)	محامي خبير قانوني
notary public	mowassaq (m)	موثّق
electrician	kahrabā'y (m)	كهربائي
plumber	samkary (m)	سمكري
carpenter	naggār (m)	نجّار
masseur	modallek (m)	مدلّك
masseuse	modalleka (f)	مدلّكة
doctor	doktore (m)	دكتور
taxi driver	sawwā' taksi (m)	سوّاق تاكسي
driver	sawwā' (m)	سوّاق
delivery man	rāgel el delivery (m)	راجل الديلفري
chambermaid	'āmela tandīf ɣoraf (f)	عاملة تنظيف غرف
security guard	ḥāres amn (m)	حارس أمن
flight attendant (fem.)	moḍīfet ṭayarān (f)	مضيفة طيران
schoolteacher	modarres madrasa (m)	مدرّس مدرسة
librarian	amīn maktaba (m)	أمين مكتبة
translator	motargem (m)	مترجم
interpreter	motargem fawwry (m)	مترجم فوّري
guide	morʃed (m)	مرشد
hairdresser	ḥallā' (m)	حلّاق
postman	sā'y el barīd (m)	ساعي البريد
salesman (store staff)	bayā' (m)	بيّاع
gardener	bostāny (m)	بستاني
domestic servant	χādema (m)	خادمة
maid (female servant)	χadema (f)	خادمة
cleaner (cleaning lady)	'āmela tandīf (f)	عاملة تنظيف

126. Military professions and ranks

private	gondy (m)	جنّدي
sergeant	raqīb tāny (m)	رقيب تاني
lieutenant	molāzem tāny (m)	ملازم تاني
captain	naqīb (m)	نقيب
major	rā'ed (m)	رائد
colonel	'aqīd (m)	عقيد
general	ʒenerāl (m)	جنرال
marshal	marʃāl (m)	مارشال
admiral	amerāl (m)	أميرال
military (n)	'askary (m)	عسكري
soldier	gondy (m)	جنّدي

officer	ḍābeṭ (m)	ضابط
commander	qā'ed (m)	قائد
border guard	ḥaras ḥodūd (m)	حرس حدود
radio operator	'āmel lāselky (m)	عامل لاسلكي
scout (searcher)	rā'ed mostakʃef (m)	رائد مستكشف
pioneer (sapper)	mohandes 'askary (m)	مهندس عسكري
marksman	rāmy (m)	رامي
navigator	mallāḥ (m)	ملاّح

127. Officials. Priests

king	malek (m)	ملك
queen	maleka (f)	ملكة
prince	amīr (m)	أمير
princess	amīra (f)	أميرة
czar	qayṣar (m)	قيصر
czarina	qayṣara (f)	قيصرة
president	ra'īs (m)	رئيس
Secretary (minister)	wazīr (m)	وزير
prime minister	ra'īs wozarā' (m)	رئيس وزراء
senator	'oḍw magles el ʃoyūχ (m)	عضو مجلس الشيوخ
diplomat	deblomāsy (m)	دبلوماسي
consul	qonṣol (m)	قنصل
ambassador	safīr (m)	سفير
counselor (diplomatic officer)	mostaʃār (m)	مستشار
official, functionary (civil servant)	mowazzaf (m)	موظّف
prefect	ra'īs edāret el ḥayī (m)	رئيس إدارة الحي
mayor	ra'īs el baladiya (m)	رئيس البلديّة
judge	qāḍy (m)	قاضي
prosecutor	el na'eb el 'ām (m)	النائب العام
missionary	mobasʃer (m)	مبشّر
monk	rāheb (m)	راهب
abbot	ra'īs el deyr (m)	رئيس الدير
rabbi	ḥaχām (m)	حاخام
vizier	wazīr (m)	وزير
shah	ʃāh (m)	شاه
sheikh	ʃɛyχ (m)	شيخ

128. Agricultural professions

beekeeper	naḥḥāl (m)	نحّال
shepherd	rā'y (m)	راعي

agronomist	mohandes zerā'y (m)	مهندس زراعي
cattle breeder	morabby el mawāʃy (m)	مربّي المواشي
veterinary surgeon	doktore beṭary (m)	دكتور بيطري
farmer	mozāre' (m)	مزارع
winemaker	ṣāne' el χamr (m)	صانع الخمر
zoologist	χabīr fe 'elm el ḥayawān (m)	خبير في علم الحيوان
cowboy	rā'y el ba'ar (m)	راعي البقر

129. Art professions

actor	momassel (m)	ممثّل
actress	momassela (f)	ممثّلة
singer (masc.)	moṭreb (m)	مطرب
singer (fem.)	moṭreba (f)	مطربة
dancer (masc.)	rāqeṣ (m)	راقص
dancer (fem.)	ra'āṣa (f)	راقصة
performer (masc.)	fannān (m)	فنّان
performer (fem.)	fannāna (f)	فنّانة
musician	'āzef (m)	عازف
pianist	'āzef biano (m)	عازف بيانو
guitar player	'āzef guitar (m)	عازف جيتار
conductor (orchestra ~)	qā'ed orkestra (m)	قائد أوركسترا
composer	molaḥḥen (m)	ملحّن
impresario	modīr fer'a (m)	مدير فرقة
film director	moχreg aflām (m)	مخرج أفلام
producer	monteg (m)	منتج
scriptwriter	kāteb senario (m)	كاتب سيناريو
critic	nāqed (m)	ناقد
writer	kāteb (m)	كاتب
poet	ʃā'er (m)	شاعر
sculptor	naḥḥāt (m)	نحّات
artist (painter)	rassām (m)	رسّام
juggler	bahlawān (m)	بهلوان
clown	aragoze (m)	أراجوز
acrobat	bahlawān (m)	بهلوان
magician	sāḥer (m)	ساحر

130. Various professions

doctor	doktore (m)	دكتور
nurse	momarreḍa (f)	ممرّضة
psychiatrist	doktore nafsāny (m)	دكتور نفساني
dentist	doktore asnān (m)	دكتور أسنان

surgeon	garrāḥ (m)	جرّاح
astronaut	rā'ed faḍā' (m)	رائد فضاء
astronomer	'ālem falak (m)	عالم فلك
pilot	ṭayār (m)	طيّار
driver (of a taxi, etc.)	sawwā' (m)	سوّاق
train driver	sawwā' (m)	سوّاق
mechanic	mikanīky (m)	ميكانيكي
miner	'āmel mangam (m)	عامل منجم
worker	'āmel (m)	عامل
locksmith	'affāl (m)	قفّال
joiner (carpenter)	naggār (m)	نجّار
turner (lathe operator)	χarrāṭ (m)	خرّاط
building worker	'āmel benā' (m)	عامل بناء
welder	laḥḥām (m)	لحّام
professor (title)	brofessor (m)	بروفيسور
architect	mohandes me'māry (m)	مهندس معماري
historian	mo'arreχ (m)	مؤرّخ
scientist	'ālem (m)	عالم
physicist	fizyā'y (m)	فيزيائي
chemist (scientist)	kemyā'y (m)	كيميائي
archaeologist	'ālem'āsār (m)	عالم آثار
geologist	ʒeoloʒy (m)	جيولوجي
researcher (scientist)	bāḥes (m)	باحث
babysitter	dāda (f)	دادة
teacher, educator	mo'allem (m)	معلّم
editor	moḥarrer (m)	محرّر
editor-in-chief	ra'īs taḥrīr (m)	رئيس تحرير
correspondent	morāsel (m)	مراسل
typist (fem.)	kāteba 'ala el 'āla el kāteba (f)	كاتبة على الآلة الكاتبة
designer	moṣammem (m)	مصمّم
computer expert	motaχaṣṣeṣ bel kombuter (m)	متخصص بالكمبيوتر
programmer	mobarmeg (m)	مبرمج
engineer (designer)	mohandes (m)	مهندس
sailor	baḥḥār (m)	بحّار
seaman	baḥḥār (m)	بحّار
rescuer	monqez (m)	منقذ
firefighter	rāgel el maṭāfy (m)	راجل المطافئ
police officer	ʃorṭy (m)	شرطي
watchman	ḥāres (m)	حارس
detective	moḥaqqeq (m)	محقّق
customs officer	mowazzaf el gamārek (m)	موظّف الجمارك
bodyguard	ḥāres ʃaχṣy (m)	حارس شخصي
prison officer	ḥāres segn (m)	حارس سجن
inspector	mofatteʃ (m)	مفتّش
sportsman	reyāḍy (m)	رياضي
trainer, coach	modarreb (m)	مدرّب

butcher	gazzār (m)	جزّار
cobbler (shoe repairer)	eskāfy (m)	إسكافي
merchant	tāger (m)	تاجر
loader (person)	ʃayāl (m)	شيّال
fashion designer	moṣammem azyā' (m)	مصمّم أزياء
model (fem.)	modeyl (f)	موديل

131. Occupations. Social status

schoolboy	talmīz (m)	تلميذ
student (college ~)	ṭāleb (m)	طالب
philosopher	faylasūf (m)	فيلسوف
economist	eqtiṣādy (m)	إقتصادي
inventor	moχtare' (m)	مخترع
unemployed (n)	'āṭel (m)	عاطل
retiree, pensioner	motaqā'ed (m)	متقاعد
spy, secret agent	gasūs (m)	جاسوس
prisoner	sagīn (m)	سجين
striker	moḍrab (m)	مضرب
bureaucrat	buroqrāṭy (m)	بيوروقراطي
traveller (globetrotter)	raḥḥāla (m)	رحّالة
gay, homosexual (n)	ʃāz (m)	شاذ
hacker	haker (m)	هاكر
hippie	hippi (m)	هيبي
bandit	qāṭe' ṭarī' (m)	قاطع طريق
hit man, killer	qātel ma'gūr (m)	قاتل مأجور
drug addict	modmen moχaddarāt (m)	مدمن مخدّرات
drug dealer	tāger moχaddarāt (m)	تاجر مخدّرات
prostitute (fem.)	mommos (f)	مومس
pimp	qawwād (m)	قوّاد
sorcerer	sāḥer (m)	ساحر
sorceress (evil ~)	sāḥera (f)	ساحرة
pirate	'orṣān (m)	قرصان
slave	'abd (m)	عبد
samurai	samuray (m)	ساموراي
savage (primitive)	motawaḥḥeʃ (m)	متوحّش

Sports

132. Kinds of sports. Sportspersons

sportsman	reyāḍy (m)	رياضي
kind of sport	nū' men el reyāḍa (m)	نوع من الرياضة
basketball	koret el salla (f)	كرة السلّة
basketball player	lā'eb korat el salla (m)	لاعب كرة السلّة
baseball	baseball (m)	بيسبول
baseball player	lā'eb basebāl (m)	لاعب بيسبول
football	koret el qadam (f)	كرة القدم
football player	lā'eb korat qadam (m)	لاعب كرة القدم
goalkeeper	ḥāres el marma (m)	حارس المرمى
ice hockey	hoky (m)	هوكي
ice hockey player	lā'eb hoky (m)	لاعب هوكي
volleyball	voliball (m)	فولي بول
volleyball player	lā'eb volly bal (m)	لاعب فولي بول
boxing	molakma (f)	ملاكمة
boxer	molākem (m)	ملاكم
wrestling	moṣar'a (f)	مصارعة
wrestler	moṣāre' (m)	مصارع
karate	karate (m)	كاراتيه
karate fighter	lā'eb karateyh (m)	لاعب كاراتيه
judo	ʒudo (m)	جودو
judo athlete	lā'eb ʒudo (m)	لاعب جودو
tennis	tennis (m)	تنسّ
tennis player	lā'eb tennis (m)	لاعب تنس
swimming	sebāḥa (f)	سباحة
swimmer	sabbāḥ (m)	سبّاح
fencing	mobarza (f)	مبارزة
fencer	mobārez (m)	مبارز
chess	ʃaṭarang (m)	شطرنج
chess player	lā'eb ʃaṭarang (m)	لاعب شطرنج
alpinism	tasalloq el gebāl (m)	تسلّق الجبال
alpinist	motasalleq el gebāl (m)	متسلّق الجبال
running	garyī (m)	جريّ

runner	'addā' (m)	عدّاء
athletics	al'āb el qowa (pl)	ألعاب القوى
athlete	lā'eb reyāḍy (m)	لاعب رياضي
horse riding	reyāḍa el forūsiya (f)	رياضة الفروسيّة
horse rider	fāres (m)	فارس
figure skating	tazallog fanny 'alal galīd (m)	تزلّج فنّي على الجليد
figure skater (masc.)	motazalleg rāqeṣ (m)	متزلّج راقص
figure skater (fem.)	motazallega rāqeṣa (f)	متزلّجة راقصة
powerlifting	raf' el asqāl (m)	رفع الأثقال
powerlifter	rāfe' el asqāl (m)	رافع الأثقال
car racing	sebā' el sayarāt (m)	سباق السيارات
racer (driver)	sawwā' sebā' (m)	سائق سباق
cycling	rokūb el darragāt (m)	ركوب الدرّاجات
cyclist	lā'eb el darrāga (m)	لاعب الدرّاجة
long jump	el qafz el 'āly (m)	القفز العالي
pole vaulting	el qafz bel 'aṣa (m)	القفز بالعصا
jumper	qāfez (m)	قافز

133. Kinds of sports. Miscellaneous

American football	koret el qadam (f)	كرة القدم
badminton	el rīʃa (m)	الريشة
biathlon	el biatlon (m)	البياتلون
billiards	bilyardo (m)	بلياردو
bobsleigh	zalāga gama'iya (f)	زلاجة جماعية
bodybuilding	body building (m)	بادي بيلدنج
water polo	koret el maya (f)	كرة الميّة
handball	koret el yad (f)	كرة اليد
golf	golf (m)	جولف
rowing	tagdīf (m)	تجديف
scuba diving	ɣoṣe (m)	غوص
cross-country skiing	reyāḍa el ski (f)	رياضة الإسكي
table tennis (ping-pong)	koret el ṭawla (f)	كرة الطاولة
sailing	reyāḍa ebḥār el marākeb (f)	رياضة إبحارالمراكب
rally	sebā' el sayarāt (m)	سباق السيارات
rugby	rugby (m)	رجبي
snowboarding	el tazallog 'lal galīd (m)	التزلّج على الجليد
archery	remāya (f)	رماية

134. Gym

barbell	bār ḥadīd (m)	بار حديد
dumbbells	dumbbells (m)	دمبلز

training machine	gehāz tadrīb (m)	جهاز تدريب
exercise bicycle	ʿagalet tadrīb (f)	عجلة تدريب
treadmill	trīdmil (f)	تريد ميل
horizontal bar	ʿoʾla (f)	عقلة
parallel bars	el motawaziyīn (pl)	المتوازيين
vault (vaulting horse)	manaṣṣet el qafz (f)	منصّة القفز
mat (exercise ~)	ḥaṣīra (f)	حصيرة
skipping rope	ḥabl el naṭṭ (m)	حبل النطّ
aerobics	aerobiks (m)	ايروبيكس
yoga	yoga (f)	يوجا

135. Ice hockey

ice hockey	hoky (m)	هوكي
ice hockey player	lāʿeb hoky (m)	لاعب هوكي
to play ice hockey	leʿeb el hoky	لعب الهوكي
ice	galīd (m)	جليد
puck	ʾorṣ el hoky (m)	قرص الهوكي
ice hockey stick	maḍrab el hoky (m)	مضرب الهوكي
ice skates	zallagāt (pl)	زلّاجات
board (ice hockey rink ~)	ḥalabet el hokky (f)	حلبة الهوكي
shot	ramya (f)	رمية
goaltender	ḥāres el marma (m)	حارس المرمى
goal (score)	hadaf (m)	هدف
to score a goal	gāb hadaf	جاب هدف
period	ʃoṭe (m)	شوط
second period	el ʃoṭe el tāni (m)	الشوط التاني
substitutes bench	dekket el eḥtiāṭy (f)	دكّة الإحتياطي

136. Football

football	koret el qadam (f)	كرة القدم
football player	lāʿeb korat qadam (m)	لاعب كرة القدم
to play football	leʿeb korret el qadam	لعب كرة القدم
major league	el dawry el kebīr (m)	الدوّري الكبير
football club	nādy koret el qadam (m)	نادي كرة القدم
coach	modarreb (m)	مدرّب
owner, proprietor	ṣāḥeb (m)	صاحب
team	farīʾ (m)	فريق
team captain	kabten el farīʾ (m)	كابتن الفريق
player	lāʿeb (m)	لاعب
substitute	lāʿeb eḥteyāṭy (m)	لاعب إحتياطي
forward	lāʿeb hogūm (m)	لاعب هجوم
centre forward	wasaṭ el hogūm (m)	وسط الهجوم

scorer	haddāf (m)	هدّاف
defender, back	modāfeʿ (m)	مدافع
midfielder, halfback	lāʿeb χaṭṭ wasaṭ (m)	لاعب خطّ وسط
match	mobarā (f)	مباراة
to meet (vi, vt)	ʾābel	قابل
final	mobarāh neha'iya (f)	مباراة نهائيّة
semi-final	el dore el neṣf el nehāʾy (m)	الدور النصف النهائي
championship	boṭūla (f)	بطولة
period, half	ʃoṭe (m)	شوط
first period	el ʃoṭe el awwal (m)	الشوط الأوّل
half-time	beyn el ʃoṭeyn	بين الشوطين
goal	marma (m)	مرمى
goalkeeper	ḥāres el marma (m)	حارس المرمى
goalpost	ʿārḍa (f)	عارضة
crossbar	ʿārḍa (f)	عارضة
net	ʃabaka (f)	شبكة
to concede a goal	samaḥ be eṣābet el hadaf	سمح بإصابة الهدف
ball	kora (f)	كرة
pass	tamrīra (f)	تمريرة
kick	ḍarba (f)	ضربة
to kick (~ the ball)	ʃāt	شات
free kick (direct ~)	ḍarba ḥorra (f)	ضربة حرّة
corner kick	ḍarba rokniya (f)	ضربة ركنيّة
attack	hogūm (m)	هجوم
counterattack	hagma moḍāda (f)	هجمة مضادّة
combination	tarkīb (m)	تركيب
referee	ḥakam (m)	حكم
to blow the whistle	ṣaffar	صفّر
whistle (sound)	ṣoffāra (f)	صفّارة
foul, misconduct	moχalfa (f)	مخالفة
to commit a foul	χālef	خالف
to send off	ṭarad men el malʿab	طرد من الملعب
yellow card	el kart el aṣfar (m)	الكارت الأصفر
red card	el kart el aḥmar (m)	الكارت الأحمر
disqualification	ḥermān (m)	حرمان
to disqualify (vt)	ḥaram	حرم
penalty kick	ḍarbet gazāʾ (f)	ضربة جزاء
wall	ḥāʾeṭ (m)	حائط
to score (vi, vt)	gāb hadaf	جاب هدف
goal (score)	hadaf (m)	هدف
to score a goal	gāb hadaf	جاب هدف
substitution	tabdīl (m)	تبديل
to replace (a player)	baddal	بدّل
rules	qawāʿed (pl)	قواعد
tactics	taktīk (m)	تكتيك
stadium	malʿab (m)	ملعب
terrace	modarrag (m)	مدرّج

fan, supporter	moʃaggeʿ (m)	مشجّع
to shout (vi)	ṣarraχ	صرّخ
scoreboard	lawḥet el natīga (f)	لوحة النتيجة
score	natīga (f)	نتيجة
defeat	hazīma (f)	هزيمة
to lose (not win)	χeser	خسر
draw	taʿādol (m)	تعادل
to draw (vi)	taʿādal	تعادل
victory	foze (m)	فوز
to win (vi, vt)	fāz	فاز
champion	baṭal (m)	بطل
best (adj)	aḥsan	أحسن
to congratulate (vt)	hanna	هنّأ
commentator	moʿalleq (m)	معلّق
to commentate (vt)	ʿallaʾ	علّق
broadcast	ezāʿa (f)	إذاعة

137. Alpine skiing

skis	zallagāt (pl)	زلّاجات
to ski (vi)	tazallag	تزلّج
mountain-ski resort	montagaʿ gabaly lel tazaḥloq (m)	منتجع جبلي للتزلج
ski lift	meṣʿad (m)	مصعد
ski poles	ʿeṣyān el tazallog (pl)	عصيان التزلّج
slope	monḥadar (m)	منحدر
slalom	el tazallog el motaʿarreg (m)	التزلّج المتعرّج

138. Tennis. Golf

golf	golf (m)	جولف
golf club	nādy golf (m)	نادي جولف
golfer	lāʿeb golf (m)	لاعب جولف
hole	tagwīf (m)	تجويف
club	maḍrab (m)	مضرب
golf trolley	ʿaraba lel golf (f)	عربة للجولف
tennis	tennis (m)	تنسّ
tennis court	malʿab tennis (m)	ملعب تنسّ
serve	monawla (f)	مناولة
to serve (vt)	nāwel	ناول
racket	maḍrab (m)	مضرب
net	ʃabaka (f)	شبكة
ball	kora (f)	كرة

139. Chess

chess	ʃaṭarang (m)	شطرنج
chessmen	aḥgār el ʃaṭarang (pl)	أحجار الشطرنج
chess player	lā'eb ʃaṭarang (m)	لاعب شطرنج
chessboard	lawḥet el ʃaṭarang (f)	لوحة الشطرنج
chessman	ḥagar (m)	حجر
White (white pieces)	aḥgār bayḍā' (pl)	أحجار بيضاء
Black (black pieces)	aḥgār sawdā' (pl)	أحجار سوداء
pawn	bayda' (m)	بيدق
bishop	fīl (m)	فيل
knight	ḥoṣān (m)	حصان
rook	rakχ (m)	رخّ
queen	el maleka (f)	الملكة
king	el malek (m)	الملك
move	χaṭwa (f)	خطوة
to move (vi, vt)	ḥarrak	حرّك
to sacrifice (vt)	ḍaḥḥa	ضحّى
castling	χaṭwa el raχ wel ʃah (f)	خطوة الرخ والشاه
check	kesʃ	كشّ
checkmate	kesʃ malek	كشّ ملك
chess tournament	boṭūlet ʃaṭarang (f)	بطولة شطرنج
Grand Master	grand master (m)	جراند ماستر
combination	tarkīb (m)	تركيب
game (in chess)	dore (m)	دور
draughts	dama (f)	داما

140. Boxing

boxing	molakma (f)	ملاكمة
fight (bout)	molakma (f)	ملاكمة
boxing match	mobarāt molakma (f)	مباراة ملاكمة
round (in boxing)	gawla (f)	جولة
ring	ḥalaba (f)	حلبة
gong	naqūs (m)	ناقوس
punch	ḍarba (f)	ضربة
knockdown	ḍarba ḥasema (f)	ضربة حاسمة
knockout	ḍarba 'āḍya (f)	ضربة قاضية
to knock out	ḍarab ḍarba qāḍiya	ضرب ضربة قاضية
boxing glove	qoffāz el molakma (m)	قفّاز الملاكمة
referee	ḥakam (m)	حكم
lightweight	el wazn el χafīf (m)	الوزن الخفيف
middleweight	el wazn el motawasseṭ (m)	الوزن المتوسط
heavyweight	el wazn el te'īl (m)	الوزن الثقيل

141. Sports. Miscellaneous

Olympic Games	al'āb olombiya (pl)	ألعاب أولمبيّة
winner	fā'ez (m)	فائز
to be winning	fāz	فاز
to win (vi)	fāz	فاز
leader	za'īm (m)	زعيم
to lead (vi)	ta'addam	تقدّم
first place	el martaba el ūla (f)	المرتبة الأولى
second place	el martaba el tanya (f)	المرتبة الثانية
third place	el martaba el talta (f)	المرتبة الثالثة
medal	medalya (f)	ميدالية
trophy	ka's (f)	كأس
prize cup (trophy)	ka's (f)	كأس
prize (in game)	gayza (f)	جائزة
main prize	akbar gayza (f)	أكبر جائزة
record	raqam qeyāsy (m)	رقم قياسي
to set a record	fāz be raqam qeyāsy	فاز برقم قياسي
final	mobarāh neha'iya (f)	مباراة نهائيّة
final (adj)	nehā'y	نهائي
champion	baṭal (m)	بطل
championship	boṭūla (f)	بطولة
stadium	mal'ab (m)	ملعب
terrace	modarrag (m)	مدرّج
fan, supporter	moʃagge' (m)	مشجّع
opponent, rival	'adeww (m)	عدو
start (start line)	xaṭṭ el bedāya (m)	خطّ البداية
finish line	xaṭṭ el nehāya (m)	خطّ النهاية
defeat	hazīma (f)	هزيمة
to lose (not win)	xeser	خسر
referee	ḥakam (m)	حكم
jury (judges)	hay'et el ḥokm (f)	هيئة الحكم
score	natīga (f)	نتيجة
draw	ta'ādol (m)	تعادل
to draw (vi)	ta'ādal	تعادل
point	no'ṭa (f)	نقطة
result (final score)	natīga neha'iya (f)	نتيجة نهائية
period	ʃoṭe (m)	شوط
half-time	beyn el ʃoṭeyn	بين الشوطين
doping	monasʃeṭāt (pl)	منشّطات
to penalise (vt)	'āqab	عاقب
to disqualify (vt)	ḥaram	حرم
apparatus	adah (f)	أداة
javelin	remḥ (m)	رمح

shot (metal ball)	kora maʿdaniya (f)	كرة معدنية
ball (snooker, etc.)	kora (f)	كرة
aim (target)	hadaf (m)	هدف
target	hadaf (m)	هدف
to shoot (vi)	ḍarab bel nār	ضرب بالنار
accurate (~ shot)	maḍbūṭ	مضبوط
trainer, coach	modarreb (m)	مدرّب
to train (sb)	darrab	درّب
to train (vi)	etdarrab	إتدرّب
training	tadrīb (m)	تدريب
gym	gīm (m)	جيم
exercise (physical)	tamrīn (m)	تمرين
warm-up (athlete ~)	tasχīn (m)	تسخين

Education

142. School

school	madrasa (f)	مدرسة
headmaster	modīr el madrasa (m)	مدير المدرسة
student (m)	talmīz (m)	تلميذ
student (f)	telmīza (f)	تلميذة
schoolboy	talmīz (m)	تلميذ
schoolgirl	telmīza (f)	تلميذة
to teach (sb)	ʿallem	علّم
to learn (language, etc.)	taʿallam	تعلّم
to learn by heart	ḥafaẓ	حفظ
to learn (~ to count, etc.)	taʿallam	تعلّم
to be at school	daras	درس
to go to school	rāḥ el madrasa	راح المدرسة
alphabet	abgadiya (f)	أبجدية
subject (at school)	madda (f)	مادّة
classroom	faṣl (m)	فصل
lesson	dars (m)	درس
playtime, break	estrāḥa (f)	إستراحة
school bell	garas el madrasa (m)	جرس المدرسة
school desk	disk el madrasa (m)	ديسك المدرسة
blackboard	sabbūra (f)	سبّورة
mark	daraga (f)	درجة
good mark	daraga kewayesa (f)	درجة كويسة
bad mark	daraga meʃ kewayesa (f)	درجة مش كويسة
to give a mark	edda daraga	إدّى درجة
mistake, error	χaṭaʾ (m)	خطأ
to make mistakes	aχṭaʾ	أخطأ
to correct (an error)	ṣaḥḥaḥ	صحّح
crib	berʃām (m)	برشام
homework	wāgeb (m)	واجب
exercise (in education)	tamrīn (m)	تمرين
to be present	ḥaḍar	حضر
to be absent	ɣāb	غاب
to miss school	taɣeyyab ʿan el madrasa	تغيّب عن المدرسة
to punish (vt)	ʿāqab	عاقب
punishment	ʿeqāb (m)	عقاب
conduct (behaviour)	solūk (m)	سلوك

school report	el taqrīr el madrasy (m)	التقرير المدرسي
pencil	'alam roṣāṣ (m)	قلم رصاص
rubber	astīka (f)	استيكة
chalk	ṭabaʃīr (m)	طباشير
pencil case	ma'lama (f)	مقلمة
schoolbag	ʃanṭet el madrasa (f)	شنطة المدرسة
pen	'alam (m)	قلم
exercise book	daftar (m)	دفتر
textbook	ketāb ta'līm (m)	كتاب تعليم
compasses	bargal (m)	برجل
to make technical drawings	rasam rasm teqany	رسم رسم تقني
technical drawing	rasm teqany (m)	رسم تقني
poem	'aṣīda (f)	قصيدة
by heart (adv)	'an ẓahr qalb	عن ظهر قلب
to learn by heart	ḥafaẓ	حفظ
school holidays	agāza (f)	أجازة
to be on holiday	'ando agāza	عنده أجازة
to spend holidays	'aḍa el agāza	قضى الأجازة
test (at school)	emteḥān (m)	إمتحان
essay (composition)	enʃā' (m)	إنشاء
dictation	emlā' (m)	إملاء
exam (examination)	emteḥān (m)	إمتحان
to do an exam	'amal emteḥān	عمل إمتحان
experiment (e.g., chemistry ~)	tagreba (f)	تجربة

143. College. University

academy	akademiya (f)	أكاديميّة
university	gam'a (f)	جامعة
faculty (e.g., ~ of Medicine)	kolliya (f)	كلّيّة
student (masc.)	ṭāleb (m)	طالب
student (fem.)	ṭāleba (f)	طالبة
lecturer (teacher)	muḥāḍer (m)	محاضر
lecture hall, room	modarrag (m)	مدرّج
graduate	motaχarreg (m)	متخرج
diploma	dibloma (f)	دبلومة
dissertation	resāla 'elmiya (f)	رسالة علميّة
study (report)	derāsa (f)	دراسة
laboratory	moχtabar (m)	مختبر
lecture	moḥaḍra (f)	محاضرة
coursemate	zamīl fel ṣaff (m)	زميل في الصفّ
scholarship, bursary	menḥa derāsiya (f)	منحة دراسيّة
academic degree	daraga 'elmiya (f)	درجة علميّة

144. Sciences. Disciplines

mathematics	reyāḍīāt (pl)	رياضيّات
algebra	el gabr (m)	الجبر
geometry	handasa (f)	هندسة
astronomy	'elm el falak (m)	علم الفلك
biology	al aḥya' (m)	الأحياء
geography	goɣrafia (f)	جغرافيا
geology	ʒeoloʒia (f)	جيولوجيا
history	tarīx (m)	تاريخ
medicine	ṭebb (m)	طبّ
pedagogy	tarbeya (f)	تربية
law	qanūn (m)	قانون
physics	fezya' (f)	فيزياء
chemistry	kemya' (f)	كيمياء
philosophy	falsafa (f)	فلسفة
psychology	'elm el nafs (m)	علم النفس

145. Writing system. Orthography

grammar	el naḥw wel ṣarf (m)	النحو والصرف
vocabulary	mofradāt el loɣa (pl)	مفردات اللغة
phonetics	ṣawtīāt (pl)	صوتيات
noun	esm (m)	اسم
adjective	ṣefa (f)	صفة
verb	fe'l (m)	فعل
adverb	ẓarf (m)	ظرف
pronoun	ḍamīr (m)	ضمير
interjection	oslūb el ta'aggob (m)	أسلوب التعجّب
preposition	ḥarf el garr (m)	حرف الجرّ
root	gezr el kelma (m)	جذر الكلمة
ending	nehāya (f)	نهاية
prefix	sabaeqa (f)	سابقة
syllable	maqṭa' lafzy (m)	مقطع لفظي
suffix	lāḥeqa (f)	لاحقة
stress mark	nabra (f)	نبرة
apostrophe	'alāmet ḥazf (f)	علامة حذف
full stop	no'ṭa (f)	نقطة
comma	faṣla (f)	فاصلة
semicolon	no'ṭa w faṣla (f)	نقطة وفاصلة
colon	no'ṭeteyn (pl)	نقطتين
ellipsis	talat no'aṭ (pl)	ثلاث نقط
question mark	'alāmet estefhām (f)	علامة إستفهام
exclamation mark	'alāmet ta'aggob (f)	علامة تعجّب

inverted commas	ʿalamāt el eqtebās (pl)	علامات الإقتباس
in inverted commas	beyn ʿalamaty el eqtebās	بين علامتي الاقتباس
parenthesis	qoseyn (du)	قوسين
in parenthesis	beyn el qoseyn	بين القوسين
hyphen	ʿalāmet waṣl (f)	علامة وصل
dash	ʃorṭa (f)	شرطة
space (between words)	farāɣ (m)	فراغ
letter	ḥarf (m)	حرف
capital letter	ḥarf kebīr (m)	حرف كبير
vowel (n)	ḥarf ṣauty (m)	حرف صوتي
consonant (n)	ḥarf sāken (m)	حرف ساكن
sentence	gomla (f)	جملة
subject	fāʿel (m)	فاعل
predicate	mosnad (m)	مسند
line	saṭr (m)	سطر
on a new line	men bedāyet el saṭr	من بداية السطر
paragraph	faqra (f)	فقرة
word	kelma (f)	كلمة
group of words	magmūʿa men el kelamāt (pl)	مجموعة من الكلمات
expression	moṣṭalaḥ (m)	مصطلح
synonym	morādef (m)	مرادف
antonym	motaḍād loɣawy (m)	متضاد لغوي
rule	qaʿeda (f)	قاعدة
exception	estesnāʾ (m)	إستثناء
correct (adj)	ṣaḥīḥ	صحيح
conjugation	ṣarf (m)	صرف
declension	taṣrīf el asmāʾ (m)	تصريف الأسماء
nominal case	ḥāla esmiya (f)	حالة أسمية
question	soʾāl (m)	سؤال
to underline (vt)	ḥaṭṭ χaṭṭ taḥt	حطّ خطّ تحت
dotted line	χaṭṭ menaʾʾaṭ (m)	خطّ منقّط

146. Foreign languages

language	loɣa (f)	لغة
foreign (adj)	agnaby	أجنبيّ
foreign language	loɣa agnabiya (f)	لغة أجنبية
to study (vt)	daras	درس
to learn (language, etc.)	taʿallam	تعلّم
to read (vi, vt)	ʾara	قرأ
to speak (vi, vt)	kallem	كلّم
to understand (vt)	fehem	فهم
to write (vt)	katab	كتب
fast (adv)	bosorʿa	بسرعة
slowly (adv)	bo boṭʾ	ببطء

fluently (adv)	beṭalāqa	بطلاقة
rules	qawā'ed (pl)	قواعد
grammar	el naḥw wel ṣarf (m)	النحو والصرف
vocabulary	mofradāt el loɣa (pl)	مفردات اللغة
phonetics	ṣawtīāt (pl)	صوتيات
textbook	ketāb ta'līm (m)	كتاب تعليم
dictionary	qamūs (m)	قاموس
teach-yourself book	ketāb ta'līm zāty (m)	كتاب تعليم ذاتي
phrasebook	ketāb lel 'ebarāt el ʃā'e'a (m)	كتاب للعبارت الشائعة
cassette, tape	kasett (m)	كاسيت
videotape	ʃerī'ṭ video (m)	شريط فيديو
CD, compact disc	sidī (m)	سي دي
DVD	dividī (m)	دي في دي
alphabet	abgadiya (f)	أبجدية
to spell (vt)	tahagga	تهجّى
pronunciation	noṭ' (m)	نطق
accent	lahga (f)	لهجة
with an accent	be lahga	بـ لهجة
without an accent	men ɣeyr lahga	من غير لهجة
word	kelma (f)	كلمة
meaning	ma'na (m)	معنى
course (e.g. a French ~)	dawra (f)	دورة
to sign up	saggel esmo	سجّل إسمه
teacher	modarres (m)	مدرّس
translation (process)	targama (f)	ترجمة
translation (text, etc.)	targama (f)	ترجمة
translator	motargem (m)	مترجم
interpreter	motargem fawwry (m)	مترجم فوّري
polyglot	'alīm be'eddet loɣāt (m)	عليم بعدّة لغات
memory	zākera (f)	ذاكرة

147. Fairy tale characters

Father Christmas	baba neweyl (m)	بابا نويل
Cinderella	sindrīla	سيندريلا
mermaid	'arūset el baḥr (f)	عروسة البحر
Neptune	nibtūn (m)	نبتون
magician, wizard	sāḥer (m)	ساحر
fairy	genniya (f)	جنّيّة
magic (adj)	seḥry	سحري
magic wand	el 'aṣāya el seḥriya (f)	العصاية السحرية
fairy tale	ḥekāya xayaliya (f)	حكاية خيالية
miracle	mo'geza (f)	معجزة
dwarf	qazam (m)	قزم

to turn into ...	taḥawwal ela ...	تحوّل إلى...
ghost	ʃabaḥ (m)	شبح
phantom	ʃabaḥ (m)	شبح
monster	waḥʃ (m)	وحش
dragon	tennīn (m)	تنّين
giant	ʿemlāq (m)	عملاق

148. Zodiac Signs

Aries	borg el ḥaml (m)	برج الحمل
Taurus	borg el sore (m)	برج الثور
Gemini	borg el gawzāʾ (m)	برج الجوزاء
Cancer	borg el saraṭān (m)	برج السرطان
Leo	borg el asad (m)	برج الأسد
Virgo	borg el ʿazrāʾ (m)	برج العذراء
Libra	borg el mezān (m)	برج الميزان
Scorpio	borg el ʿaʾrab (m)	برج العقرب
Sagittarius	borg el qose (m)	برج القوس
Capricorn	borg el gady (m)	برج الجدي
Aquarius	borg el dalw (m)	برج الدلو
Pisces	borg el ḥūt (m)	برج الحوت
character	ʃaχṣiya (f)	شخصية
character traits	el ṣefāt el ʃaχṣiya (pl)	الصفات الشخصية
behaviour	solūk (m)	سلوك
to tell fortunes	ʾara el ṭāleʿ	قرأ الطالع
fortune-teller	ʿarrāfa (f)	عرّافة
horoscope	tawaqqoʿāt el abrāg (pl)	توقّعات الأبراج

Arts

149. Theatre

theatre	masraḥ (m)	مسرح
opera	obra (f)	أوبرا
operetta	obrette (f)	أوبريت
ballet	baleyh (m)	باليه
theatre poster	molṣaq (m)	ملصق
theatre company	fer'a (f)	فرقة
tour	gawlet fananīn (f)	جولة فنّانين
to be on tour	tagawwal	تجوّل
to rehearse (vi, vt)	ʿamal brova	عمل بروفة
rehearsal	brova (f)	بروفة
repertoire	barnāmeg el masraḥ (m)	برنامج المسرح
performance	adāʾ (m)	أداء
theatrical show	ʿarḍ masraḥy (m)	عرض مسرحي
play	masraḥiya (f)	مسرحيّة
ticket	tazkara (f)	تذكرة
booking office	ʃebbāk el tazāker (m)	شبّاك التذاكر
lobby, foyer	ṣāla (f)	صالة
coat check (cloakroom)	ɣorfet īdāʿ el maʿāṭef (f)	غرفة إيداع المعاطف
cloakroom ticket	beṭāʾet edāʿ el maʿaṭef (f)	بطاقة إيداع المعاطف
binoculars	naḍḍāra moʿaẓẓema lel obera (f)	نظارة معظمة للأوبرا
usher	ḥāgeb el sinema (m)	حاجب السينما
stalls (orchestra seats)	karāsy el orkestra (pl)	كراسي الأوركسترا
balcony	balakona (f)	بلكونة
dress circle	ʃorfa (f)	شرفة
box	log (m)	لوج
row	ṣaff (m)	صفّ
seat	meqʿad (m)	مقعد
audience	gomhūr (m)	جمهور
spectator	moʃāhed (m)	مشاهد
to clap (vi, vt)	ṣaffaʾ	صفّق
applause	taṣfīʾ (m)	تصفيق
ovation	taṣfīʾ ḥār (m)	تصفيق حار
stage	χaʃabet el masraḥ (f)	خشبة المسرح
curtain	setāra (f)	ستارة
scenery	dekor (m)	ديكور
backstage	kawalīs (pl)	كواليس
scene (e.g. the last ~)	maʃ-had (m)	مشهد
act	faṣl (m)	فصل
interval	estrāḥa (f)	استراحة

150. Cinema

actor	momassel (m)	ممثّل
actress	momassela (f)	ممثّلة
cinema (industry)	el aflām (m)	الأفلام
film	film (m)	فيلم
episode	goz' (m)	جزء
detective film	film bolīsy (m)	فيلم بوليسي
action film	film akʃen (m)	فيلم أكشن
adventure film	film moɣamarāt (m)	فيلم مغامرات
science fiction film	film χayāl 'elmy (m)	فيلم خيال علمي
horror film	film ro'b (m)	فيلم رعب
comedy film	film komedia (f)	فيلم كوميديا
melodrama	melodrama (m)	ميلودراما
drama	drama (f)	دراما
fictional film	film χayāly (m)	فيلم خيالي
documentary	film wasā'eqy (m)	فيلم وثائقي
cartoon	kartōn (m)	كرتون
silent films	sinema ṣāmeta (f)	سينما صامتة
role (part)	dore (m)	دور
leading role	dore ra'īsy (m)	دور رئيسي
to play (vi, vt)	massel	مثّل
film star	negm senamā'y (m)	نجم سينمائي
well-known (adj)	ma'rūf	معروف
famous (adj)	maʃ-hūr	مشهور
popular (adj)	maḥbūb	محبوب
script (screenplay)	senario (m)	سيناريو
scriptwriter	kāteb senario (m)	كاتب سيناريو
film director	moχreg (m)	مخرج
producer	monteg (m)	منتج
assistant	mosā'ed (m)	مساعد
cameraman	moṣawwer (m)	مصوّر
stuntman	mo'addy maʃāhed χaṭīra (m)	مؤدي مشاهد خطيرة
double (body double)	momassel badīl (m)	ممثّل بديل
to shoot a film	ṣawwar film	صوّر فيلم
audition, screen test	tagreba adā' (f)	تجربة أداء
shooting	taṣwīr (m)	تصوير
film crew	ṭāqem el film (m)	طاقم الفيلم
film set	mante'et taṣwīr (f)	منطقة التصوير
camera	kamera (f)	كاميرا
cinema	sinema (f)	سينما
screen (e.g. big ~)	ʃāʃa (f)	شاشة
to show a film	'araḍ film	عرض فيلم
soundtrack	mosīqa taṣweriya (f)	موسيقى تصويرية
special effects	mo'asserāt χāṣa (pl)	مؤثّرات خاصّة

subtitles	targamet el ḥewār (f)	ترجمة الحوار
credits	ʃāret el nehāya (f)	شارة النهاية
translation	targama (f)	ترجمة

151. Painting

art	fann (m)	فنّ
fine arts	fonūn gamīla (pl)	فنون جميلة
art gallery	maʿraḍ fonūn (m)	معرض فنون
art exhibition	maʿraḍ fanny (m)	معرض فنّي
painting (art)	lawḥa (f)	لوحة
graphic art	fann taṣwīry (m)	فن تصويري
abstract art	fann tagrīdy (m)	فنّ تجريدي
impressionism	el enṭebāʿiya (f)	الإنطباعيّة
picture (painting)	lawḥa (f)	لوحة
drawing	rasm (m)	رسم
poster	boster (m)	بوستر
illustration (picture)	rasm tawḍīḥy (m)	رسم توضيحي
miniature	ṣūra moṣaɣyara (f)	صورة مصغّرة
copy (of painting, etc.)	nosχa (f)	نسخة
reproduction	nosχa ṭebʾ el aṣl (f)	نسخة طبق الأصل
mosaic	fosayfesāʾ (f)	فسيفساء
stained glass window	ʃebbāk ʾezāz mlawwen (m)	شبّاك قزاز ملوّن
fresco	taṣwīr gaṣṣy (m)	تصوير جصي
engraving	naʾʃ (m)	نقش
bust (sculpture)	temsāl neṣfy (m)	تمثال نصفي
sculpture	naḥt (m)	نحت
statue	temsāl (m)	تمثال
plaster of Paris	gibss (m)	جيبس
plaster (as adj)	men el gebs	من الجيبس
portrait	bortreyh (m)	بورتريه
self-portrait	bortreyh ʃaχṣy (m)	بورتريه شخصي
landscape painting	lawḥet manzar ṭabeeʿy (f)	لوحة منظر طبيعي
still life	ṭabeeʿa ṣāmeta (f)	طبيعة صامتة
caricature	ṣūra karikatoriya (f)	صورة كاريكاتورية
sketch	rasm tamhīdy (m)	رسم تمهيدي
paint	lone (m)	لون
watercolor paint	alwān maya (m)	ألوان ميّة
oil (paint)	zeyt (m)	زيت
pencil	ʾalam roṣāṣ (m)	قلم رصاص
Indian ink	ḥebr hendy (m)	حبر هندي
charcoal	faḥm (m)	فحم
to draw (vi, vt)	rasam	رسم
to paint (vi, vt)	rasam	رسم
to pose (vi)	ʾaʿad	قعد
artist's model (masc.)	modeyl ḥayī amām el rassām (m)	موديل حيّ أمام الرسّام

artist's model (fem.)	modeyl ḥayī amām el rassām (m)	موديل حيّ أمام الرسّام
artist (painter)	rassām (m)	رسّام
work of art	'amal fanny (m)	عمل فنّي
masterpiece	toḥfa faniya (f)	تحفة فنية
studio (artist's workroom)	warʃa (f)	ورشة
canvas (cloth)	kanava (f)	كانفا
easel	masnad el loḥe (m)	مسند اللوح
palette	lawḥet el alwān (f)	لوحة الألوان
frame (picture ~, etc.)	eṭār (m)	إطار
restoration	tarmīm (m)	ترميم
to restore (vt)	rammem	رمّم

152. Literature & Poetry

literature	adab (m)	أدب
author (writer)	mo'allef (m)	مؤلّف
pseudonym	esm mosta'ār (m)	اسم مستعار
book	ketāb (m)	كتاب
volume	mogallad (m)	مجلّد
table of contents	gadwal el moḥtawayāt (m)	جدوَل المحتويات
page	ṣafḥa (f)	صفحة
main character	el ʃaχṣiya el ra'esiya (f)	الشخصية الرئيسية
autograph	tawqee' el mo'allef (m)	توقيع المؤلّف
short story	qeṣṣa 'aṣīra (f)	قصّة قصيرة
story (novella)	'oṣṣa (f)	قصّة
novel	rewāya (f)	رواية
work (writing)	mo'allef (m)	مؤلّف
fable	ḥekāya (f)	حكاية
detective novel	rewāya bolesiya (f)	رواية بوليسية
poem (verse)	'aṣīda (f)	قصيدة
poetry	ʃe'r (m)	شعر
poem (epic, ballad)	'aṣīda (f)	قصيدة
poet	ʃā'er (m)	شاعر
fiction	χayāl (m)	خيال
science fiction	χayāl 'elmy (m)	خيال علمي
adventures	adab el moɣamrāt (m)	أدب المغامرات
educational literature	adab tarbawy (m)	أدب تربوّي
children's literature	adab el aṭfāl (m)	أدب الأطفال

153. Circus

circus	serk (m)	سيرك
travelling circus	serk motana''el (m)	سيرك متنقّل
programme	barnāmeg (m)	برنامج
performance	adā' (m)	أداء

act (circus ~)	ʿarḍ (m)	عرض
circus ring	ḥalabet el serk (f)	حلبة السيرك
pantomime (act)	momassel īmāʾy (m)	ممثّل إيمائي
clown	aragoze (m)	أراجوز
acrobat	bahlawān (m)	بهلوان
acrobatics	alʿab bahlawaniya (f)	ألعاب بهلوانية
gymnast	lāʿeb gombāz (m)	لاعب جمباز
acrobatic gymnastics	gombāz (m)	جمباز
somersault	ḥarakāt ʃaʾlaba (pl)	حركات شقلبة
strongman	el ragl el qawy (m)	الرجل القوي
tamer (e.g., lion ~)	morawweḍ (m)	مروّض
rider (circus horse ~)	fāres (m)	فارس
assistant	mosāʿed (m)	مساعد
stunt	ḥeyla (f)	حيلة
magic trick	χedʿa seḥriya (f)	خدعة سحرية
conjurer, magician	sāḥer (m)	ساحر
juggler	bahlawān (m)	بهلوان
to juggle (vi, vt)	leʿeb be korāt ʿadīda	لعب بكرات عديدة
animal trainer	modarreb ḥayawanāt (m)	مدرّب حيوانات
animal training	tadrīb el ḥayawanāt (m)	تدريب الحيوانات
to train (animals)	darrab	درّب

154. Music. Pop music

music	mosīqa (f)	موسيقى
musician	ʿāzef (m)	عازف
musical instrument	ʾāla moseqiya (f)	آلة موسيقيّة
to play ...	ʿazaf ...	عزف...
guitar	guitar (m)	جيتار
violin	kamān (m)	كمان
cello	el tʃello (m)	التشيلو
double bass	kamān kebīr (m)	كمان كبير
harp	qesār (m)	قيثار
piano	biano (m)	بيانو
grand piano	biano kebīr (m)	بيانو كبير
organ	arɣan (m)	أرغن
wind instruments	ʾālāt el nafχ (pl)	آلات النفخ
oboe	mezmār (m)	مزمار
saxophone	saksofon (m)	ساكسوفون
clarinet	klarinet (m)	كلارنيت
flute	flute (m)	فلوت
trumpet	būʾ (m)	بوق
accordion	okordiōn (m)	أكورديون
drum	ṭabla (f)	طبلة
duo	sonāʾy (m)	ثنائي

trio	solāsy (m)	ثلاثي
quartet	robā'y (m)	رباعي
choir	korale (m)	كورال
orchestra	orkestra (f)	أوركسترا
pop music	mosīqa el bob (f)	موسيقى البوب
rock music	mosīqa el rok (f)	موسيقى الروك
rock group	fer'et el rokk (f)	فرقة الروك
jazz	ʒāzz (m)	جاز
idol	ma'būd (m)	معبود
admirer, fan	mo'gab (m)	معجب
concert	ḥafla mūsiqiya (f)	حفلة موسيقيّة
symphony	semfoniya (f)	سمفونيّة
composition	'eṭ'a mosiqiya (f)	قطعة موسيقيّة
to compose (write)	allaf	ألّف
singing (n)	ɣenā' (m)	غناء
song	oɣniya (f)	أغنيّة
tune (melody)	laḥn (m)	لحن
rhythm	eqā' (m)	إيقاع
blues	mosīqa el blues (f)	موسيقى البلوز
sheet music	notāt (pl)	نوتات
baton	'aṣa el maystro (m)	عصا المايسترو
bow	qose (m)	قوس
string	watar (m)	وتر
case (e.g. guitar ~)	ʃanṭa (f)	شنطة

Rest. Entertainment. Travel

155. Trip. Travel

tourism, travel	seyāḥa (f)	سياحة
tourist	sā'eḥ (m)	سائح
trip, voyage	reḥla (f)	رحلة
adventure	moɣamra (f)	مغامرة
trip, journey	reḥla (f)	رحلة
holiday	agāza (f)	أجازة
to be on holiday	kān fi agāza	كان في أجازة
rest	estrāḥa (f)	إستراحة
train	qeṭār, 'aṭṭr (m)	قطار
by train	bel qeṭār - bel aṭṭr	بالقطار
aeroplane	ṭayāra (f)	طيّارة
by aeroplane	bel ṭayāra	بالطيّارة
by car	bel sayāra	بالسيّارة
by ship	bel safīna	بالسفينة
luggage	el ʃonaṭ (pl)	الشنط
suitcase	ʃanṭa (f)	شنطة
luggage trolley	'arabet ʃonaṭ (f)	عربة شنط
passport	basbore (m)	باسبور
visa	ta'ʃīra (f)	تأشيرة
ticket	tazkara (f)	تذكرة
air ticket	tazkara ṭayarān (f)	تذكرة طيران
guidebook	dalīl (m)	دليل
map (tourist ~)	χarīṭa (f)	خريطة
area (rural ~)	mante'a (f)	منطقة
place, site	makān (m)	مكان
exotica (n)	ɣarāba (f)	غرابة
exotic (adj)	ɣarīb	غريب
amazing (adj)	mod-heʃ	مدهش
group	magmū'a (f)	مجموعة
excursion, sightseeing tour	gawla (f)	جولة
guide (person)	morʃed (m)	مرشد

156. Hotel

hotel	fondo' (m)	فندق
motel	motel (m)	موتيل
three-star (~ hotel)	talat nogūm	ثلاث نجوم

five-star	χamas nogūm	خمس نجوم
to stay (in a hotel, etc.)	nezel	نزل
room	oḍa (f)	أوضة
single room	owḍa le ʃaχṣ wāḥed (f)	أوضة لشخص واحد
double room	oḍa le ʃaχṣeyn (f)	أوضة لشخصين
to book a room	ḥagaz owḍa	حجز أوضة
half board	wagbeteyn fel yome (du)	وجبتين في اليوم
full board	talat wagabāt fel yome	ثلاث وجبات في اليوم
with bath	bel banyo	بـ البانيو
with shower	bel doʃ	بالدوش
satellite television	televizion be qanawāt faḍā'iya (m)	تليفزيون بقنوات فضائية
air-conditioner	takyīf (m)	تكييف
towel	fūṭa (f)	فوطة
key	meftāḥ (m)	مفتاح
administrator	modīr (m)	مدير
chambermaid	'āmela tandīf γoraf (f)	عاملة تنظيف غرف
porter	ʃayāl (m)	شيّال
doorman	bawwāb (m)	بوّاب
restaurant	maṭ'am (m)	مطعم
pub, bar	bār (m)	بار
breakfast	foṭūr (m)	فطور
dinner	'aʃā' (m)	عشاء
buffet	bofeyh (m)	بوفيه
lobby	rad-ha (f)	ردهة
lift	asanseyr (m)	اسانسير
DO NOT DISTURB	nargu 'adam el ez'āg	نرجو عدم الإزعاج
NO SMOKING	mamnū' el tadχīn	ممنوع التدخين

157. Books. Reading

book	ketāb (m)	كتاب
author	mo'allef (m)	مؤلّف
writer	kāteb (m)	كاتب
to write (~ a book)	allaf	ألّف
reader	qāre' (m)	قارئ
to read (vi, vt)	'ara	قرأ
reading (activity)	qerā'a (f)	قراءة
silently (to oneself)	beṣamt	بصمت
aloud (adv)	beṣote 'āly	بصوت عالي
to publish (vt)	naʃar	نشر
publishing (process)	naʃr (m)	نشر
publisher	nāʃer (m)	ناشر
publishing house	dar el ṭebā'a wel naʃr (f)	دار الطباعة والنشر

to come out (be released)	ṣadar	صدر
release (of a book)	ṣodūr (m)	صدور
print run	'adad el nosaχ (m)	عدد النسخ
bookshop	maḥal kotob (m)	محل كتب
library	maktaba (f)	مكتبة
story (novella)	'oṣṣa (f)	قصّة
short story	qeṣṣa 'aṣīra (f)	قصّة قصيرة
novel	rewāya (f)	رواية
detective novel	rewāya bolesiya (f)	رواية بوليسية
memoirs	mozakkerāt (pl)	مذكّرات
legend	osṭūra (f)	أسطورة
myth	χorāfa (f)	خرافة
poetry, poems	ʃe'r (m)	شعر
autobiography	sīret ḥayah (f)	سيرة حياة
selected works	muχtarāt (pl)	مختارات
science fiction	χayāl 'elmy (m)	خيال علمي
title	'enwān (m)	عنوان
introduction	moqaddema (f)	مقدّمة
title page	ṣafḥet 'enwān (f)	صفحة العنوان
chapter	faṣl (m)	فصل
extract	χolāṣa (f)	خلاصة
episode	maʃ-had (m)	مشهد
plot (storyline)	ḥabka (f)	حبكة
contents	moḥtawayāt (pl)	محتويات
table of contents	gadwal el moḥtawayāt (m)	جدول المحتويات
main character	el ʃaχṣiya el ra'esiya (f)	الشخصية الرئيسية
volume	mogallad (m)	مجلّد
cover	ɣelāf (m)	غلاف
binding	taglīd (m)	تجليد
bookmark	ʃerīṭ (m)	شريط
page	ṣafḥa (f)	صفحة
to page through	'alleb el ṣafaḥāt	قلّب الصفحات
margins	hāmeʃ (m)	هامش
annotation (marginal note, etc.)	molaḥza (f)	ملاحظة
footnote	molaḥza (f)	ملاحظة
text	noṣṣ (m)	نصّ
type, fount	nū' el χaṭṭ (m)	نوع الخطّ
misprint, typo	χaṭa' maṭba'y (m)	خطأ مطبعيّ
translation	targama (f)	ترجمة
to translate (vt)	targem	ترجم
original (n)	aṣliya (f)	أصلية
famous (adj)	maʃ-hūr	مشهور
unknown (not famous)	meʃ ma'rūf	مش معروف

interesting (adj)	moʃawweq	مشوّق
bestseller	aktar mabee'an (m)	أكثر مبيعاً
dictionary	qamūs (m)	قاموس
textbook	ketāb ta'līm (m)	كتاب تعليم
encyclopedia	ensayklopedia (f)	إنسيكلوبيديا

158. Hunting. Fishing

hunting	ṣeyd (m)	صيد
to hunt (vi, vt)	eṣṭād	إصطاد
hunter	ṣayād (m)	صيّاد
to shoot (vi)	ḍarab bel nār	ضرب بالنار
rifle	bondoqiya (f)	بندقيّة
bullet (shell)	roṣāṣa (f)	رصاصة
shot (lead balls)	'eyār (m)	عيار
steel trap	maṣyada (f)	مصيّدة
snare (for birds, etc.)	fakχ (m)	فخّ
to fall into the steel trap	we'e' fe fakχ	وقع في فخّ
to lay a steel trap	naṣb fakχ	نصب فخّ
poacher	sāre' el ṣeyd (m)	سارق الصيد
game (in hunting)	ṣeyd (m)	صيد
hound dog	kalb ṣeyd (m)	كلب صيد
safari	safāry (m)	سفاري
mounted animal	ḥayawān moḥannaṭ (m)	حيوان محنّط
fisherman	ṣayād el samak (m)	صيّاد السمك
fishing (angling)	ṣeyd el samak (m)	صيد السمك
to fish (vi)	eṣṭād samak	إصطاد سمك
fishing rod	ṣennāra (f)	صنّارة
fishing line	χeyṭ (m)	خيط
hook	ʃaṣ el garīma (m)	شص الصيد
float	'awwāma (f)	عوّامة
bait	ṭa'm (m)	طعم
to cast a line	ṭaraḥ el ṣennāra	طرح الصنّارة
to bite (ab. fish)	'aḍḍ	عضّ
catch (of fish)	el samak el moṣṭād (m)	السمك المصطاد
ice-hole	fat-ḥa fel galīd (f)	فتحة في الجليد
fishing net	ʃabaket el ṣeyd (f)	شبكة الصيد
boat	markeb (m)	مركب
to net (to fish with a net)	eṣṭād bel ʃabaka	إصطاد بالشبكة
to cast[throw] the net	rama ʃabaka	رمى شبكة
to haul the net in	aχrag ʃabaka	أخرج شبكة
to fall into the net	we'e' fe ʃabaka	وقع في شبكة
whaler (person)	ṣayād el ḥūt (m)	صيّاد الحوت
whaleboat	safīna ṣeyd ḥitān (f)	سفينة صيد الحيتان
harpoon	ḥerba (f)	حربة

159. Games. Billiards

billiards	bilyardo (m)	بلياردو
billiard room, hall	qā'a bilyardo (m)	قاعة بلياردو
ball (snooker, etc.)	kora (f)	كرة
to pocket a ball	dakχal kora	دخّل كرة
cue	'aṣāyet bilyardo (f)	عصاية بلياردو
pocket	geyb bilyardo (m)	جيب بلياردو

160. Games. Playing cards

diamonds	el dinary (m)	الديناري
spades	el bastūny (m)	البستوني
hearts	el koba (f)	الكوبة
clubs	el sebāty (m)	السباتي
ace	'āss (m)	آس
king	malek (m)	ملك
queen	maleka (f)	ملكة
jack, knave	walad (m)	ولد
playing card	wara'a (f)	ورقة
cards	wara' (m)	ورق
trump	wara'a rābeḥa (f)	ورقة رابحة
pack of cards	desta wara' 'enab (f)	دستة ورق اللعب
point	nu'ṭa (f)	نقطة
to deal (vi, vt)	farra'	فرّق
to shuffle (cards)	χalaṭ	خلط
lead, turn (n)	dore (m)	دور
cardsharp	moḥtāl fel 'omār (m)	محتال في القمار

161. Casino. Roulette

casino	kazino (m)	كازينو
roulette (game)	rulett (m)	روليت
bet	rahān (m)	رهان
to place bets	qāmar	قامر
red	aḥmar (m)	أحمر
black	aswad (m)	أسود
to bet on red	rāhen 'ala el aḥmar	راهن على الأحمر
to bet on black	rāhen 'ala el aswad	راهن على الأسود
croupier (dealer)	mowazzaf nādy el 'omār (m)	موظّف نادى القمار
to spin the wheel	dawwar el 'agala	دوّر العجلة
rules (~ of the game)	qawā'ed (pl)	قواعد
chip	fīʃa (f)	فيشة
to win (vi, vt)	keseb	كسب
win (winnings)	rebḥ (m)	ربح

to lose (~ 100 dollars)	xeser	خسر
loss (losses)	xesāra (f)	خسارة
player	lā'eb (m)	لاعب
blackjack (card game)	blɛkdʒɛk (m)	بلاك جاك
craps (dice game)	le'bet el nard (f)	لعبة النرد
dice (a pair of ~)	zahr el nard (m)	زهر النرد
fruit machine	'ālet qomār (f)	آلة قمار

162. Rest. Games. Miscellaneous

to stroll (vi, vt)	tamasʃa	تمشّى
stroll (leisurely walk)	tamʃeya (f)	تمشيّة
car ride	gawla bel sayāra (f)	جولة بالسيّارة
adventure	moɣamra (f)	مغامرة
picnic	nozha (f)	نزهة
game (chess, etc.)	le'ba (f)	لعبة
player	lā'eb (m)	لاعب
game (one ~ of chess)	dore (m)	دور
collector (e.g. philatelist)	gāme' (m)	جامع
to collect (stamps, etc.)	gamma'	جمّع
collection	magmū'a (f)	مجموعة
crossword puzzle	kalemāt motaqaṭ'a (pl)	كلمات متقاطعة
racecourse (hippodrome)	ḥalabet el sebā' (f)	حلبة السباق
disco (discotheque)	disko (m)	ديسكو
sauna	sauna (f)	ساونا
lottery	yanaṣīb (m)	يانصيب
camping trip	reḥlet taxyīm (f)	رحلة تخييم
camp	moxayam (m)	مخيّم
tent (for camping)	xeyma (f)	خيمة
compass	boṣla (f)	بوصلة
camper	moxayam (m)	مخيّم
to watch (film, etc.)	ʃāhed	شاهد
viewer	moʃāhed (m)	مشاهد
TV show (TV program)	barnāmeg televiziony (m)	برنامج تليفزيوني

163. Photography

camera (photo)	kamera (f)	كاميرا
photo, picture	ṣūra (f)	صورة
photographer	moṣawwer (m)	مصوّر
photo studio	estudio taṣwīr (m)	إستوديو تصوير
photo album	albūm el ṣewar (m)	ألبوم الصور
camera lens	'adaset kamera (f)	عدسة الكاميرا
telephoto lens	'adasa teleskopiya (f)	عدسة تلسكوبيّة

filter	filter (m)	فلتر
lens	ʿadasa (f)	عدسة
optics (high-quality ~)	baṣrīāt (pl)	بصريات
diaphragm (aperture)	saddāda (f)	سدّادة
exposure time (shutter speed)	moddet el taʿarroḍ (f)	مدّة التعرض
viewfinder	el ʿeyn el faḥeṣa (f)	العين الفاحصة
digital camera	kamera diʒital (f)	كاميرا ديجيتال
tripod	tribod (m)	ترايبود
flash	flāʃ (m)	فلاش
to photograph (vt)	ṣawwar	صوّر
to take pictures	ṣawwar	صوّر
to have one's picture taken	etṣawwar	إتصوّر
focus	tarkīz (m)	تركيز
to focus	rakkez	ركّز
sharp, in focus (adj)	ḥādda	حادّة
sharpness	ḥedda (m)	حدّة
contrast	tabāyon (m)	تباين
contrast (as adj)	motabāyen	متباين
picture (photo)	ṣūra (f)	صورة
negative (n)	el nosχa el salba (f)	النسخة السالبة
film (a roll of ~)	film (m)	فيلم
frame (still)	eṭār (m)	إطار
to print (photos)	ṭabaʿ	طبع

164. Beach. Swimming

beach	ʃāṭeʾ (m)	شاطئ
sand	raml (m)	رمل
deserted (beach)	mahgūr	مهجور
suntan	esmerār el baʃra (m)	إسمرار البشرة
to get a tan	etʃammes	إتشمّس
tanned (adj)	asmar	أسمر
sunscreen	krīm wāqy men el ʃams (m)	كريم واقي من الشمس
bikini	bikini (m)	بكيني
swimsuit, bikini	mayo (m)	مايّوه
swim trunks	mayo regāly (m)	مايوه رجالي
swimming pool	ḥammām sebāḥa (m)	حمّام سباحة
to swim (vi)	ʿām, sabaḥ	عام, سبح
shower	doʃ (m)	دوش
to change (one's clothes)	ɣayar lebso	غيّر لبسه
towel	fūṭa (f)	فوطة
boat	markeb (m)	مركب
motorboat	lunʃ (m)	لنش

water ski	tazallog ʿalal mā' (m)	تزلّج على الماء
pedalo	el baddāl (m)	البدّال
surfing	surfing (m)	سيرفينج
surfer	rākeb el amwāg (m)	راكب الأمواج
scuba set	gehāz el tanaffos (m)	جهاز التنفّس
flippers (swim fins)	zaʿānef el sebāḥa (pl)	زعانف السباحة
mask (diving ~)	kamāma (f)	كمامة
diver	ɣawwāṣ (m)	غوّاص
to dive (vi)	ɣāṣ	غاص
underwater (adv)	taḥt el maya	تحت المايّة
beach umbrella	ʃamsiya (f)	شمسيّة
beach chair (sun lounger)	korsy blāʒ (m)	كرسي بلاج
sunglasses	naḍḍāret ʃams (f)	نضّارة شمس
air mattress	martaba hawa'iya (f)	مرتبة هوائية
to play (amuse oneself)	leʿeb	لعب
to go for a swim	sebeḥ	سبح
beach ball	koret ʃaṭṭ (f)	كرة شطّ
to inflate (vt)	nafaχ	نفخ
inflatable, air (adj)	qābel lel nafχ	قابل للنفخ
wave	mouga (f)	موجة
buoy (line of ~s)	ʃamandūra (f)	شمندورة
to drown (ab. person)	ɣere'	غرق
to save, to rescue	anqaz	أنقذ
life jacket	sotret nagah (f)	سترة نجاة
to observe, to watch	rāqab	راقب
lifeguard	ḥāres ʃāṭe' (m)	حارس شاطئ

TECHNICAL EQUIPMENT. TRANSPORT

Technical equipment

165. Computer

computer	kombuter (m)	كمبيوتر
notebook, laptop	lab tob (m)	لابتوب
to turn on	fataḥ, ʃagɣal	فتح, شغّل
to turn off	ṭaffa	طفّى
keyboard	lawḥet el mafatīḥ (f)	لوحة المفاتيح
key	meftāḥ (m)	مفتاح
mouse	maws (m)	ماوس
mouse mat	maws bād (m)	ماوس باد
button	zerr (m)	زرّ
cursor	mo'asʃer (m)	مؤشّر
monitor	ʃāʃa (f)	شاشة
screen	ʃāʃa (f)	شاشة
hard disk	hard disk (m)	هارد ديسك
hard disk capacity	se'et el hard disk (f)	سعة الهارد ديسك
memory	zākera (f)	ذاكرة
random access memory	zākerat el woṣūl el 'aʃwā'y (f)	ذاكرة الوصول العشوائي
file	malaff (m)	ملفّ
folder	ḥāfeza (m)	حافظة
to open (vt)	fataḥ	فتح
to close (vt)	'afal	قفل
to save (vt)	ḥafaẓ	حفظ
to delete (vt)	masaḥ	مسح
to copy (vt)	nasaχ	نسخ
to sort (vt)	ṣannaf	صنّف
to transfer (copy)	na'al	نقل
programme	barnāmeg (m)	برنامج
software	barmagīāt (pl)	برمجيّات
programmer	mobarmeg (m)	مبرمج
to program (vt)	barmag	برمج
hacker	haker (m)	هاكر
password	kelmet el serr (f)	كلمة السرّ
virus	virūs (m)	فيروس
to find, to detect	la'a	لقى
byte	byte (m)	بايت

megabyte	megabayt (m)	ميجا بايت
data	bayanāt (pl)	بيانات
database	qa'edet bayanāt (f)	قاعدة بيانات
cable (USB, etc.)	kabl (m)	كابل
to disconnect (vt)	faṣal	فصل
to connect (sth to sth)	waṣṣal	وصّل

166. Internet. E-mail

Internet	internet (m)	إنترنت
browser	motaṣaffeḥ (m)	متصفّح
search engine	moḥarrek baḥs (m)	محرك بحث
provider	ʃerket el internet (f)	شركة الإنترنت
webmaster	modīr el mawqeʿ (m)	مدير الموقع
website	mawqeʿ elektrony (m)	موقع الكتروني
web page	ṣafḥet web (f)	صفحة ويب
address (e-mail ~)	ʿenwān (m)	عنوان
address book	daftar el ʿanawīn (m)	دفتر العناوين
postbox	ṣandūʾ el barīd (m)	صندوق البريد
post	barīd (m)	بريد
full (adj)	mumtaliʾ	ممتلىء
message	resāla (f)	رسالة
incoming messages	rasaʾel wārda (pl)	رسائل واردة
outgoing messages	rasaʾel ṣādra (pl)	رسائل صادرة
sender	morsel (m)	مرسل
to send (vt)	arsal	أرسل
sending (of mail)	ersāl (m)	إرسال
receiver	morsel elayh (m)	مرسل إليه
to receive (vt)	estalam	إستلم
correspondence	morasla (f)	مراسلة
to correspond (vi)	tarāsal	تراسل
file	malaff (m)	ملفّ
to download (vt)	ḥammel	حمّل
to create (vt)	ʿamal	عمل
to delete (vt)	masaḥ	مسح
deleted (adj)	mamsūḥ	ممسوح
connection (ADSL, etc.)	etteṣāl (m)	إتّصال
speed	sorʿa (f)	سرعة
modem	modem (m)	مودم
access	woṣūl (m)	وصول
port (e.g. input ~)	maχrag (m)	مخرج
connection (make a ~)	etteṣāl (m)	إتّصال
to connect to ... (vi)	yuwṣel	يوصل
to select (vt)	eχtār	إختار
to search (for ...)	baḥs	بحث

167. Electricity

electricity	kahraba' (m)	كهرباء
electric, electrical (adj)	kahrabā'y	كهربائي
electric power station	maḥaṭṭa kahraba'iya (f)	محطّة كهربائيّة
energy	ṭāqa (f)	طاقة
electric power	ṭāqa kahraba'iya (f)	طاقة كهربائيّة
light bulb	lammba (f)	لمّبة
torch	kasʃāf el nūr (m)	كشّاف النور
street light	ʿamūd el nūr (m)	عمود النور
light	nūr (m)	نور
to turn on	fataḥ, ʃagɣal	فتح, شغّل
to turn off	ṭaffa	طفّى
to turn off the light	ṭaffa el nūr	طفّى النور
to burn out (vi)	etṭafa	إتّطفى
short circuit	dayra kahraba'iya 'aṣīra (f)	دائرة كهربائية قصيرة
broken wire	selk ma'ṭūʿ (m)	سلك مقطوع
contact (electrical ~)	talāmos (m)	تلامس
light switch	meftāḥ el nūr (m)	مفتاح النور
socket outlet	bareza el kaharaba' (f)	بريزة الكهرباء
plug	fīʃet el kahraba' (f)	فيشة الكهرباء
extension lead	selk tawṣīl (m)	سلك توصيل
fuse	fetīl (m)	فتيل
cable, wire	selk (m)	سلك
wiring	aslāk (pl)	أسلاك
ampere	ambere (m)	أمبير
amperage	ʃeddet el tayār (f)	شدّة التيّار
volt	volt (m)	فولت
voltage	el gohd el kaharab'y (m)	الجهد الكهربائي
electrical device	gehāz kahrabā'y (m)	جهاز كهربائي
indicator	mo'asʃer (m)	مؤشّر
electrician	kahrabā'y (m)	كهربائي
to solder (vt)	laḥam	لحم
soldering iron	adat laḥm (f)	إداة لحم
electric current	tayār kahrabā'y (m)	تيّاركهربائي

168. Tools

tool, instrument	adah (f)	أداة
tools	adawāt (pl)	أدوات
equipment (factory ~)	moʿeddāt (pl)	معدّات
hammer	ʃakūʃ (m)	شاكوش
screwdriver	mefakk (m)	مفكّ
axe	fa's (m)	فأس

saw	monʃār (m)	منشار
to saw (vt)	naʃar	نشر
plane (tool)	meshāg (m)	مسحاج
to plane (vt)	saḥag	سحج
soldering iron	adat laḥm (f)	إداة لحم
to solder (vt)	laḥam	لحم
file (tool)	mabrad (m)	مبرد
carpenter pincers	kamʃa (f)	كمشة
combination pliers	zardiya (f)	زرديّة
chisel	ezmīl (m)	إزميل
drill bit	mesqāb (m)	مثقاب
electric drill	drill kahrabā'y (m)	دريل كهربائي
to drill (vi, vt)	ḥafar	حفر
knife	sekkīna (f)	سكّينة
pocket knife	sekkīnet gīb (m)	سكّينة جيب
blade	ʃafra (f)	شفرة
sharp (blade, etc.)	ḥād	حاد
dull, blunt (adj)	telma	تلمة
to get blunt (dull)	kānet telma	كانت تلمة
to sharpen (vt)	sann	سنّ
bolt	mesmār 'alawoze (m)	مسمار قلاووظ
nut	ṣamūla (f)	صامولة
thread (of a screw)	χaʃχana (f)	خشخنة
wood screw	'alawūz (m)	قلاووظ
nail	mesmār (m)	مسمار
nailhead	rās el mesmār (m)	رأس المسمار
ruler (for measuring)	masṭara (f)	مسطرة
tape measure	ʃerīṭ el 'eyās (m)	شريط القياس
spirit level	mizān el maya (m)	ميزان الميّة
magnifying glass	'adasa mokabbera (f)	عدسة مكبّرة
measuring instrument	gehāz 'eyās (m)	جهاز قياس
to measure (vt)	'ās	قاس
scale (temperature ~, etc.)	me'yās (m)	مقياس
readings	qerā'a (f)	قراءة
compressor	kombressor (m)	كومبرسور
microscope	mikroskob (m)	ميكروسكوب
pump (e.g. water ~)	ṭolommba (f)	طلمّبة
robot	robot (m)	روبوت
laser	laser (m)	ليزر
spanner	meftāḥ rabṭ (m)	مفتاح ربط
adhesive tape	laz' (m)	لزق
glue	ṣamχ (m)	صمغ
sandpaper	wara' ṣanfara (m)	ورق صنفرة
spring	sosta (f)	سوستة

magnet	meɣnaṭīs (m)	مغنطيس
gloves	gwanty (m)	جوانتي
rope	ḥabl (m)	حبل
cord	selk (m)	سلك
wire (e.g. telephone ~)	selk (m)	سلك
cable	kabl (m)	كابل
sledgehammer	marzaba (f)	مرزبة
prybar	ʿatala (f)	عتلة
ladder	sellem (m)	سلّم
stepladder	sellem naʾāl (m)	سلّم نقال
to screw (tighten)	aḥkam el ʃadd	أحكم الشدّ
to unscrew (lid, filter, etc.)	fataḥ	فتح
to tighten (e.g. with a clamp)	kamaʃ	كمش
to glue, to stick	alṣaq	ألصق
to cut (vt)	ʾaṭaʿ	قطع
malfunction (fault)	ʿoṭl (m)	عطل
repair (mending)	taṣlīḥ (m)	تصليح
to repair, to fix (vt)	ṣallaḥ	صلّح
to adjust (machine, etc.)	ḍabaṭ	ضبط
to check (to examine)	eχtabar	إختبر
checking	faḥṣ (m)	فحص
readings	qerāʾa (f)	قراءة
reliable, solid (machine)	matīn	متين
complex (adj)	morakkab	مركّب
to rust (get rusted)	ṣadaʾ	صدئ
rusty (adj)	meṣaddy	مصدّي
rust	ṣadaʾ (m)	صدأ

Transport

169. Aeroplane

aeroplane	ṭayāra (f)	طيّارة
air ticket	tazkara ṭayarān (f)	تذكرة طيران
airline	ʃerket ṭayarān (f)	شركة طيران
airport	maṭār (m)	مطار
supersonic (adj)	χāreq lel ṣote	خارق للصوت
captain	kabten (m)	كابتن
crew	ṭa'm (m)	طقم
pilot	ṭayār (m)	طيّار
stewardess	moḍīfet ṭayarān (f)	مضيفة طيران
navigator	mallāḥ (m)	ملاّح
wings	agneḥa (pl)	أجنحة
tail	deyl (m)	ذيل
cockpit	kabīna (f)	كابينة
engine	motore (m)	موتور
undercarriage (landing gear)	'agalāt el hobūṭ (pl)	عجلات الهبوط
turbine	torbīna (f)	توربينة
propeller	marwaḥa (f)	مروّحة
black box	mosaggel el ṭayarān (m)	مسجّل الطيران
yoke (control column)	moqawwed el ṭayāra (m)	مقوّد الطيّارة
fuel	woqūd (m)	وقود
safety card	beṭā'et el salāma (f)	بطاقة السلامة
oxygen mask	mask el oksyʒīn (m)	ماسك الاوكسيجين
uniform	zayī muwaḥḥad (m)	زيّ موحّد
lifejacket	sotret nagah (f)	سترة نجاة
parachute	baraʃot (m)	باراشوت
takeoff	eqlā' (m)	إقلاع
to take off (vi)	aqla'et	أقلعت
runway	modarrag el ṭa'erāṭ (m)	مدرّج الطائرات
visibility	ro'ya (f)	رؤية
flight (act of flying)	ṭayarān (m)	طيران
altitude	ertefā' (m)	إرتفاع
air pocket	geyb hawā'y (m)	جيب هوائي
seat	meq'ad (m)	مقعد
headphones	samma'āt ra'siya (pl)	سمّاعات رأسية
folding tray (tray table)	ṣeniya qabela lel ṭayī (f)	صينية قابلة للطيّ
airplane window	ʃebbāk el ṭayāra (m)	شبّاك الطيّارة
aisle	mamarr (m)	ممرّ

170. Train

train	qeṭār, 'aṭṭr (m)	قطار
commuter train	qeṭār rokkāb (m)	قطار ركّاب
express train	qeṭār saree' (m)	قطار سريع
diesel locomotive	qāṭeret dīzel (f)	قاطرة ديزل
steam locomotive	qāṭera boχariya (f)	قاطرة بخاريّة
coach, carriage	'araba (f)	عربة
buffet car	'arabet el ṭa'ām (f)	عربة الطعام
rails	qoḍbān (pl)	قضبان
railway	sekka ḥadīdiya (f)	سكّة حديديّة
sleeper (track support)	'āreḍa sekket ḥadīd (f)	عارضة سكّة الحديد
platform (railway ~)	raṣīf (m)	رصيف
platform (~ 1, 2, etc.)	χaṭṭ (m)	خطّ
semaphore	semafore (m)	سيمافور
station	maḥaṭṭa (f)	محطّة
train driver	sawwā' (m)	سوّاق
porter (of luggage)	ʃayāl (m)	شيّال
carriage attendant	mas'ūl 'arabet el qeṭār (m)	مسؤول عربة القطار
passenger	rākeb (m)	راكب
ticket inspector	kamsary (m)	كمسري
corridor (in train)	mamarr (m)	ممرّ
emergency brake	farāmel el ṭawāre' (pl)	فرامل الطوارئ
compartment	ɣorfa (f)	غرفة
berth	serīr (m)	سرير
upper berth	serīr 'olwy (m)	سرير علويّ
lower berth	serīr sofly (m)	سرير سفلي
bed linen, bedding	aɣṭeyet el serīr (pl)	أغطية السرير
ticket	tazkara (f)	تذكرة
timetable	gadwal (m)	جدوّل
information display	lawḥet ma'lomāt (f)	لوحة معلومات
to leave, to depart	ɣādar	غادر
departure (of a train)	moɣadra (f)	مغادرة
to arrive (ab. train)	weṣel	وصل
arrival	woṣūl (m)	وصول
to arrive by train	weṣel bel qeṭār	وصل بالقطار
to get on the train	rekeb el qeṭār	ركب القطار
to get off the train	nezel men el qeṭār	نزل من القطار
train crash	ḥeṭām qeṭār (m)	حطام قطار
to derail (vi)	χarag 'an χaṭṭ sīru	خرج عن خطّ سيره
steam locomotive	qāṭera boχariya (f)	قاطرة بخاريّة
stoker, fireman	'atʃagy (m)	عطشجي
firebox	forn el moḥarrek (m)	فرن المحرّك
coal	faḥm (m)	فحم

171. Ship

ship	safīna (f)	سفينة
vessel	safīna (f)	سفينة
steamship	baχera (f)	باخرة
riverboat	baχera nahriya (f)	باخرة نهرية
cruise ship	safīna seyaḥiya (f)	سفينة سياحيّة
cruiser	ṭarrād safīna baḥariya (m)	طرّاد سفينة بحريّة
yacht	yaχt (m)	يخت
tugboat	qāṭera baḥariya (f)	قاطرة بحريّة
barge	ṣandal (m)	صندل
ferry	ʿabbāra (f)	عبّارة
sailing ship	safīna ʃeraʿiya (m)	سفينة شراعيّة
brigantine	markeb ʃerāʿy (m)	مركب شراعي
ice breaker	moḥaṭṭemet galīd (f)	محطّمة جليد
submarine	ɣawwāṣa (f)	غوّاصة
boat (flat-bottomed ~)	markeb (m)	مركب
dinghy (lifeboat)	zawraʾ (m)	زورق
lifeboat	qāreb nagah (m)	قارب نجاة
motorboat	lunʃ (m)	لنش
captain	ʾobṭān (m)	قبطان
seaman	baḥḥār (m)	بحّار
sailor	baḥḥār (m)	بحّار
crew	ṭāqem (m)	طاقم
boatswain	rabbān (m)	ربّان
ship's boy	ṣaby el safīna (m)	صبي السفينة
cook	ṭabbāχ (m)	طبّاخ
ship's doctor	ṭabīb el safīna (m)	طبيب السفينة
deck	saṭ-ḥ el safīna (m)	سطح السفينة
mast	sāreya (f)	سارية
sail	ʃerāʿ (m)	شراع
hold	ʿanbar (m)	عنبر
bow (prow)	moʾaddema (m)	مقدّمة
stern	moʾaχeret el safīna (f)	مؤخّرة السفينة
oar	megdāf (m)	مجذاف
screw propeller	marwaḥa (f)	مروحة
cabin	kabīna (f)	كابينة
wardroom	ɣorfet el ṭaʿām wel rāḥa (f)	غرفة الطعام والراحة
engine room	qesm el ʾālāt (m)	قسم الآلات
bridge	borg el qeyāda (m)	برج القيادة
radio room	ɣorfet el lāselky (f)	غرفة اللاسلكي
wave (radio)	mouga (f)	موجة
logbook	segel el safīna (m)	سجل السفينة
spyglass	monzār (m)	منظار
bell	garas (m)	جرس

flag	ʿalam (m)	علم
hawser (mooring ~)	ḥabl (m)	حبل
knot (bowline, etc.)	ʿoʾda (f)	عقدة
deckrails	drabzīn saṭ-ḥ el safīna (m)	درابزين سطح السفينة
gangway	sellem (m)	سلّم
anchor	marsāh (f)	مرساة
to weigh anchor	rafaʿ morsah	رفع مرساة
to drop anchor	rasa	رسا
anchor chain	selselet morsah (f)	سلسلة مرساة
port (harbour)	mināʾ (m)	ميناء
quay, wharf	marsa (m)	مرسى
to berth (moor)	rasa	رسا
to cast off	aqlaʿ	أقلع
trip, voyage	reḥla (f)	رحلة
cruise (sea trip)	reḥla baḥariya (f)	رحلة بحريّة
course (route)	masār (m)	مسار
route (itinerary)	ṭarīʾ (m)	طريق
fairway (safe water channel)	magra melāḥy (m)	مجرى ملاحيّ
shallows	meyāh ḍaḥla (f)	مياه ضحلة
to run aground	ganaḥ	جنح
storm	ʿāṣefa (f)	عاصفة
signal	eʃara (f)	إشارة
to sink (vi)	ɣereʾ	غرق
Man overboard!	saʾaṭ rāgil min el sefīna!	سقط راجل من السفينة!
SOS (distress signal)	nedāʾ eɣāsa (m)	نداء إغاثة
ring buoy	ṭoʾe nagah (m)	طوق نجاة

172. Airport

airport	maṭār (m)	مطار
aeroplane	ṭayāra (f)	طيّارة
airline	ʃerket ṭayarān (f)	شركة طيران
air traffic controller	marākeb el ḥaraka el gawiya (m)	مراكب الحركة الجويّة
departure	moɣadra (f)	مغادرة
arrival	woṣūl (m)	وصول
to arrive (by plane)	weṣel	وصل
departure time	waʾt el moɣadra (m)	وقت المغادرة
arrival time	waʾt el woṣūl (m)	وقت الوصول
to be delayed	taʾakχar	تأخّر
flight delay	taʾaχor el reḥla (m)	تأخّر الرحلة
information board	lawḥet el maʿlomāt (f)	لوحة المعلومات
information	esteʿlamāt (pl)	إستعلامات
to announce (vt)	aʿlan	أعلن

flight (e.g. next ~)	reḥlet ṭayarān (f)	رحلة طيران
customs	gamārek (pl)	جمارك
customs officer	mowazzaf el gamārek (m)	موظّف الجمارك
customs declaration	taṣrīḥ gomroky (m)	تصريح جمركي
to fill in (vt)	mala	ملا
to fill in the declaration	mala el taṣrīḥ	ملأ التصريح
passport control	taftīʃ el gawazāt (m)	تفتيش الجوازات
luggage	el ʃonaṭ (pl)	الشنط
hand luggage	ʃonaṭ el yad (pl)	شنط اليد
luggage trolley	ʿarabet ʃonaṭ (f)	عربة شنط
landing	hobūṭ (m)	هبوط
landing strip	mamarr el hobūṭ (m)	ممرّ الهبوط
to land (vi)	habaṭ	هبط
airstair (passenger stair)	sellem el ṭayāra (m)	سلّم الطيّارة
check-in	tasgīl (m)	تسجيل
check-in counter	makān tasgīl (m)	مكان تسجيل
to check-in (vi)	saggel	سجّل
boarding card	beṭāqet el rokūb (f)	بطاقة الركوب
departure gate	bawwābet el moɣadra (f)	بوّابة المغادرة
transit	tranzīt (m)	ترانزيت
to wait (vt)	estanna	إستنّى
departure lounge	ṣālet el moɣadra (f)	صالة المغادرة
to see off	waddaʿ	ودّع
to say goodbye	waddaʿ	ودّع

173. Bicycle. Motorcycle

bicycle	beskeletta (f)	بسكلتّة
scooter	fezba (f)	فزبة
motorbike	motosekl (m)	موتوسيكل
to go by bicycle	rāḥ bel beskeletta	راح بالبسكلتّة
handlebars	moqawwed (m)	مقود
pedal	dawwāsa (f)	دوّاسة
brakes	farāmel (pl)	فرامل
bicycle seat (saddle)	korsy (m)	كرسي
pump	ṭolommba (f)	طلمبة
pannier rack	raff el amteʿa (m)	رفّ الأمتعة
front lamp	el meṣbāḥ el amāmy (m)	المصباح الأمامي
helmet	xawza (f)	خوذة
wheel	ʿagala (f)	عجلة
mudguard	refrāf (m)	رفراف
rim	eṭār (m)	إطار
spoke	mekbaḥ el ʿagala (m)	مكبح العجلة

Cars

174. Types of cars

car	sayāra (f)	سيّارة
sports car	sayāra reyāḍiya (f)	سيّارة رياضيّة
limousine	limozīn (m)	ليموزين
off-road vehicle	sayāret ṭoro' wa'ra (f)	سيّارة طرق وعرة
drophead coupé (convertible)	kabryoleyh (m)	كابريوليه
minibus	mikrobāṣ (m)	ميكروباص
ambulance	es'āf (m)	إسعاف
snowplough	garrāfet talg (f)	جرّافة ثلج
lorry	ʃāḥena (f)	شاحنة
road tanker	nāqelet betrūl (f)	ناقلة بترول
van (small truck)	'arabiyet na'l (f)	عربيّة نقل
tractor unit	garrār (m)	جرّار
trailer	ma'ṭūra (f)	مقطورة
comfortable (adj)	morīḥ	مريح
used (adj)	mosta'mal	مستعمل

175. Cars. Bodywork

bonnet	kabbūt (m)	كبّوت
wing	refrāf (m)	رفراف
roof	sa'f (m)	سقف
windscreen	ezāz amāmy (f)	إزاز أمامي
rear-view mirror	merāya daχeliya (f)	مراية داخليّة
windscreen washer	monazzef el ezāz el amāmy (m)	منظّف الإزاز الأمامي
windscreen wipers	massāḥāt (pl)	مسّاحات
side window	ʃebbāk gāneby (m)	شبّاك جانبي
electric window	ezāz kahrabā'y (m)	إزاز كهربائي
aerial	hawā'y (m)	هوائي
sunroof	fat-ḥet el sa'f (f)	فتحة السقف
bumper	ekṣedām (m)	اكصدام
boot	ʃanṭet el 'arabiya (f)	شنطة العربيّة
roof luggage rack	raff sa'f el 'arabiya (m)	رفّ سقف العربيّة
door	bāb (m)	باب
door handle	okret el bāb (f)	اوكرة الباب
door lock	'efl el bāb (m)	قفل الباب
number plate	lawḥet raqam el sayāra (f)	لوحة رقم السيارة

silencer	kātem lel ṣote (m)	كاتم للصوت
petrol tank	χazzān el banzīn (m)	خزّان البنزين
exhaust pipe	anbūb el ʿādem (m)	أنبوب العادم
accelerator	ɣāz (m)	غاز
pedal	dawwāsa (f)	دوّاسة
accelerator pedal	dawwāset el banzīn (f)	دوّاسة البنزين
brake	farāmel (pl)	فرامل
brake pedal	dawwāset el farāmel (m)	دوّاسة الفرامل
to brake (use the brake)	farmel	فرمل
handbrake	farāmel el enteẓār (pl)	فرامل الإنتظار
clutch	klatʃ (m)	كلتش
clutch pedal	dawwāset el klatʃ (f)	دوّاسة الكلتش
clutch disc	ʾorṣ el klatʃ (m)	قرص الكلتش
shock absorber	momtaṣṣ lel ṣadamāt (m)	ممتصّ للصدمات
wheel	ʿagala (f)	عجلة
spare tyre	ʿagala eḥteyāṭy (f)	عجلة إحتياطية
tyre	eṭār (m)	إطار
wheel cover (hubcap)	ṭīs (m)	طيس
driving wheels	ʿagalāt el qeyāda (pl)	عجلات القيادة
front-wheel drive (as adj)	dafʿ amāmy (m)	دفع أمامي
rear-wheel drive (as adj)	dafʿ χalfy (m)	دفع خلفي
all-wheel drive (as adj)	dafʿ kāmel (m)	دفع كامل
gearbox	gearboks (m)	جير بوكس
automatic (adj)	otomatīky	أوتوماتيكي
mechanical (adj)	mikanīky	ميكانيكي
gear lever	meqbaḍ nāqel lel ḥaraka (m)	مقبض ناقل الحركة
headlamp	el meṣbāḥ el amāmy (m)	المصباح الأمامي
headlights	el maṣabīḥ el amamiya (pl)	المصابيح الأمامية
dipped headlights	nūr moʾaʃer monχafeḍ (pl)	نور مؤشر منخفض
full headlights	nūr moʾasʃer ʿāly (m)	نور مؤشر عالي
brake light	nūr el farāmel (m)	نور الفرامل
sidelights	lambet el enteẓār (f)	لمبة الإنتظار
hazard lights	eʃārāt el taḥzīr (pl)	إشارات التحذير
fog lights	kasʃāf el ḍabāb (m)	كشّاف الضباب
turn indicator	eʃāret el enʿeṭāf (f)	إشارة الإنعطاف
reversing light	ḍūʾ el rogūʿ lel χalf (m)	ضوء الرجوع للخلف

176. Cars. Passenger compartment

car interior	ṣalone el sayāra (m)	صالون السيارة
leather (as adj)	men el geld	من الجلد
velour (as adj)	men el moχmal	من المخمل
upholstery	tangīd (m)	تنجيد
instrument (gage)	gehāz (m)	جهاز
dashboard	lawḥet ag-heza (f)	لوحة أجهزة

speedometer	me'yās sor'a (m)	مقياس سرعة
needle (pointer)	mo'asʃer (m)	مؤشّر
mileometer	'addād el mesafāt (m)	عدّاد المسافات
indicator (sensor)	'addād (m)	عدّاد
level	mostawa (m)	مستوى
warning light	lammbet enzār (f)	لمّبة إنذار
steering wheel	moqawwed (m)	مقوّد
horn	kalaks (m)	كلاكس
button	zerr (m)	زرّ
switch	nāqel, meftāḥ (m)	ناقل, مفتاح
seat	korsy (m)	كرسي
backrest	masnad el ḍahr (m)	مسند الظهر
headrest	masnad el ra's (m)	مسند الرأس
seat belt	ḥezām el amān (m)	حزام الأمان
to fasten the belt	rabaṭ el ḥezām	ربط الحزام
adjustment (of seats)	ḍabṭ (m)	ضبط
airbag	wesāda hawa'iya (f)	وسادة هوائية
air-conditioner	takyīf (m)	تكييف
radio	radio (m)	راديو
CD player	moʃagɣel sidi (m)	مشغّل سي دي
to turn on	fataḥ, ʃagɣal	فتح, شغّل
aerial	hawā'y (m)	هوائي
glove box	dorg (m)	درج
ashtray	ṭa'ṭū'a (f)	طقطوقة

177. Cars. Engine

engine	moḥarrek (m)	محرّك
motor	motore (m)	موتور
diesel (as adj)	'alal diesel	على الديزل
petrol (as adj)	'alal banzīn	على البنزين
engine volume	ḥagm el moḥarrek (m)	حجم المحرّك
power	'owwa (f)	قوّة
horsepower	ḥoṣān (m)	حصان
piston	mekbas (m)	مكبس
cylinder	esṭewāna (f)	أسطوانة
valve	ṣamām (m)	صمام
injector	baχāχa (f)	بخّاخة
generator (alternator)	mowalled (m)	مولّد
carburettor	karburetor (m)	كاربراتير
motor oil	zeyt el moḥarrek (m)	زيت المحرّك
radiator	radiator (m)	رادياتير
coolant	mobarred (m)	مبرّد
cooling fan	marwaḥa (f)	مروحة
battery (accumulator)	baṭṭariya (f)	بطّاريّة
starter	meftāḥ el taʃɣīl (m)	مفتاح التشغيل

ignition	nezām taʃɣīl (m)	نظام تشغيل
sparking plug	ʃam'et el eḥterāq (f)	شمعة الإحتراق
terminal (battery ~)	ṭaraf tawṣīl (m)	طرف توصيل
positive terminal	ṭaraf muwgeb (m)	طرف موجب
negative terminal	ṭaraf sāleb (m)	طرف سالب
fuse	fetīl (m)	فتيل
air filter	ṣaffāyet el hawā' (f)	صفّاية الهواء
oil filter	ṣaffāyet el zeyt (f)	صفّاية الزيت
fuel filter	ṣaffāyet el banzīn (f)	صفّاية البنزين

178. Cars. Crash. Repair

car crash	ḥadset sayāra (f)	حادثة سيارة
traffic accident	ḥādes morūry (m)	حادث مروري
to crash (into the wall, etc.)	xabaṭ	خبط
to get smashed up	daʃdaʃ	دشدش
damage	xesāra (f)	خسارة
intact (unscathed)	salīm	سليم
to break down (vi)	ta'aṭṭal	تعطّل
towrope	ḥabl el saḥb	حبل السحب
puncture	soqb (m)	ثقب
to have a puncture	fasʃ	فشّ
to pump up	nafax	نفخ
pressure	ḍaɣṭ (m)	ضغط
to check (to examine)	extabar	إختبر
repair	taṣlīḥ (m)	تصليح
garage (auto service shop)	warʃet taṣlīḥ 'arabīāt (f)	ورشة تصليح عربيات
spare part	'eṭ'et ɣeyār (f)	قطعة غيار
part	'eṭ'a (f)	قطعة
bolt (with nut)	mesmār 'alawoze (m)	مسمار قلاووظ
screw (fastener)	mesmār (m)	مسمار
nut	ṣamūla (f)	صامولة
washer	warda (f)	وردة
bearing (e.g. ball ~)	maḥmal (m)	محمل
tube	anbūba (f)	أنبوبة
gasket (head ~)	'az'a (f)	عزقة
cable, wire	selk (m)	سلك
jack	'afrīṭa (f)	عفريطة
spanner	meftāḥ rabṭ (m)	مفتاح ربط
hammer	ʃakūʃ (m)	شاكوش
pump	ṭolommba (f)	طلمبة
screwdriver	mefakk (m)	مفك
fire extinguisher	ṭaffayet harī' (f)	طفّاية حريق
warning triangle	eʃāret taḥzīr (f)	إشارة تحذير
to stall (vi)	et'aṭṭal	إتعطّل

stall (n)	tawaqqof (m)	توقّف
to be broken	kān maksūr	كان مكسور
to overheat (vi)	soxn aktar men el lāzem	سخن أكثر من اللازم
to be clogged up	kān masdūd	كان مسدود
to freeze up (pipes, etc.)	etgammed	إتجمّد
to burst (vi, ab. tube)	enqaṭa' - ett'aṭṭa'	إنقطع
pressure	ḍaɣṭ (m)	ضغط
level	mostawa (m)	مستوى
slack (~ belt)	ḍa'īf	ضعيف
dent	ṭa'ga (f)	طعجة
knocking noise (engine)	da'' (m)	دقّ
crack	ʃa'' (m)	شقّ
scratch	xadʃ (m)	خدش

179. Cars. Road

road	ṭarī' (m)	طريق
motorway	ṭarī' saree' (m)	طريق سريع
highway	otostrad (m)	اوتوستراد
direction (way)	ettegāh (m)	إتّجاه
distance	masāfa (f)	مسافة
bridge	kobry (m)	كبري
car park	maw'ef el 'arabeyāt (m)	موقف العربيات
square	medān (m)	ميدان
road junction	taqāṭo' ṭoro' (m)	تقاطع طرق
tunnel	nafa' (m)	نفق
petrol station	maḥaṭṭet banzīn (f)	محطّة بنزين
car park	maw'ef el 'arabeyāt (m)	موقف العربيات
petrol pump	maḍaxet banzīn (f)	مضخّة بنزين
auto repair shop	warʃet taṣlīḥ 'arabīāt (f)	ورشة تصليح عربيات
to fill up	mala banzīn	ملى بنزين
fuel	woqūd (m)	وقود
jerrycan	ʒerken (m)	جركن
asphalt, tarmac	asfalt (m)	اسفلت
road markings	'alamāt el ṭarī' (pl)	علامات الطريق
kerb	bardora (f)	بردورة
crash barrier	sūr (m)	سور
ditch	ter'a (f)	ترعة
roadside (shoulder)	ḥaffet el ṭarī' (f)	حافّة الطريق
lamppost	'amūd nūr (m)	عمود نور
to drive (a car)	sā'	ساق
to turn (e.g., ~ left)	ḥād	حاد
to make a U-turn	laff fe u-turn	لفّ في يو تيرن
reverse (~ gear)	ḥaraka ela al warā' (f)	حركة إلى الوراء
to honk (vi)	zammar	زمّر
honk (sound)	kalaks (m)	كلاكس

to get stuck (in the mud, etc.)	ɣaraz	غرز
to spin the wheels	dawwar	دور
to cut, to turn off (vt)	awqaf	أوقف
speed	sorʿa (f)	سرعة
to exceed the speed limit	ʿadda el sorʿa	عدّى السرعة
to give a ticket	farad ɣarāma	فرض غرامة
traffic lights	eʃārāt el morūr (pl)	إشارات المرور
driving licence	roxṣet el qeyāda (f)	رخصة قيادة
level crossing	maʿbar (m)	معبر
crossroads	taqāṭoʿ (m)	تقاطع
zebra crossing	maʿbar (m)	معبر
bend, curve	monʿaṭaf (m)	منعطف
pedestrian precinct	manteʾa lel moʃāh (f)	منطقة للمشاة

180. Signs

Highway Code	qawāʿed el ṭarīʾ (pl)	قواعد الطريق
road sign (traffic sign)	ʿalāma (f)	علامة
overtaking	tagāwuz (m)	تجاوز
curve	monʿaṭaf (m)	منعطف
U-turn	malaff (m)	ملفّ
roundabout	dawarān morūry (m)	دوّران مروري
No entry	mamnūʿ el doxūl	ممنوع الدخول
All vehicles prohibited	mamnūʿ morūr el sayārāt	ممنوع مرور السيارات
No overtaking	mamnūʿ el morūr	ممنوع المرور
No parking	mamnūʿ el woʾūf	ممنوع الوقوف
No stopping	mamnūʿ el woʾūf	ممنوع الوقوف
dangerous curve	monʿaṭaf xaṭar (m)	منعطف خطر
steep descent	monḥadar ʃedīd (m)	منحدر شديد
one-way traffic	ṭarīʾ etegāh wāḥed	طريق إتجاه واحد
zebra crossing	maʿbar (m)	معبر
slippery road	ṭarīʾ zaleq (m)	طريق زلق
GIVE WAY	eʃāret el awlawiya	إشارة الأولوية

PEOPLE. LIFE EVENTS

181. Holidays. Event

celebration, holiday	ʿīd (m)	عيد
national day	ʿīd waṭany (m)	عيد وطني
public holiday	agāza rasmiya (f)	أجازة رسميّة
to commemorate (vt)	eḥtafal be zekra	إحتفل بذكرى
event (happening)	ḥadass (m)	حدث
event (organized activity)	monasba (f)	مناسبة
banquet (party)	walīma (f)	وليمة
reception (formal party)	ḥaflet esteʾbāl (f)	حفلة إستقبال
feast	walīma (f)	وليمة
anniversary	zekra sanawiya (f)	ذكرى سنوية
jubilee	yobeyl (m)	يوبيل
to celebrate (vt)	eḥtafal	إحتفل
New Year	raʾs el sanna (m)	رأس السنة
Happy New Year!	koll sana wenta ṭayeb!	كلّ سنة وأنت طيّب!
Father Christmas	baba neweyl (m)	بابا نويل
Christmas	ʿīd el melād (m)	عيد الميلاد
Merry Christmas!	ʿīd melād saʿīd!	عيد ميلاد سعيد!
Christmas tree	ʃagaret el kresmas (f)	شجرة الكريسمس
fireworks (fireworks show)	alʿāb nāriya (pl)	ألعاب ناريّة
wedding	faraḥ (m)	فرح
groom	ʿarīs (m)	عريس
bride	ʿarūsa (f)	عروسة
to invite (vt)	ʿazam	عزم
invitation card	beṭāʾet daʿwa (f)	بطاقة دعوة
guest	ḍeyf (m)	ضيف
to visit (~ your parents, etc.)	zār	زار
to meet the guests	estaʾbal ḍoyūf	إستقبل ضيوف
gift, present	hediya (f)	هديّة
to give (sth as present)	edda	إدّى
to receive gifts	estalam hadāya	إستلم هدايا
bouquet (of flowers)	bokeyh (f)	بوكيه
congratulations	tahneʾa (f)	تهنئة
to congratulate (vt)	hanna	هنّأ
greetings card	beṭāʾet tahneʾa (f)	بطاقة تهنئة
to send a postcard	baʿat beṭāʾet tahneʾa	بعت بطاقة تهنئة
to get a postcard	estalam beṭāʾa tahneʾa	استلم بطاقة تهنئة

toast	naχab (m)	نخب
to offer (a drink, etc.)	ḍayaf	ضيّف
champagne	ʃambania (f)	شمبانيا
to enjoy oneself	estamtaʿ	إستمتع
merriment (gaiety)	bahga (f)	بهجة
joy (emotion)	saʿāda (f)	سعادة
dance	ra'ṣa (f)	رقصة
to dance (vi, vt)	ra'aṣ	رقص
waltz	valles (m)	فالس
tango	tango (m)	تانجو

182. Funerals. Burial

cemetery	maqbara (f)	مقبرة
grave, tomb	'abr (m)	قبر
cross	ṣalīb (m)	صليب
gravestone	ḥagar el ma''bara (m)	حجر المقبرة
fence	sūr (m)	سور
chapel	kenīsa saɣīra (f)	كنيسة صغيرة
death	mote (m)	موت
to die (vi)	māt	مات
the deceased	el motawaffy (m)	المتوّفي
mourning	ḥedād (m)	حداد
to bury (vt)	dafan	دفن
undertakers	maktab motaʿahhed el dafn (m)	مكتب متعهّد الدفن
funeral	ganāza (f)	جنازة
wreath	eklīl (m)	إكليل
coffin	tabūt (m)	تابوت
hearse	naʿʃ (m)	نعش
shroud	kafan (m)	كفن
funeral procession	ganāza (f)	جنازة
funerary urn	garra gana'eziya (f)	جرّة جنائزية
crematorium	maḥra'et gosas el mawta (f)	محرقة جثث الموتى
obituary	segel el wafīāt (m)	سجل الوفيات
to cry (weep)	baka	بكى
to sob (vi)	nawwaḥ	نوّح

183. War. Soldiers

platoon	faṣīla (f)	فصيلة
company	serriya (f)	سريّة
regiment	foge (m)	فوج
army	geyʃ (m)	جيش

division	fer'a (f)	فرقة
section, squad	weḥda (f)	وحدة
host (army)	geyʃ (m)	جيش
soldier	gondy (m)	جنّدي
officer	ḍābeṭ (m)	ضابط
private	gondy (m)	جنّدي
sergeant	raqīb tāny (m)	رقيب تاني
lieutenant	molāzem tāny (m)	ملازم تاني
captain	naqīb (m)	نقيب
major	rā'ed (m)	رائد
colonel	ʿaqīd (m)	عقيد
general	ʒenerāl (m)	جنرال
sailor	baḥḥār (m)	بحّار
captain	'obṭān (m)	قبطان
boatswain	rabbān (m)	ربّان
artilleryman	gondy fe selāḥ el madfaʿiya (m)	جنّدي في سلاح المدفعيّة
paratrooper	selāḥ el maẓallāt (m)	سلاح المظلّلات
pilot	ṭayār (m)	طيّار
navigator	mallāḥ (m)	ملاّح
mechanic	mikanīky (m)	ميكانيكي
pioneer (sapper)	mohandes ʿaskary (m)	مهندس عسكري
parachutist	gondy el baraʃot (m)	جنّدي الباراشوت
reconnaissance scout	kaʃāfet el esteṭlāʿ (f)	كشّافة الإستطلاع
sniper	qannāṣ (m)	قنّاص
patrol (group)	dawriya (f)	دوريّة
to patrol (vt)	'ām be dawriya	قام بدوريّة
sentry, guard	ḥāres (m)	حارس
warrior	muḥāreb (m)	محارب
patriot	waṭany (m)	وطني
hero	baṭal (m)	بطل
heroine	baṭala (f)	بطلة
traitor	xāyen (m)	خاين
to betray (vt)	xān	خان
deserter	hāreb men el gondiya (m)	هارب من الجنديّة
to desert (vi)	farr men el geyʃ	فرّ من الجيش
mercenary	ma'gūr (m)	مأجور
recruit	gondy gedīd (m)	جنّدي جديد
volunteer	motaṭawweʿ (m)	متطوّع
dead (n)	'atīl (m)	قتيل
wounded (n)	garīḥ (m)	جريح
prisoner of war	asīr ḥarb (m)	أسير حرب

184. War. Military actions. Part 1

war	ḥarb (f)	حرب
to be at war	ḥārab	حارب
civil war	ḥarb ahliya (f)	حرب أهليّة
treacherously (adv)	ɣadran	غدراً
declaration of war	eʿlān ḥarb (m)	إعلان حرب
to declare (~ war)	aʿlan	أعلن
aggression	ʿedwān (m)	عدوان
to attack (invade)	hagam	هجم
to invade (vt)	eḥtall	إحتلّ
invader	moḥtell (m)	محتلّ
conqueror	fāteḥ (m)	فاتح
defence	defāʿ (m)	دفاع
to defend (a country, etc.)	dāfaʿ	دافع
to defend (against ...)	dāfaʿ ʿan ...	دافع عن ...
enemy	ʿadeww (m)	عدوّ
foe, adversary	χeṣm (m)	خصم
enemy (as adj)	ʿadeww	عدوّ
strategy	estrateʒiya (f)	إستراتيجيّة
tactics	taktīk (m)	تكتيك
order	amr (m)	أمر
command (order)	amr (m)	أمر
to order (vt)	amar	أمر
mission	mohemma (f)	مهمّة
secret (adj)	serry	سرّي
battle	maʿraka (f)	معركة
combat	ʾetāl (m)	قتال
attack	hogūm (m)	هجوم
charge (assault)	enqeḍāḍ (m)	إنقضاض
to storm (vt)	enqaḍḍ	إنقضّ
siege (to be under ~)	ḥeṣār (m)	حصار
offensive (n)	hogūm (m)	هجوم
to go on the offensive	hagam	هجم
retreat	enseḥāb (m)	إنسحاب
to retreat (vi)	ensaḥab	إنسحب
encirclement	eḥāṭa (f)	إحاطة
to encircle (vt)	aḥāṭ	أحاط
bombing (by aircraft)	ʾaṣf (m)	قصف
to drop a bomb	asqaṭ qonbola	أسقط قنبلة
to bomb (vt)	ʾaṣaf	قصف
explosion	enfegār (m)	إنفجار
shot	ṭalʾa (f)	طلقة

to fire (~ a shot)	aṭlaq el nār	أطلق النار
firing (burst of ~)	eṭlāq nār (m)	إطلاق نار
to aim (to point a weapon)	ṣawwab ʿala …	... صوّب على
to point (a gun)	ṣawwab	صوّب
to hit (the target)	aṣāb el hadaf	أصاب الهدف
to sink (~ a ship)	aɣraʾ	أغرق
hole (in a ship)	soqb (m)	ثقب
to founder, to sink (vi)	ɣereʾ	غرق
front (war ~)	gabha (f)	جبهة
evacuation	exlāʾ (m)	إخلاء
to evacuate (vt)	axla	أخلى
trench	xondoq (m)	خندق
barbed wire	aslāk ʃāʾeka (pl)	أسلاك شائكة
barrier (anti tank ~)	ḥāgez (m)	حاجز
watchtower	borg moraʾba (m)	برج مراقبة
military hospital	mostaʃfa ʿaskary (m)	مستشفى عسكري
to wound (vt)	garaḥ	جرح
wound	garḥ (m)	جرح
wounded (n)	garīḥ (m)	جريح
to be wounded	oṣīb bel garḥ	أصيب بالجرح
serious (wound)	xaṭīr	خطير

185. War. Military actions. Part 2

captivity	asr (m)	أسر
to take captive	asar	أسر
to be held captive	etʾasar	أتأسر
to be taken captive	weʾeʿ fel asr	وقع في الأسر
concentration camp	moʿaskar eʿteqāl (m)	معسكر إعتقال
prisoner of war	asīr ḥarb (m)	أسير حرب
to escape (vi)	hereb	هرب
to betray (vt)	xān	خان
betrayer	xāyen (m)	خاين
betrayal	xeyāna (f)	خيانة
to execute (by firing squad)	aʿdam ramyan bel roṣāṣ	أعدم رمياً بالرصاص
execution (by firing squad)	eʿdām ramyan bel roṣāṣ (m)	إعدام رمياً بالرصاص
equipment (military gear)	el ʿetād el ʿaskary (m)	العتاد العسكري
shoulder board	kattāfa (f)	كتافة
gas mask	qenāʿ el ɣāz (m)	قناع الغاز
field radio	gehāz lāselky (m)	جهاز لاسلكي
cipher, code	ʃafra (f)	شفرة
secrecy	serriya (f)	سرّية
password	kelmet el morūr (f)	كلمة مرور
land mine	loɣz arāḍy (m)	لغم أرضي

to mine (road, etc.)	lagɣam	لغّم
minefield	ḥaql alɣām (m)	حقل ألغام
air-raid warning	enzār gawwy (m)	إنذار جوّي
alarm (alert signal)	enzār (m)	إنذار
signal	eʃara (f)	إشارة
signal flare	eʃāra moḍī'a (f)	إشارة مضيئة
headquarters	maqarr (m)	مقرّ
reconnaissance	kaʃāfet el esteṭlā' (f)	كشّافة الإستطلاع
situation	ḥāla (f), waḍ' (m)	حالة, وضع
report	ta'rīr (m)	تقرير
ambush	kamīn (m)	كمين
reinforcement (army)	emdadāt 'askariya (pl)	إمدادات عسكريّة
target	hadaf (m)	هدف
training area	arḍ eχtebār (m)	أرض إختبار
military exercise	monawrāt 'askariya (pl)	مناورات عسكريّة
panic	zo'r (m)	ذعر
devastation	damār (m)	دمار
destruction, ruins	ḥeṭām (pl)	حطام
to destroy (vt)	dammar	دمّر
to survive (vi, vt)	negy	نجي
to disarm (vt)	garrad men el selāḥ	جرّد من السلاح
to handle (~ a gun)	esta'mel	إستعمل
Attention!	entebāh!	!إنتباه
At ease!	estareḥ!	!إسترح
feat, act of courage	ma'sara (f)	مأثرة
oath (vow)	qasam (m)	قسم
to swear (an oath)	aqsam	أقسم
decoration (medal, etc.)	wesām (m)	وسام
to award (give a medal to)	manaḥ	منح
medal	medalya (f)	ميدالية
order (e.g. ~ of Merit)	wesām 'askary (m)	وسام عسكري
victory	enteṣār - foze (m)	إنتصار, فوز
defeat	hazīma (f)	هزيمة
armistice	hodna (f)	هدنة
standard (battle flag)	rāyet el ma'raka (f)	راية المعركة
glory (honour, fame)	magd (m)	مجد
parade	mawkeb (m)	موكب
to march (on parade)	sār	سار

186. Weapons

weapons	asleḥa (pl)	أسلحة
firearms	asleḥa nāriya (pl)	أسلحة ناريّة
cold weapons (knives, etc.)	asleḥa bayḍā' (pl)	أسلحة بيضاء

chemical weapons	asleḥa kemawiya (pl)	أسلحة كيماويّة
nuclear (adj)	nawawy	نوويّ
nuclear weapons	asleḥa nawawiya (pl)	أسلحة نوويّة
bomb	qonbela (f)	قنبلة
atomic bomb	qonbela nawawiya (f)	قنبلة نوويّة
pistol (gun)	mosaddas (m)	مسدّس
rifle	bondoqiya (f)	بندقيّة
submachine gun	mosaddas rasʃāʃ (m)	مسدّس رشّاش
machine gun	rasʃāʃ (m)	رشّاش
muzzle	fawha (f)	فوهة
barrel	anbūba (f)	أنبوبة
calibre	ʿeyār (m)	عيار
trigger	zanād (m)	زناد
sight (aiming device)	moṣawweb (m)	مصوّب
magazine	maχzan (m)	مخزن
butt (shoulder stock)	ʿaqab el bondoʾiya (m)	عقب البندقيّة
hand grenade	qonbela yadawiya (f)	قنبلة يدويّة
explosive	mawād motafaggera (pl)	مواد متفجّرة
bullet	roṣāṣa (f)	رصاصة
cartridge	χarṭūʃa (f)	خرطوشة
charge	ḥaʃwa (f)	حشوة
ammunition	zaχīra (f)	ذخيرة
bomber (aircraft)	qazefet qanābel (f)	قاذفة قنابل
fighter	ṭayāra muqātela (f)	طيّارة مقاتلة
helicopter	heliokobter (m)	هليكوبتر
anti-aircraft gun	madfaʿ moḍād lel ṭaʾerāṭ (m)	مدفع مضاد للطائرات
tank	dabbāba (f)	دبّابة
tank gun	madfaʿ el dabbāba (m)	مدفع الدبّابة
artillery	madfaʿiya (f)	مدفعيّة
gun (cannon, howitzer)	madfaʿ (m)	مدفع
to lay (a gun)	ṣawwab	صوّب
shell (projectile)	qazīfa (f)	قذيفة
mortar bomb	qonbela hawn (f)	قنبلة هاون
mortar	hawn (m)	هاون
splinter (shell fragment)	ʃazya (f)	شظية
submarine	ɣawwāṣa (f)	غوّاصة
torpedo	ṭorbīd (m)	طوربيد
missile	ṣarūχ (m)	صاروخ
to load (gun)	ʿammar	عمّر
to shoot (vi)	ḍarab bel nār	ضرب بالنار
to point at (the cannon)	ṣawwab ʿala ...	صوّب على ...
bayonet	ḥerba (f)	حربة
rapier	seyf zu ḥaddeyn (m)	سيف ذو حدّين
sabre (e.g. cavalry ~)	seyf monḥany (m)	سيف منحني

spear (weapon)	remḥ (m)	رمح
bow	qose (m)	قوس
arrow	sahm (m)	سهم
musket	musket (m)	مسكيت
crossbow	qose mostaʿraḍ (m)	قوس مستعرض

187. Ancient people

primitive (prehistoric)	bedāʾy	بدائي
prehistoric (adj)	ma qabl el tarīχ	ما قبل التاريخ
ancient (~ civilization)	ʾadīm	قديم
Stone Age	el ʿaṣr el ḥagary (m)	العصر الحجري
Bronze Age	el ʿaṣr el bronzy (m)	العصر البرونزي
Ice Age	el ʿaṣr el galīdy (m)	العصر الجليدي
tribe	qabīla (f)	قبيلة
cannibal	ʾākel loḥūm el baʃar (m)	آكل لحوم البشر
hunter	ṣayād (m)	صيّاد
to hunt (vi, vt)	eṣṭād	إصطاد
mammoth	mamūθ (m)	ماموث
cave	kahf (m)	كهف
fire	nār (f)	نار
campfire	nār moχayem (m)	نار مخيّم
cave painting	rasm fel kahf (m)	رسم في الكهف
tool (e.g. stone axe)	adah (f)	أداة
spear	remḥ (m)	رمح
stone axe	faʾs ḥagary (m)	فأس حجري
to be at war	ḥārab	حارب
to domesticate (vt)	estaʾnas	استئنس
idol	ṣanam (m)	صنم
to worship (vt)	ʿabad	عبد
superstition	χorāfa (f)	خرافة
rite	mansak (m)	منسك
evolution	taṭṭawwor (m)	تطوّر
development	nomoww (m)	نموّ
disappearance (extinction)	enqerāḍ (m)	إنقراض
to adapt oneself	takayaf (maʿ)	تكيّف (مع)
archaeology	ʿelm el ʾāsār (m)	علم الآثار
archaeologist	ʿālem āsār (m)	عالم آثار
archaeological (adj)	asary	أثري
excavation site	mawqeʿ ḥafr (m)	موقع حفر
excavations	tanqīb (m)	تنقيب
find (object)	ekteʃāf (m)	إكتشاف
fragment	ʾeṭʿa (f)	قطعة

188. Middle Ages

people (ethnic group)	ʃaʿb (m)	شعب
peoples	ʃoʿūb (pl)	شعوب
tribe	qabīla (f)	قبيلة
tribes	qabāʾel (pl)	قبائل
barbarians	el barabra (pl)	البرابرة
Gauls	el ɣaliyūn (pl)	الغاليّون
Goths	el qūṭiyūn (pl)	القوطيون
Slavs	el selāf (pl)	السلاف
Vikings	el viking (pl)	الفايكينج
Romans	el romān (pl)	الرومان
Roman (adj)	romāny	روماني
Byzantines	bizanṭiyūn (pl)	بيزنطيون
Byzantium	bīzanṭa (f)	بيزنطة
Byzantine (adj)	bīzanṭy	بيزنطي
emperor	embraṭore (m)	إمبراطور
leader, chief (tribal ~)	zaʿīm (m)	زعيم
powerful (~ king)	gabbār	جبّار
king	malek (m)	ملك
ruler (sovereign)	ḥākem (m)	حاكم
knight	fāres (m)	فارس
feudal lord	eqṭāʿy (m)	إقطاعي
feudal (adj)	eqṭāʿy	إقطاعي
vassal	ḥākem tābeʿ (m)	حاكم تابع
duke	dūʾ (m)	دوق
earl	earl (m)	ايرل
baron	barūn (m)	بارون
bishop	asqof (m)	أسقف
armour	derʿ (m)	درع
shield	derʿ (m)	درع
sword	seyf (m)	سيف
visor	ḥaffa amamiya lel χoza (f)	حافة أماميّة للخوذة
chainmail	derʿ el zard (m)	درع الزرد
Crusade	ḥamla ṣalībiya (f)	حملة صليبيّة
crusader	ṣalīby (m)	صليبي
territory	arḍ (f)	أرض
to attack (invade)	hagam	هجم
to conquer (vt)	fataḥ	فتح
to occupy (invade)	eḥtall	إحتلّ
siege (to be under ~)	ḥeṣār (m)	حصار
besieged (adj)	moḥāṣar	محاصر
to besiege (vt)	ḥāṣar	حاصر
inquisition	maḥākem el taftīʃ (pl)	محاكم التفتيش
inquisitor	mofatteʃ (m)	مفتّش

torture	ta'zīb (m)	تعذيب
cruel (adj)	waḥʃy	وحشي
heretic	moharṭeq (m)	مهرطق
heresy	harṭa'a (f)	هرطقة
seafaring	el safar bel baḥr (m)	السفر بالبحر
pirate	'orṣān (m)	قرصان
piracy	'arṣana (f)	قرصنة
boarding (attack)	mohagmet safīna (f)	مهاجمة سفينة
loot, booty	ɣanīma (f)	غنيمة
treasure	konūz (pl)	كنوز
discovery	ekteʃāf (m)	إكتشاف
to discover (new land, etc.)	ektaʃaf	إكتشف
expedition	be'sa (f)	بعثة
musketeer	fāres (m)	فارس
cardinal	kardinal (m)	كاردينال
heraldry	ʃe'ārāt el nabāla (pl)	شعارات النبالة
heraldic (adj)	χāṣṣ be ʃe'arāt el nebāla	خاصّ بشعارات النبالة

189. Leader. Chief. Authorities

king	malek (m)	ملك
queen	maleka (f)	ملكة
royal (adj)	malaky	ملكي
kingdom	mamlaka (f)	مملكة
prince	amīr (m)	أمير
princess	amīra (f)	أميرة
president	ra'īs (m)	رئيس
vice-president	nā'eb el ra'īs (m)	نائب الرئيس
senator	'oḍw magles el ʃoyūχ (m)	عضو مجلس الشيوخ
monarch	'āhel (m)	عاهل
ruler (sovereign)	ḥākem (m)	حاكم
dictator	dektatore (m)	ديكتاتور
tyrant	ṭāɣeya (f)	طاغية
magnate	ra'smāly kebīr (m)	رأسمالي كبير
director	modīr (m)	مدير
chief	ra'īs (m)	رئيس
manager (director)	modīr (m)	مدير
boss	ra'īs (m)	رئيس
owner	ṣāḥeb (m)	صاحب
leader	za'īm (m)	زعيم
head (~ of delegation)	ra'īs (m)	رئيس
authorities	solṭāt (pl)	سلطات
superiors	ro'asā' (pl)	رؤساء
governor	muḥāfeẓ (m)	محافظ
consul	qonṣol (m)	قنصل

diplomat	deblomāsy (m)	دبلوماسي
mayor	ra'īs el baladiya (m)	رئيس البلديّة
sheriff	ʃerīf (m)	شريف
emperor	embratore (m)	إمبراطور
tsar, czar	qayṣar (m)	قيصر
pharaoh	fer'one (m)	فرعون
khan	χān (m)	خان

190. Road. Way. Directions

road	ṭarī' (m)	طريق
way (direction)	ṭarī' (m)	طريق
highway	otostrad (m)	اوتوستراد
motorway	ṭarī' saree' (m)	طريق سريع
trunk road	ṭarī' waṭany (m)	طريق وطني
main road	ṭarī' ra'īsy (m)	طريق رئيسي
dirt road	ṭarī' torāby (m)	طريق ترابي
pathway	mamarr (m)	ممرّ
footpath (troddenpath)	mamarr (m)	ممرّ
Where?	feyn?	فين؟
Where (to)?	feyn?	فين؟
From where?	meneyn?	منين؟
direction (way)	ettegāh (m)	إتّجاه
to point (~ the way)	ʃāwer	شاور
to the left	lel ʃemāl	للشمال
to the right	lel yemīn	لليمين
straight ahead (adv)	'ala ṭūl	على طول
back (e.g. to turn ~)	wara'	وراء
bend, curve	mon'aṭaf (m)	منعطف
to turn (e.g., ~ left)	ḥād	حاد
to make a U-turn	laff fe u-turn	لفّ في يو تيرن
to be visible (mountains, castle, etc.)	ẓahar	ظهر
to appear (come into view)	ẓahar	ظهر
stop, halt (e.g., during a trip)	estrāḥa ṭawīla (f)	إستراحة طويلة
to rest, to pause (vi)	rayaḥ	ريّح
rest (pause)	rāḥa (f)	راحة
to lose one's way	tāh	تاه
to lead to ... (ab. road)	adda ela ...	أدّى إلى...
to came out (e.g., on the highway)	weṣel ela ...	وصل إلى...
stretch (of the road)	emtedād (m)	إمتداد
asphalt	asfalt (m)	اسفلت

kerb	bardora (f)	بردورة
ditch	ter'a (f)	ترعة
manhole	fat-ḥa (f)	فتحة
roadside (shoulder)	ḥaffet el ṭarī' (f)	حافّة الطريق
pit, pothole	ḥofra (f)	حفرة
to go (on foot)	meʃy	مشي
to overtake (vt)	egtāz	إجتاز
step (footstep)	xaṭwa (f)	خطوة
on foot (adv)	maʃyī	مشيِ
to block (road)	sadd	سدّ
boom gate	ḥāgez ṭarī' (m)	حاجز طريق
dead end	ṭarī' masdūd (m)	طريق مسدود

191. Breaking the law. Criminals. Part 1

bandit	qāṭe' ṭarī' (m)	قاطع طريق
crime	garīma (f)	جريمة
criminal (person)	mogrem (m)	مجرم
thief	sāre' (m)	سارق
to steal (vi, vt)	sara'	سرق
stealing, theft	ser'a (f)	سرقة
to kidnap (vt)	xaṭaf	خطف
kidnapping	xaṭf (m)	خطف
kidnapper	xāṭef (m)	خاطف
ransom	fedya (f)	فدية
to demand ransom	ṭalab fedya	طلب فدية
to rob (vt)	nahab	نهب
robbery	nahb (m)	نهب
robber	nahhāb (m)	نهّاب
to extort (vt)	balṭag	بلطج
extortionist	balṭagy (m)	بلطجي
extortion	balṭaga (f)	بلطجة
to murder, to kill	'atal	قتل
murder	'atl (m)	قتل
murderer	qātel (m)	قاتل
gunshot	ṭal'et nār (f)	طلقة نار
to fire (~ a shot)	aṭlaq el nār	أطلق النار
to shoot to death	'atal bel roṣāṣ	قتل بالرصاص
to shoot (vi)	ḍarab bel nār	ضرب بالنار
shooting	ḍarb nār (m)	ضرب نار
incident (fight, etc.)	ḥādes (m)	حادث
fight, brawl	xenā'a (f)	خناقة
Help!	sā'idni	ساعدني!

victim	ḍaḥiya (f)	ضحيّة
to damage (vt)	χarrab	خرّب
damage	χesāra (f)	خسارة
dead body, corpse	gossa (f)	جثّة
grave (~ crime)	χaṭīra	خطيرة
to attack (vt)	hagam	هجم
to beat (to hit)	ḍarab	ضرب
to beat up	ḍarab	ضرب
to take (rob of sth)	salab	سلب
to stab to death	ṭaʿan ḥatta el mote	طعن حتّى الموت
to maim (vt)	ʃawwah	شوّه
to wound (vt)	garaḥ	جرح
blackmail	ebtezāz (m)	إبتزاز
to blackmail (vt)	ebtazz	إبتزّ
blackmailer	mobtazz (m)	مبتزّ
protection racket	balṭaga (f)	بلطجة
racketeer	mobtazz (m)	مبتزّ
gangster	ragol ʿeṣāba (m)	رجل عصابة
mafia	mafia (f)	مافيا
pickpocket	nasʃāl (m)	نشّال
burglar	leṣṣ beyūt (m)	لص بيوت
smuggling	tahrīb (m)	تهريب
smuggler	moharreb (m)	مهرّب
forgery	tazwīr (m)	تزوير
to forge (counterfeit)	zawwar	زوّر
fake (forged)	mozawwara	مزوّرة

192. Breaking the law. Criminals. Part 2

rape	eɣteṣāb (m)	إغتصاب
to rape (vt)	eɣtaṣab	إغتصب
rapist	moɣtaṣeb (m)	مغتصب
maniac	mahwūs (m)	مهووس
prostitute (fem.)	mommos (f)	مومّس
prostitution	daʿāra (f)	دعارة
pimp	qawwād (m)	قوّاد
drug addict	modmen moχaddarāt (m)	مدمن مخدّرات
drug dealer	tāger moχaddarāt (m)	تاجر مخدّرات
to blow up (bomb)	faggar	فجّر
explosion	enfegār (m)	إنفجار
to set fire	aʃʿal el nār	أشعل النار
arsonist	moʃʿel ḥarīq ʿan ʿamd (m)	مشعل حريق عن عمد
terrorism	erhāb (m)	إرهاب
terrorist	erhāby (m)	إرهابي
hostage	rahīna (m)	رهينة

to swindle (deceive)	eḥtāl	إحتال
swindle, deception	eḥteyāl (m)	إحتيال
swindler	moḥtāl (m)	محتال
to bribe (vt)	raʃa	رشا
bribery	erteʃāʾ (m)	إرتشاء
bribe	raʃwa (f)	رشوة
poison	semm (m)	سمّ
to poison (vt)	sammem	سمّم
to poison oneself	sammem nafsoh	سمّم نفسه
suicide (act)	enteḥār (m)	إنتحار
suicide (person)	montaḥer (m)	منتحر
to threaten (vt)	hadded	هدّد
threat	tahdīd (m)	تهديد
to make an attempt	ḥāwel eɣteyāl	حاول إغتيال
attempt (attack)	moḥawlet eɣteyāl (f)	محاولة إغتيال
to steal (a car)	saraʾ	سرق
to hijack (a plane)	eχtaṭaf	إختطف
revenge	enteqām (m)	إنتقام
to avenge (get revenge)	entaqam	إنتقم
to torture (vt)	ʿazzeb	عذّب
torture	taʿzīb (m)	تعذيب
to torment (vt)	ʿazzeb	عذّب
pirate	ʾorṣān (m)	قرصان
hooligan	wabaʃ (m)	وبش
armed (adj)	mosallaḥ	مسلّح
violence	ʿonf (m)	عنف
illegal (unlawful)	meʃ qanūniy	مش قانونيّ
spying (espionage)	tagassas (m)	تجسّس
to spy (vi)	tagassas	تجسّس

193. Police. Law. Part 1

justice	qaḍāʾ (m)	قضاء
court (see you in ~)	maḥkama (f)	محكمة
judge	qāḍy (m)	قاضي
jurors	moḥallafīn (pl)	محلّفين
jury trial	qaḍāʾ el muḥallafīn (m)	قضاء المحلّفين
to judge, to try (vt)	ḥakam	حكم
lawyer, barrister	muḥāmy (m)	محامي
defendant	moddaʿy ʿaleyh (m)	مدّعي عليه
dock	ʾafaṣ el ettehām (m)	قفص الإتّهام
charge	ettehām (m)	إتّهام
accused	mottaham (m)	متّهم

sentence	ḥokm (m)	حكم
to sentence (vt)	ḥakam	حكم
guilty (culprit)	gāny (m)	جاني
to punish (vt)	ʿāqab	عاقب
punishment	ʿeqāb (m)	عقاب
fine (penalty)	ɣarāma (f)	غرامة
life imprisonment	segn mada el ḥayah (m)	سجن مدى الحياة
death penalty	ʿoqūbet ʾeʿdām (f)	عقوبة إعدام
electric chair	el korsy el kaharabāʾy (m)	الكرسي الكهربائي
gallows	maʃnaʾa (f)	مشنقة
to execute (vt)	aʿdam	أعدم
execution	eʿdām (m)	إعدام
prison	segn (m)	سجن
cell	zenzāna (f)	زنزانة
escort (convoy)	ḥerāsa (f)	حراسة
prison officer	ḥāres segn (m)	حارس سجن
prisoner	sagīn (m)	سجين
handcuffs	kalabʃāt (pl)	كلابشات
to handcuff (vt)	kalbeʃ	كلبش
prison break	horūb men el segn (m)	هروب من السجن
to break out (vi)	hereb	هرب
to disappear (vi)	eχtafa	إختفى
to release (from prison)	aχla sabīl	أخلى سبيل
amnesty	ʿafw ʿām (m)	عفو عام
police	ʃorṭa (f)	شرطة
police officer	ʃorṭy (m)	شرطي
police station	qesm ʃorṭa (m)	قسم شرطة
truncheon	ʿaṣāya maṭṭāṭiya (f)	عصاية مطّاطية
megaphone (loudhailer)	būʾ (m)	بوق
patrol car	ʿarabiyet dawrīāt (f)	عربيّة دوريات
siren	sarīna (f)	سرينة
to turn on the siren	wallaʿ el sarīna	ولّع السرينة
siren call	ṣote sarīna (m)	صوت سرينة
crime scene	masraḥ el garīma (m)	مسرح الجريمة
witness	ʃāhed (m)	شاهد
freedom	ḥorriya (f)	حرّيّة
accomplice	ʃerīk fel garīma (m)	شريك في الجريمة
to flee (vi)	hereb	هرب
trace (to leave a ~)	asar (m)	أثر

194. Police. Law. Part 2

search (investigation)	baḥs (m)	بحث
to look for ...	dawwar ʿala	دوّر على

suspicion	ʃobha (f)	شبهة
suspicious (e.g., ~ vehicle)	maʃbūh	مشبوه
to stop (cause to halt)	awqaf	أوقف
to detain (keep in custody)	eʿtaqal	إعتقل
case (lawsuit)	ʾaḍiya (f)	قضيّة
investigation	taḥʾīʾ (m)	تحقيق
detective	moḥaqqeq (m)	محقّق
investigator	mofatteʃ (m)	مفتّش
hypothesis	rewāya (f)	رواية
motive	dāfeʿ (m)	دافع
interrogation	estegwāb (m)	إستجواب
to interrogate (vt)	estagweb	إستجوّب
to question (~ neighbors, etc.)	estanṭaʾ	إستنطق
check (identity ~)	faḥṣ (m)	فحص
round-up (raid)	gamʿ (m)	جمع
search (~ warrant)	taftīʃ (m)	تفتيش
chase (pursuit)	moṭarda (f)	مطاردة
to pursue, to chase	ṭārad	طارد
to track (a criminal)	tatabbaʿ	تتبّع
arrest	eʿteqāl (m)	إعتقال
to arrest (sb)	eʿtaqal	اعتقل
to catch (thief, etc.)	ʾabaḍ ʿala	قبض على
capture	ʾabḍ (m)	قبض
document	wasīqa (f)	وثيقة
proof (evidence)	dalīl (m)	دليل
to prove (vt)	asbat	أثبت
footprint	baṣma (f)	بصمة
fingerprints	baṣamāt el aṣābeʿ (pl)	بصمات الأصابع
piece of evidence	ʾeṭʿa men el adella (f)	قطعة من الأدلّة
alibi	ḥegget ɣeyāb (f)	حجّة غياب
innocent (not guilty)	barīʾ	بريء
injustice	ẓolm (m)	ظلم
unjust, unfair (adj)	meʃ ʿādel	مش عادل
criminal (adj)	mogrem	مجرم
to confiscate (vt)	ṣādar	صادر
drug (illegal substance)	moχaddarāt (pl)	مخدّرات
weapon, gun	selāḥ (m)	سلاح
to disarm (vt)	garrad men el selāḥ	جرّد من السلاح
to order (command)	amar	أمر
to disappear (vi)	eχtafa	إختفى
law	qanūn (m)	قانون
legal, lawful (adj)	qanūny	قانوني
illegal, illicit (adj)	meʃ qanūny	مش قانوني
responsibility (blame)	masʾoliya (f)	مسؤوليّة
responsible (adj)	masʾūl (m)	مسؤول

NATURE

The Earth. Part 1

195. Outer space

space	faḍā' (m)	فضاء
space (as adj)	faḍā'y	فضائي
outer space	el faḍā' el χāregy (m)	الفضاء الخارجي
world	ʿālam (m)	عالم
universe	el kōn (m)	الكون
galaxy	el magarra (f)	المجرّة
star	negm (m)	نجم
constellation	borg (m)	برج
planet	kawwkab (m)	كوكب
satellite	'amar ṣenāʿy (m)	قمر صناعي
meteorite	nayzek (m)	نيزك
comet	mozannab (m)	مذنّب
asteroid	kowaykeb (m)	كويكب
orbit	madār (m)	مدار
to revolve (~ around the Earth)	dār	دار
atmosphere	el ɣelāf el gawwy (m)	الغلاف الجوّي
the Sun	el ʃams (f)	الشمس
solar system	el magmūʿa el ʃamsiya (f)	المجموعة الشمسيّة
solar eclipse	kosūf el ʃams (m)	كسوف الشمس
the Earth	el arḍ (f)	الأرض
the Moon	el 'amar (m)	القمر
Mars	el marrīχ (m)	المرّيخ
Venus	el zahra (f)	الزهرة
Jupiter	el moʃtary (m)	المشتري
Saturn	zoḥḥol (m)	زحل
Mercury	ʿaṭāred (m)	عطارد
Uranus	uranus (m)	اورانوس
Neptune	nibtūn (m)	نبتون
Pluto	bluto (m)	بلوتو
Milky Way	darb el tebbāna (m)	درب التبّانة
Great Bear (Ursa Major)	el dobb el akbar (m)	الدب الأكبر
North Star	negm el 'oṭb (m)	نجم القطب
Martian	sāken el marrīχ (m)	ساكن المرّيخ
extraterrestrial (n)	faḍā'y (m)	فضائي

alien	kā'en faḍā'y (m)	كائن فضائي
flying saucer	ṭaba' ṭā'er (m)	طبق طائر
spaceship	markaba faḍa'iya (f)	مركبة فضائية
space station	maḥaṭṭet faḍā' (f)	محطّة فضاء
blast-off	enṭelāq (m)	إنطلاق
engine	motore (m)	موتور
nozzle	manfaθ (m)	منفث
fuel	woqūd (m)	وقود
cockpit, flight deck	kabīna (f)	كابينة
aerial	hawā'y (m)	هوائي
porthole	kowwa mostadīra (f)	كوّة مستديرة
solar panel	lawḥa ʃamsiya (f)	لوحة شمسيّة
spacesuit	badlet el faḍā' (f)	بدّلة الفضاء
weightlessness	en'edām wazn (m)	إنعدام الوزن
oxygen	oksiʒīn (m)	أوكسجين
docking (in space)	rasw (m)	رسو
to dock (vi, vt)	rasa	رسى
observatory	marṣad (m)	مرصد
telescope	teleskop (m)	تلسكوب
to observe (vt)	rāqab	راقب
to explore (vt)	estakʃef	إستكشف

196. The Earth

the Earth	el arḍ (f)	الأرض
the globe (the Earth)	el kora el arḍiya (f)	الكرة الأرضيّة
planet	kawwkab (m)	كوّكب
atmosphere	el ɣelāf el gawwy (m)	الغلاف الجوّي
geography	goɣrafia (f)	جغرافيا
nature	ṭabee'a (f)	طبيعة
globe (table ~)	namūzag lel kora el arḍiya (m)	نموذج للكرة الأرضيّة
map	χarīṭa (f)	خريطة
atlas	aṭlas (m)	أطلس
Europe	orobba (f)	أوروبّا
Asia	asya (f)	آسيا
Africa	afreqia (f)	أفريقيا
Australia	ostorālya (f)	أستراليا
America	amrīka (f)	أمريكا
North America	amrīka el ʃamaliya (f)	أمريكا الشماليّة
South America	amrīka el ganūbiya (f)	أمريكا الجنوبيّة
Antarctica	el qoṭb el ganūby (m)	القطب الجنوبي
the Arctic	el qoṭb el ʃamāly (m)	القطب الشمالي

197. Cardinal directions

north	ʃemāl (m)	شمال
to the north	lel ʃamāl	للشمال
in the north	fel ʃamāl	في الشمال
northern (adj)	ʃamāly	شمالي
south	ganūb (m)	جنوب
to the south	lel ganūb	للجنوب
in the south	fel ganūb	في الجنوب
southern (adj)	ganūby	جنوبي
west	ɣarb (m)	غرب
to the west	lel ɣarb	للغرب
in the west	fel ɣarb	في الغرب
western (adj)	ɣarby	غربي
east	ʃarʾ (m)	شرق
to the east	lel ʃarʾ	للشرق
in the east	fel ʃarʾ	في الشرق
eastern (adj)	ʃarʾy	شرقي

198. Sea. Ocean

sea	baḥr (m)	بحر
ocean	moḥīṭ (m)	محيط
gulf (bay)	χalīg (m)	خليج
straits	maḍīq (m)	مضيق
land (solid ground)	barr (m)	برّ
continent (mainland)	qārra (f)	قارّة
island	gezīra (f)	جزيرة
peninsula	ʃebh gezeyra (f)	شبه جزيرة
archipelago	magmūʿet gozor (f)	مجموعة جزر
bay, cove	χalīg (m)	خليج
harbour	mināʾ (m)	ميناء
lagoon	lagūn (m)	لاجون
cape	raʾs (m)	رأس
atoll	gezīra morganiya estwaʾiya (f)	جزيرة مرجانيّة إستوائيّة
reef	ʃoʿāb (pl)	شعاب
coral	morgān (m)	مرجان
coral reef	ʃoʿāb morganiya (pl)	شعاب مرجانية
deep (adj)	ʿamīq	عميق
depth (deep water)	ʿomq (m)	عمق
abyss	el ʿomq el saḥīq (m)	العمق السحيق
trench (e.g. Mariana ~)	χondoq (m)	خندق
current (Ocean ~)	tayār (m)	تيّار
to surround (bathe)	ḥāṭ	حاط
shore	sāḥel (m)	ساحل

coast	sāḥel (m)	ساحل
flow (flood tide)	tayār (m)	تيّار
ebb (ebb tide)	gozor (m)	جزر
shoal	meyāh ḍaḥla (f)	مياه ضحلة
bottom (~ of the sea)	qāʿ (m)	قاع
wave	mouga (f)	موجة
crest (~ of a wave)	qemma (f)	قمّة
spume (sea foam)	zabad el baḥr (m)	زبد البحر
storm (sea storm)	ʿāṣefa (f)	عاصفة
hurricane	eʿṣār (m)	إعصار
tsunami	tsunāmy (m)	تسونامي
calm (dead ~)	hodūʾ (m)	هدوء
quiet, calm (adj)	hady	هادئ
pole	ʾoṭb (m)	قطب
polar (adj)	ʾoṭby	قطبي
latitude	ʿarḍ (m)	عرض
longitude	χaṭṭ ṭūl (m)	خطّ طول
parallel	motawāz (m)	متواز
equator	χaṭṭ el estewāʾ (m)	خطّ الإستواء
sky	samāʾ (f)	سماء
horizon	ofoq (m)	أفق
air	hawāʾ (m)	هواء
lighthouse	manāra (f)	منارة
to dive (vi)	ɣāṣ	غاص
to sink (ab. boat)	ɣereʾ	غرق
treasure	konūz (pl)	كنوز

199. Seas & Oceans names

Atlantic Ocean	el moḥeyṭ el aṭlanṭy (m)	المحيط الأطلنطي
Indian Ocean	el moḥeyṭ el hendy (m)	المحيط الهندي
Pacific Ocean	el moḥeyṭ el hādy (m)	المحيط الهادي
Arctic Ocean	el moḥeyṭ el motagammed el ʃamāly (m)	المحيط المتجمّد الشمالي
Black Sea	el baḥr el aswad (m)	البحر الأسود
Red Sea	el baḥr el aḥmar (m)	البحر الأحمر
Yellow Sea	el baḥr el aṣfar (m)	البحر الأصفر
White Sea	el baḥr el abyaḍ (m)	البحر الأبيض
Caspian Sea	baḥr qazwīn (m)	بحر قزوين
Dead Sea	el baḥr el mayet (m)	البحر الميّت
Mediterranean Sea	el baḥr el abyaḍ el motawasseṭ (m)	البحر الأبيض المتوسّط
Aegean Sea	baḥr eygah (m)	بحر إيجة
Adriatic Sea	el baḥr el adreyatīky (m)	البحر الأدرياتيكي
Arabian Sea	baḥr el ʿarab (m)	بحر العرب

Sea of Japan	baḥr el yabān (m)	بحر اليابان
Bering Sea	baḥr bering (m)	بحر بيرينغ
South China Sea	baḥr el ṣeyn el ganūby (m)	بحر الصين الجنوبي
Coral Sea	baḥr el morgān (m)	بحر المرجان
Tasman Sea	baḥr tazman (m)	بحر تسمان
Caribbean Sea	el baḥr el karību (m)	البحر الكاريبي
Barents Sea	baḥr barents (m)	بحر بارنتس
Kara Sea	baḥr kara (m)	بحر كارا
North Sea	baḥr el ʃamāl (m)	بحر الشمال
Baltic Sea	baḥr el balṭīq (m)	بحر البلطيق
Norwegian Sea	baḥr el nerwīg (m)	بحر النرويج

200. Mountains

mountain	gabal (m)	جبل
mountain range	selselet gebāl (f)	سلسلة جبال
mountain ridge	notū' el gabal (m)	نتوء الجبل
summit, top	qemma (f)	قمّة
peak	qemma (f)	قمّة
foot (~ of the mountain)	asfal (m)	أسفل
slope (mountainside)	monḥadar (m)	منحدر
volcano	borkān (m)	بركان
active volcano	borkān naʃeṭ (m)	بركان نشط
dormant volcano	borkān χāmed (m)	بركان خامد
eruption	sawarān (m)	ثوَران
crater	fawhet el borkān (f)	فوهة البركان
magma	magma (f)	ماجما
lava	ḥomam borkāniya (pl)	حمم بركانية
molten (~ lava)	monṣahera	منصهرة
canyon	wādy ḍaye' (m)	وادي ضيّق
gorge	mamarr ḍaye' (m)	ممرّ ضيّق
crevice	ʃa'' (m)	شقّ
abyss (chasm)	hāwya (f)	هاوية
pass, col	mamarr gabaly (m)	ممرّ جبلي
plateau	haḍaba (f)	هضبة
cliff	garf (m)	جرف
hill	tall (m)	تلّ
glacier	nahr galīdy (m)	نهر جليدي
waterfall	ʃallāl (m)	شلّال
geyser	nabʿ maya ḥāra (m)	نبع ميّة حارة
lake	boḥeyra (f)	بحيرة
plain	sahl (m)	سهل
landscape	manzar ṭabeeʿy (m)	منظر طبيعي
echo	ṣada (m)	صدى

alpinist	motasalleq el gebāl (m)	متسلّق الجبال
rock climber	motasalleq ṣoχūr (m)	متسلّق صخور
to conquer (in climbing)	taɣallab ʿala	تغلّب على
climb (an easy ~)	tasalloq (m)	تسلّق

201. Mountains names

The Alps	gebāl el alb (pl)	جبال الألب
Mont Blanc	mōn blōn (m)	مون بلون
The Pyrenees	gebāl el barānes (pl)	جبال البرانس
The Carpathians	gebāl el karbāt (pl)	جبال الكاربات
The Ural Mountains	gebāl el urāl (pl)	جبال الأورال
The Caucasus Mountains	gebāl el qoqāz (pl)	جبال القوقاز
Mount Elbrus	gabal elbrus (m)	جبل إلبروس
The Altai Mountains	gebāl altāy (pl)	جبال ألتاي
The Tian Shan	gebāl tian ʃan (pl)	جبال تيان شان
The Pamirs	gebāl bamir (pl)	جبال بامير
The Himalayas	himalāya (pl)	هيمالايا
Mount Everest	gabal everest (m)	جبل افرست
The Andes	gebāl el andīz (pl)	جبال الأنديز
Mount Kilimanjaro	gabal kilimanʒaro (m)	جبل كليمنجارو

202. Rivers

river	nahr (m)	نهر
spring (natural source)	ʿeyn (m)	عين
riverbed (river channel)	magra el nahr (m)	مجرى النهر
basin (river valley)	ḥoḍe (m)	حوض
to flow into …	ṣabb fe …	صبّ في...
tributary	rāfed (m)	رافد
bank (river ~)	ḍaffa (f)	ضفّة
current (stream)	tayār (m)	تيّار
downstream (adv)	maʿ ettigāh magra el nahr	مع إتّجاه مجرى النهر
upstream (adv)	ḍed el tayār	ضد التيار
inundation	ɣamr (m)	غمر
flooding	fayaḍān (m)	فيضان
to overflow (vi)	fāḍ	فاض
to flood (vt)	ɣamar	غمر
shallow (shoal)	meyāh ḍaḥla (f)	مياه ضحلة
rapids	monḥadar el nahr (m)	منحدر النهر
dam	sadd (m)	سدّ
canal	qanah (f)	قناة
reservoir (artificial lake)	χazzān mā'y (m)	خزّان مائي
sluice, lock	bawwāba qanṭara (f)	بوّابة قنطرة

water body (pond, etc.)	berka (f)	بركة
swamp (marshland)	mostanqaʿ (m)	مستنقع
bog, marsh	mostanqaʿ (m)	مستنقع
whirlpool	dawwāma (f)	دوّامة
stream (brook)	gadwal (m)	جدول
drinking (ab. water)	el ʃorb	الشرب
fresh (~ water)	ʿazb	عذب
ice	galīd (m)	جليد
to freeze over (ab. river, etc.)	etgammed	إتجمّد

203. Rivers names

Seine	el seyn (m)	السين
Loire	el lua:r (m)	اللوار
Thames	el teymz (m)	التيمز
Rhine	el rayn (m)	الراين
Danube	el danūb (m)	الدانوب
Volga	el volga (m)	الفولغا
Don	el done (m)	الدون
Lena	lena (m)	لينا
Yellow River	el nahr el aṣfar (m)	النهر الأصفر
Yangtze	el yangesty (m)	اليانغستي
Mekong	el mekong (m)	الميكونغ
Ganges	el ɣang (m)	الغانج
Nile River	el nīl (m)	النيل
Congo River	el kongo (m)	الكونغو
Okavango River	okavango (m)	أوكافانجو
Zambezi River	el zambizi (m)	الزمبيزي
Limpopo River	limbobo (m)	ليمبوبو
Mississippi River	el mississibbi (m)	الميسيسيبي

204. Forest

forest, wood	ɣāba (f)	غابة
forest (as adj)	ɣāba	غابة
thick forest	ɣāba kasīfa (f)	غابة كثيفة
grove	bostān (m)	بستان
forest clearing	ezālet el ɣābāt (f)	إزالة الغابات
thicket	agama (f)	أجمة
scrubland	arāḍy el ʃogayrāt (pl)	أراضي الشجيرات
footpath (troddenpath)	mamarr (m)	ممرّ
gully	wādy ḍayeʾ (m)	وادي ضيّق
tree	ʃagara (f)	شجرة

leaf	wara'a (f)	ورقة
leaves (foliage)	wara' (m)	ورق
fall of leaves	tasā'oṭ el awrā' (m)	تساقط الأوراق
to fall (ab. leaves)	saqaṭ	سقط
top (of the tree)	ra's (m)	رأس
branch	ɣoṣn (m)	غصن
bough	ɣoṣn ra'īsy (m)	غصن رئيسي
bud (on shrub, tree)	bor'om (m)	برعم
needle (of the pine tree)	ʃawka (f)	شوكة
fir cone	kūz el ṣnowbar (m)	كوز الصنوبر
tree hollow	gofe (m)	جوف
nest	'eʃ (m)	عشّ
burrow (animal hole)	goḥr (m)	جحر
trunk	gez' (m)	جذع
root	gezr (m)	جذر
bark	leḥā' (m)	لحاء
moss	ṭaḥlab (m)	طحلب
to uproot (remove trees or tree stumps)	eqtala'	إقتلع
to chop down	'aṭṭa'	قطّع
to deforest (vt)	azāl el ɣabāt	أزال الغابات
tree stump	gez' el ʃagara (m)	جذع الشجرة
campfire	nār moχayem (m)	نار مخيّم
forest fire	ḥarī' ɣāba (m)	حريق غابة
to extinguish (vt)	ṭaffa	طفّى
forest ranger	ḥāres el ɣāba (m)	حارس الغابة
protection	ḥemāya (f)	حماية
to protect (~ nature)	ḥama	حمى
poacher	sāre' el ṣeyd (m)	سارق الصيد
steel trap	maṣyada (f)	مصيّدة
to gather, to pick (vt)	gamma'	جمّع
to lose one's way	tāh	تاه

205. Natural resources

natural resources	sarawāt ṭabī'iya (pl)	ثروات طبيعيّة
minerals	ma'āden (pl)	معادن
deposits	rawāseb (pl)	رواسب
field (e.g. oilfield)	ḥaql (m)	حقل
to mine (extract)	estaχrag	إستخرج
mining (extraction)	esteχrāg (m)	إستخراج
ore	χām (m)	خام
mine (e.g. for coal)	mangam (m)	منجم
shaft (mine ~)	mangam (m)	منجم
miner	'āmel mangam (m)	عامل منجم

gas (natural ~)	ɣāz (m)	غاز
gas pipeline	χaṭṭ anabīb ɣāz (m)	خطّ أنابيب غاز
oil (petroleum)	nafṭ (m)	نفط
oil pipeline	anabīb el nafṭ (pl)	أنابيب النفط
oil well	bīr el nafṭ (m)	بير النفط
derrick (tower)	ḥaffāra (f)	حفّارة
tanker	nāqelet betrūl (f)	ناقلة بترول
sand	raml (m)	رمل
limestone	ḥagar el kals (m)	حجر الكلس
gravel	ḥaṣa (m)	حصى
peat	χaθ faḥm nabāty (m)	خث فحم نباتي
clay	ṭīn (m)	طين
coal	faḥm (m)	فحم
iron (ore)	ḥadīd (m)	حديد
gold	dahab (m)	ذهب
silver	faḍḍa (f)	فضّة
nickel	nikel (m)	نيكل
copper	neḥās (m)	نحاس
zinc	zink (m)	زنك
manganese	manganīz (m)	منجنيز
mercury	ze'baq (m)	زئبق
lead	roṣāṣ (m)	رصاص
mineral	ma'dan (m)	معدن
crystal	kristāl (m)	كريستال
marble	roχām (m)	رخام
uranium	yuranuim (m)	يورانيوم

The Earth. Part 2

206. Weather

weather	ṭa'sْ (m)	طقس
weather forecast	naʃra gawiya (f)	نشرة جويّة
temperature	ḥarāra (f)	حرارة
thermometer	termometr (m)	ترمومتر
barometer	barometr (m)	بارومتر
humid (adj)	roṭob	رطب
humidity	roṭūba (f)	رطوبة
heat (extreme ~)	ḥarāra (f)	حرارة
hot (torrid)	ḥarr	حارّ
it's hot	el gaww ḥarr	الجّو حرّ
it's warm	el gaww dafa	الجوّ دفا
warm (moderately hot)	dāfe'	دافئ
it's cold	el gaww bāred	الجوّ بارد
cold (adj)	bāred	بارد
sun	ʃams (f)	شمس
to shine (vi)	nawwar	نوّر
sunny (day)	moʃmes	مشمس
to come up (vi)	ʃara'	شرق
to set (vi)	ɣarab	غرب
cloud	saḥāba (f)	سحابة
cloudy (adj)	meɣayem	مغيّم
rain cloud	saḥābet maṭar (f)	سحابة مطر
somber (gloomy)	meɣayem	مغيّم
rain	maṭar (m)	مطر
it's raining	el donia betmaṭṭar	الدنيا بتمطّر
rainy (~ day, weather)	momṭer	ممطر
to drizzle (vi)	maṭṭaret razāz	مطّرت رذاذ
pouring rain	maṭar monhamer (f)	مطر منهمر
downpour	maṭar ɣazīr (m)	مطر غزير
heavy (e.g. ~ rain)	ʃedīd	شديد
puddle	berka (f)	بركة
to get wet (in rain)	ettbal	إتّبل
fog (mist)	ʃabbūra (f)	شبّورة
foggy	fih ʃabbūra	فيه شبّورة
snow	talg (m)	ثلج
it's snowing	fih talg	فيه ثلج

207. Severe weather. Natural disasters

thunderstorm	ʿāṣefa raʿdiya (f)	عاصفة رعدية
lightning (~ strike)	barʾ (m)	برق
to flash (vi)	baraq	برق
thunder	raʿd (m)	رعد
to thunder (vi)	dawa	دوّى
it's thundering	el samāʾ dawat raʿd (f)	السماء دوّت رعد
hail	maṭar bard (m)	مطر برد
it's hailing	maṭṭaret bard	مطّرت برد
to flood (vt)	ɣamar	غمر
flood, inundation	fayaḍān (m)	فيضان
earthquake	zelzāl (m)	زلزال
tremor, shoke	hazza arḍiya (f)	هزّة أرضية
epicentre	markaz el zelzāl (m)	مركز الزلزال
eruption	sawarān (m)	ثوّران
lava	ḥomam borkāniya (pl)	حمم بركانية
twister, tornado	eʿṣār (m)	إعصار
typhoon	tyfūn (m)	طوفان
hurricane	eʿṣār (m)	إعصار
storm	ʿāṣefa (f)	عاصفة
tsunami	tsunāmy (m)	تسونامي
cyclone	eʿṣār (m)	إعصار
bad weather	ṭaʾs sayeʾ (m)	طقس سيئ
fire (accident)	ḥarīʾ (m)	حريق
disaster	karsa (f)	كارثة
meteorite	nayzek (m)	نيّزك
avalanche	enheyār talgy (m)	إنهيار ثلجي
snowslide	enheyār talgy (m)	إنهيار ثلجي
blizzard	ʿāṣefa talgiya (f)	عاصفة ثلجيّة
snowstorm	ʿāṣefa talgiya (f)	عاصفة ثلجيّة

208. Noises. Sounds

silence (quiet)	ṣamt (m)	صمت
sound	ṣote (m)	صوت
noise	dawʃa (f)	دوشة
to make noise	ʿamal dawʃa	عمل دوشة
noisy (adj)	mozʿeg	مزعج
loudly (to speak, etc.)	beṣote ʿāly	بصوت عالي
loud (voice, etc.)	ʿāly	عالي
constant (e.g., ~ noise)	mostamerr	مستمرّ
cry, shout (n)	ṣarxa (f)	صرخة

to cry, to shout (vi)	ṣarrax	صرّخ
whisper	hamsa (f)	همسة
to whisper (vi, vt)	hamas	همس
barking (dog's ~)	nebāḥ (m)	نباح
to bark (vi)	nabaḥ	نبح
groan (of pain, etc.)	anīn (m)	أنين
to groan (vi)	ann	أنّ
cough	koḥḥa (f)	كحّة
to cough (vi)	kaḥḥ	كحّ
whistle	taṣfīr (m)	تصفير
to whistle (vi)	ṣaffar	صفّر
knock (at the door)	ṭar', da'' (m)	طرق, دقّ
to knock (on the door)	da''	دقّ
to crack (vi)	far'a'	فرقع
crack (cracking sound)	far'a'a (f)	فرقعة
siren	sarīna (f)	سرينة
whistle (factory ~, etc.)	ṣafīr (m)	صفير
to whistle (ab. train)	ṣaffar	صفّر
honk (car horn sound)	tazmīr (m)	تزمير
to honk (vi)	zammar	زمّر

209. Winter

winter (n)	ʃetā' (m)	شتاء
winter (as adj)	ʃetwy	شتوي
in winter	fel ʃetā'	في الشتاء
snow	talg (m)	ثلج
it's snowing	fih talg	فيه ثلج
snowfall	tasā'oṭ el tolūg (m)	تساقط الثلوج
snowdrift	rokma talgiya (f)	ركمة ثلجية
snowflake	nadfet talg (f)	ندفة ثلج
snowball	koret talg (f)	كرة ثلج
snowman	rāgel men el talg (m)	راجل من الثلج
icicle	'eṭ'et galīd (f)	قطعة جليد
December	desember (m)	ديسمبر
January	yanāyer (m)	يناير
February	febrāyer (m)	فبراير
frost (severe ~, freezing cold)	ṣaqee' (m)	صقيع
frosty (weather, air)	ṣā'e'	صاقع
below zero (adv)	taḥt el ṣefr	تحت الصفر
first frost	ṣaqee' (m)	صقيع
hoarfrost	ṣaqee' motagammed (m)	صقيع متجمّد
cold (cold weather)	bard (m)	برد
it's cold	el gaww bāred	الجوّ بارد

fur coat	balṭo farww (m)	بالطو فروّ
mittens	gwanty men ɣeyr aṣābe' (m)	جوانتي من غير أصابع
to fall ill	mereḍ	مرض
cold (illness)	zokām (m)	زكام
to catch a cold	gālo bard	جاله برد
ice	galīd (m)	جليد
black ice	ɣaṭā' galīdy 'lal arḍ (m)	غطاء جليدي على الأرض
to freeze over (ab. river, etc.)	etgammed	إتجمّد
ice floe	roqāqet galīd (f)	رقاقة جليد
skis	zallagāt (pl)	زلّاجات
skier	motazaḥleq 'alal galīd (m)	متزحلق على الجليد
to ski (vi)	tazallag	تزلّج
to skate (vi)	tazallag	تزلّج

Fauna

210. Mammals. Predators

predator	moftares (m)	مفترس
tiger	nemr (m)	نمر
lion	asad (m)	أسد
wolf	ze'b (m)	ذئب
fox	ta'lab (m)	ثعلب
jaguar	nemr amrīky (m)	نمر أمريكي
leopard	fahd (m)	فهد
cheetah	fahd ṣayād (m)	فهد صيّاد
black panther	nemr aswad (m)	نمر أسوّد
puma	asad el gebāl (m)	أسد الجبال
snow leopard	nemr el tolūg (m)	نمر الثلوج
lynx	waʃaq (m)	وشق
coyote	qayūṭ (m)	قيوط
jackal	ebn 'āwy (m)	ابن آوى
hyena	ḍeb' (m)	ضبع

211. Wild animals

animal	ḥayawān (m)	حيوان
beast (animal)	waḥʃ (m)	وحش
squirrel	sengāb (m)	سنجاب
hedgehog	qonfoz (m)	قنفذ
hare	arnab barry (m)	أرنب برّي
rabbit	arnab (m)	أرنب
badger	ɣarīr (m)	غرير
raccoon	rakūn (m)	راكون
hamster	hamster (m)	هامستر
marmot	marmoṭ (m)	مرموط
mole	xold (m)	خلد
mouse	fār (m)	فأر
rat	gerz (m)	جرذ
bat	xoffāʃ (m)	خفّاش
ermine	qāqem (m)	قاقم
sable	sammūr (m)	سمّور
marten	fara'īāt (m)	فرائيات
weasel	ebn 'ers (m)	ابن عرس
mink	mink (m)	منك

beaver	qondos (m)	قندس
otter	taʿlab maya (m)	ثعلب الميّة
horse	ḥoṣān (m)	حصان
moose	eyl el mūz (m)	أيّل الموظ
deer	ayl (m)	أيل
camel	gamal (m)	جمل
bison	bison (m)	بيسون
wisent	byson orobby (m)	بيسون أوروبي
buffalo	gamūs (m)	جاموس
zebra	ḥomār waḥʃy (m)	حمار وحشي
antelope	ẓaby (m)	ظبي
roe deer	yaḥmūr orobby (m)	يحمورأوروبيّ
fallow deer	eyl asmar orobby (m)	أيل أسمر أوروبي
chamois	ʃamwah (f)	شاموا ه
wild boar	χenzīr barry (m)	خنزير برّي
whale	ḥūt (m)	حوت
seal	foqma (f)	فقمة
walrus	el kabʿ (m)	الكبع
fur seal	foqmet el farāʾ (f)	فقمة الفراء
dolphin	dolfīn (m)	دولفين
bear	dobb (m)	دبّ
polar bear	dobb ʾoṭṭby (m)	دبّ قطبي
panda	banda (m)	باندا
monkey	ʾerd (m)	قرد
chimpanzee	ʃimbanzy (m)	شيمبانزي
orangutan	orangutan (m)	أورنغوتان
gorilla	ɣorella (f)	غوريلا
macaque	ʾerd el makāk (m)	قرد المكاك
gibbon	gibbon (m)	جيبون
elephant	fīl (m)	فيل
rhinoceros	χartīt (m)	خرتيت
giraffe	zarāfa (f)	زرافة
hippopotamus	faras el nahr (m)	فرس النهر
kangaroo	kangarū (m)	كانجّارو
koala (bear)	el koala (m)	الكوالا
mongoose	nems (m)	نمس
chinchilla	ʃenʃīla (f)	شنشيلة
skunk	ẓerbān (m)	ظربان
porcupine	nīṣ (m)	نيص

212. Domestic animals

cat	ʾoṭṭa (f)	قطّة
tomcat	ʾoṭṭ (m)	قطّ
dog	kalb (m)	كلب

horse	ḥoṣān (m)	حصان
stallion (male horse)	χeyl faḥl (m)	خيل فحل
mare	faras (f)	فرس
cow	ba'ara (f)	بقرة
bull	sore (m)	ثور
ox	sore (m)	ثور
sheep (ewe)	χarūf (f)	خروف
ram	kebʃ (m)	كبش
goat	me'za (f)	معزة
billy goat, he-goat	mā'ez zakar (m)	ماعز ذكر
donkey	ḥomār (m)	حمار
mule	baɣl (m)	بغل
pig	χenzīr (m)	خنزير
piglet	χannūṣ (m)	خنّوص
rabbit	arnab (m)	أرنب
hen (chicken)	farχa (f)	فرخة
cock	dīk (m)	ديك
duck	baṭṭa (f)	بطّة
drake	dakar el baṭṭ (m)	ذكر البط
goose	wezza (f)	وزّة
tom turkey, gobbler	dīk rūmy (m)	ديك رومي
turkey (hen)	dīk rūmy (m)	ديك رومي
domestic animals	ḥayawānāt dawāgen (pl)	حيوانات دواجن
tame (e.g. ~ hamster)	alīf	أليف
to tame (vt)	rawweḍ	روّض
to breed (vt)	rabba	ربى
farm	mazra'a (f)	مزرعة
poultry	dawāgen (pl)	دواجن
cattle	māʃeya (f)	ماشية
herd (cattle)	qaṭee' (m)	قطيع
stable	esṭabl χeyl (m)	إسطبل خيل
pigsty	ḥazīret χanazīr (f)	حظيرة الخنازير
cowshed	zerībet el ba'ar (f)	زريبة البقر
rabbit hutch	qan el arāneb (m)	قن الأرانب
hen house	qan el ferāχ (m)	قن الفراخ

213. Dogs. Dog breeds

dog	kalb (m)	كلب
sheepdog	kalb rā'y (m)	كلب رعي
German shepherd	kalb rā'y almāny (m)	كلب راعي ألمانيّ
poodle	būdle (m)	بودل
dachshund	daʃhund (m)	داشهند
bulldog	bulldog (m)	بولدوج

boxer	bokser (m)	بوكسر
mastiff	mastiff (m)	ماستيف
Rottweiler	rottfeyler (m)	روت فايلر
Doberman	doberman (m)	دوبرمان
basset	basset (m)	باسيت
bobtail	bobtayl (m)	بوبتيل
Dalmatian	delmāṭy (m)	دلماطي
cocker spaniel	kokker spaniel (m)	كوكر سبانييل
Newfoundland	nyu faundland (m)	نيوفاوندلاند
Saint Bernard	sant bernard (m)	سانت بيرنارد
husky	hasky (m)	هاسكي
Chow Chow	tʃaw tʃaw (m)	تشاوتشاو
spitz	esbitz (m)	إسبتز
pug	bug (m)	بج

214. Sounds made by animals

barking (n)	nebāḥ (m)	نباح
to bark (vi)	nabaḥ	نبح
to miaow (vi)	mawmaw	مومو
to purr (vi)	xarxar	خرخر
to moo (vi)	xār	خار
to bellow (bull)	xār	خار
to growl (vi)	damdam	دمدم
howl (n)	ʿawāʾ (m)	عواء
to howl (vi)	ʿawa	عوى
to whine (vi)	ann	أنّ
to bleat (sheep)	maʾmaʾ	مأمأ
to oink, to grunt (pig)	qabaʿ	قبع
to squeal (vi)	qabaʿ	قبع
to croak (vi)	naʾʾ	نقّ
to buzz (insect)	ṭann	طنّ
to chirp (crickets, grasshopper)	ʿarʿar	عرعر

215. Young animals

cub	ḥayawān ṣaɣīr (m)	حيوان صغير
kitten	ʾoṭṭa saɣīra (f)	قطّة صغيرة
baby mouse	fār ṣaɣīr (m)	فار صغير
puppy	garww (m)	جرو
leveret	xarnaʾ (m)	خرنق
baby rabbit	arnab saɣīr (m)	أرنب صغير
wolf cub	garmūza (m)	جرموزا

fox cub	hagras (m)	هجرس
bear cub	daysam (m)	ديّسم
lion cub	ʃebl el asad (m)	شبل الأسد
tiger cub	farz (m)	فرز
elephant calf	daɣfal (m)	دغفل
piglet	χannūṣ (m)	خنّوص
calf (young cow, bull)	ʿegl (m)	عجل
kid (young goat)	gady (m)	جدي
lamb	ḥaml (m)	حمل
fawn (young deer)	el raʃa (m)	الرشا
young camel	ṣaɣīr el gamal (m)	صغير الجمل
snakelet (baby snake)	ḥerbeʃ (m)	حربش
froglet (baby frog)	ḍeffḍaʿ saɣīr (m)	ضفدع صغير
baby bird	farχ (m)	فرخ
chick (of chicken)	katkūt (m)	كتكوت
duckling	baṭṭa ṣaɣīra (f)	بطّة صغيرة

216. Birds

bird	ṭāʾer (m)	طائر
pigeon	ḥamāma (f)	حمامة
sparrow	ʿaṣfūr dawri (m)	عصفور دوري
tit (great tit)	qarqaf (m)	قرقف
magpie	ʿaʾʿaʾ (m)	عقعق
raven	ɣorāb aswad (m)	غراب أسود
crow	ɣorāb (m)	غراب
jackdaw	zāɣ zarʿy (m)	زاغ زرعي
rook	ɣorāb el qeyẓ (m)	غراب القيظ
duck	baṭṭa (f)	بطّة
goose	wezza (f)	وزّة
pheasant	tadarrog (m)	تدرج
eagle	ʿeqāb (m)	عقاب
hawk	el bāz (m)	الباز
falcon	ṣaʾr (m)	صقر
vulture	nesr (m)	نسر
condor (Andean ~)	kondor (m)	كندور
swan	el temm (m)	التمّ
crane	karkiya (m)	كركية
stork	loqloq (m)	لقلق
parrot	babaɣāʾ (m)	ببغاء
hummingbird	ṭannān (m)	طنّان
peacock	ṭawūs (m)	طاووس
ostrich	naʿāma (f)	نعامة
heron	belʃone (m)	بلشون

flamingo	flamingo (m)	فلامينجو
pelican	bag'a (f)	بجعة
nightingale	'andalīb (m)	عندليب
swallow	el sonūnū (m)	السنونو
thrush	somnet el ḥoqūl (m)	سمنة الحقول
song thrush	somna moɣarreda (m)	سمنة مغرّدة
blackbird	ʃaḥrūr aswad (m)	شحرور أسود
swift	semmāma (m)	سمّامة
lark	qabra (f)	قبرة
quail	semmān (m)	سمّان
woodpecker	na'ār el χaʃab (m)	نقار الخشب
cuckoo	weqwāq (m)	وقواق
owl	būma (f)	بومة
eagle owl	būm orāsy (m)	بوم أوراسي
wood grouse	dīk el χalang (m)	ديك الخلنج
black grouse	ṭyhūg aswad (m)	طيهوج أسود
partridge	el ḥagal (m)	الحجل
starling	zerzūr (m)	زرزور
canary	kanāry (m)	كناري
hazel grouse	ṭyhūg el bondo' (m)	طيهوج البندق
chaffinch	ʃarʃūr (m)	شرشور
bullfinch	deɣnāʃ (m)	دغناش
seagull	nawras (m)	نورس
albatross	el qoṭros (m)	القطرس
penguin	beṭrīq (m)	بطريق

217. Birds. Singing and sounds

to sing (vi)	ɣanna	غنّى
to call (animal, bird)	nāda	نادى
to crow (cock)	ṣāḥ	صاح
cock-a-doodle-doo	kokokūko	كوكوكوكو
to cluck (hen)	kāky	كاكي
to caw (crow call)	na'aq	نعق
to quack (duck call)	baṭbaṭ	بطبط
to cheep (vi)	ṣawṣaw	صوصو
to chirp, to twitter	za'za'	زقزق

218. Fish. Marine animals

bream	abramīs (m)	أبراميس
carp	ʃabbūṭ (m)	شبّوط
perch	farχ (m)	فرخ
catfish	'armūṭ (m)	قرموط
pike	karāky (m)	كراكي

salmon	salamon (m)	سلمون
sturgeon	ḥafʃ (m)	حفش
herring	renga (f)	رنجة
Atlantic salmon	salamon aṭlasy (m)	سلمون أطلسي
mackerel	makerel (m)	ماكريل
flatfish	samak mefalṭah (f)	سمك مفلطح
zander, pike perch	samak sandar (m)	سمك سندر
cod	el qadd (m)	القد
tuna	tuna (f)	تونة
trout	salamon mera''aṭ (m)	سلمون مرقّط
eel	ḥankalīs (m)	حنكليس
electric ray	ra'ād (m)	رعاد
moray eel	moraya (f)	موراية
piranha	bīrana (f)	بيرانا
shark	'erʃ (m)	قرش
dolphin	dolfīn (m)	دولفين
whale	ḥūt (m)	حوت
crab	kaboria (m)	كابوريا
jellyfish	'andīl el baḥr (m)	قنديل البحر
octopus	aχṭabūṭ (m)	أخطبوط
starfish	negmet el baḥr (f)	نجمة البحر
sea urchin	qonfoz el baḥr (m)	قنفذ البحر
seahorse	ḥoṣān el baḥr (m)	حصان البحر
oyster	maḥār (m)	محار
prawn	gammbary (m)	جمّبري
lobster	estakoza (f)	استكوزا
spiny lobster	estakoza (m)	استاكوزا

219. Amphibians. Reptiles

snake	te'bān (m)	ثعبان
venomous (snake)	sām	سام
viper	af'a (f)	أفعى
cobra	kobra (m)	كوبرا
python	te'bān byton (m)	ثعبان بايثون
boa	bawā' el 'aṣera (f)	بواء العاصرة
grass snake	te'bān el 'oʃb (m)	ثعبان العشب
rattle snake	af'a megalgela (f)	أفعي مجلجلة
anaconda	anakonda (f)	أناكوندا
lizard	seḥliya (f)	سحليّة
iguana	eɣwana (f)	إغوانة
monitor lizard	warl (m)	ورل
salamander	salamander (m)	سلمندر
chameleon	ḥerbāya (f)	حرباية

scorpion	ʿaʾrab (m)	عقرب
turtle	solḥefah (f)	سلحفاة
frog	ḍeffḍaʿ (m)	ضفدع
toad	ḍeffḍaʿ el ṭeyn (m)	ضفدع الطين
crocodile	temsāḥ (m)	تمساح

220. Insects

insect	ḥaʃara (f)	حشرة
butterfly	farāʃa (f)	فراشة
ant	namla (f)	نملة
fly	debbāna (f)	دبّانة
mosquito	namūsa (f)	ناموسة
beetle	χonfesa (f)	خنفسة
wasp	dabbūr (m)	دبّور
bee	naḥla (f)	نحلة
bumblebee	naḥla ṭannāna (f)	نحلة طنّانة
gadfly (botfly)	naʿra (f)	نعرة
spider	ʿankabūt (m)	عنكبوت
spider's web	nasīg ʿankabūt (m)	نسيج عنكبوت
dragonfly	yaʿsūb (m)	يعسوب
grasshopper	garād (m)	جراد
moth (night butterfly)	ʿetta (f)	عثّة
cockroach	ṣarṣūr (m)	صرصور
tick	qarāda (f)	قرادة
flea	barɣūt (m)	برغوث
midge	baʿūḍa (f)	بعوضة
locust	garād (m)	جراد
snail	ḥalazōn (m)	حلزون
cricket	ṣarṣūr el ḥaql (m)	صرصور الحقل
firefly	yarāʿa (f)	يراعة
ladybird	χonfesa menaʾṭṭa (f)	خنفسة منقّطة
cockchafer	χonfesa motlefa lel nabāt (f)	خنفسة متلفة للنبات
leech	ʿalaqa (f)	علقة
caterpillar	yasrūʿ (m)	يسروع
earthworm	dūda (f)	دودة
larva	yaraqa (f)	يرقة

221. Animals. Body parts

beak	monqār (m)	منقار
wings	agneḥa (pl)	أجنحة
foot (of the bird)	regl (f)	رجل
feathers (plumage)	rīʃ (m)	ريش
feather	rīʃa (f)	ريشة
crest	ʿorf el dīk (m)	عرف الديك

gills	xāyaʃīm (pl)	خياشيم
spawn	beyḍ el samak (pl)	بيض السمك
larva	yaraqa (f)	يرقة
fin	za'nafa (f)	زعنفة
scales (of fish, reptile)	ḥarāfeʃ (pl)	حرافش
fang (canine)	nāb (m)	ناب
paw (e.g. cat's ~)	yad (f)	يد
muzzle (snout)	xaṭm (m)	خطم
mouth (cat's ~)	bo' (m)	بوء
tail	deyl (m)	ذيل
whiskers	ʃawāreb (pl)	شوارب
hoof	ḥāfer (m)	حافر
horn	'arn (m)	قرن
carapace	der' (m)	درع
shell (mollusk ~)	maḥāra (f)	محارة
eggshell	'eʃret beyḍa (f)	قشرة بيضة
animal's hair (pelage)	ʃa'r (m)	شعر
pelt (hide)	geld (m)	جلد

222. Actions of animals

to fly (vi)	ṭār	طار
to fly in circles	ḥallaq	حلّق
to fly away	ṭār	طار
to flap (~ the wings)	rafraf	رفرف
to peck (vi)	na'ar	نقر
to sit on eggs	'a'ad 'alal beyḍ	قعد على البيض
to hatch out (vi)	fa'as	فقس
to build a nest	bana 'esʃa	بنى عشّة
to slither, to crawl	zaḥaf	زحف
to sting, to bite (insect)	lasa'	لسع
to bite (ab. animal)	'aḍḍ	عضّ
to sniff (vt)	taʃammam	تشمّم
to bark (vi)	nabaḥ	نبح
to hiss (snake)	has-hes	هسهس
to scare (vt)	xawwef	خوّف
to attack (vt)	hagam	هجم
to gnaw (bone, etc.)	'araḍ	قرض
to scratch (with claws)	xarbeʃ	خربش
to hide (vi)	estaxabba	إستخبّى
to play (kittens, etc.)	le'eb	لعب
to hunt (vi, vt)	eṣṭād	إصطاد
to hibernate (vi)	kān di sobār el ʃetā'	كان في سبات الشتاء
to go extinct	enqaraḍ	إنقرض

223. Animals. Habitats

habitat	mawṭen (m)	موّطن
migration	hegra (f)	هجرة
mountain	gabal (m)	جبل
reef	ʃoʻāb (pl)	شعاب
cliff	garf (m)	جرف
forest	ɣāba (f)	غابة
jungle	adɣāl (pl)	أدغال
savanna	savanna (f)	سافانّا
tundra	tundra (f)	تندرا
steppe	barāry (pl)	براري
desert	ṣaḥra' (f)	صحراء
oasis	wāḥa (f)	واحة
sea	baḥr (m)	بحر
lake	boḥeyra (f)	بحيرة
ocean	moḥīṭ (m)	محيط
swamp (marshland)	mostanqaʻ (m)	مستنقع
freshwater (adj)	maya ʻazba	ميّة عذبة
pond	berka (f)	بركة
river	nahr (m)	نهر
den (bear's ~)	wekr (m)	وكر
nest	ʻeʃ (m)	عش
tree hollow	gofe (m)	جوف
burrow (animal hole)	goḥr (m)	جحر
anthill	ʻeʃ naml (m)	عش نمل

224. Animal care

zoo	ḥadīqet el ḥayawān (f)	حديقة حيوان
nature reserve	maḥmiya ṭabeʻiya (f)	محمية طبيعية
breeder (cattery, kennel, etc.)	morabby (m)	مربّي
open-air cage	'afaṣ fel hawā' el ṭal' (m)	قفص في الهواء الطلق
cage	'afaṣ (m)	قفص
kennel	beyt el kalb (m)	بيت الكلب
dovecot	borg el ḥamām (m)	برج الحمام
aquarium (fish tank)	ḥoḍe samak (m)	حوض سمك
dolphinarium	ḥoḍe dolfīn (m)	حوض دولفين
to breed (animals)	rabba	ربّى
brood, litter	zorriya (f)	ذريّة
to tame (vt)	rawweḍ	روّض
to train (animals)	darrab	درّب
feed (fodder, etc.)	ʻalaf (m)	علف
to feed (vt)	akkel	أكّل

pet shop	maḥal ḥayawanāt (m)	محل حيوانات
muzzle (for dog)	kamāma (f)	كمامة
collar (e.g., dog ~)	ṭo'e (m)	طوق
name (of an animal)	esm (m)	اسم
pedigree (dog's ~)	selselet el nasab (f)	سلسلة النسب

225. Animals. Miscellaneous

pack (wolves)	qaṭee' (m)	قطيع
flock (birds)	serb (m)	سرب
shoal, school (fish)	serb (m)	سرب
herd (horses)	qaṭee' (m)	قطيع
male (n)	dakar (m)	ذكر
female (n)	onsa (f)	أنثى
hungry (adj)	ge'ān	جعان
wild (adj)	barry	بري
dangerous (adj)	χaṭīr	خطير

226. Horses

horse	ḥoṣān (m)	حصان
breed (race)	solāla (f)	سلالة
foal	mahr (m)	مهر
mare	faras (f)	فرس
mustang	mustān (m)	موستان
pony	ḥoṣān qazam (m)	حصان قزم
draught horse	ḥoṣān el na'l (m)	حصان النقل
mane	'orf (m)	عرف
tail	deyl (m)	ذيل
hoof	ḥāfer (m)	حافر
horseshoe	na'l (m)	نعل
to shoe (vt)	na''al	نعّل
blacksmith	ḥaddād (m)	حدّاد
saddle	serg (m)	سرج
stirrup	rekāb (m)	ركاب
bridle	legām (m)	لجام
reins	'anān (m)	عنان
whip (for riding)	korbāg (m)	كرباج
rider	fāres (m)	فارس
to saddle up (vt)	asrag	أسرج
to mount a horse	rekeb ḥoṣān	ركب حصان
gallop	ramāḥa (f)	رماحة
to gallop (vi)	gery bel ḥoṣān	جري بالحصان

trot (n)	harwala (f)	هروّلة
at a trot (adv)	harwel	هروّل
to go at a trot	harwel	هروّل
racehorse	ḥoṣān sebāʾ (m)	حصان سباق
horse racing	sebāʾ el χeyl (m)	سباق الخيل
stable	esṭabl χeyl (m)	إسطبل خيل
to feed (vt)	akkel	أكّل
hay	ʾasʃ (m)	قشّ
to water (animals)	saʾa	سقى
to wash (horse)	naḍḍaf	نظّف
horse-drawn cart	ʿarabet χayl (f)	عربة خيل
to graze (vi)	ertaʿa	إرتعى
to neigh (vi)	ṣahal	صهل
to kick (to buck)	rafas	رفس

Flora

227. Trees

tree	ʃagara (f)	شجرة
deciduous (adj)	nafḍiya	نفضيّة
coniferous (adj)	ṣonoberiya	صنوبرية
evergreen (adj)	dā'emet el χoḍra	دائمة الخضرة
apple tree	ʃagaret toffāḥ (f)	شجرة تفّاح
pear tree	ʃagaret komettra (f)	شجرة كمثّرى
cherry tree	ʃagaret karaz (f)	شجرة كرز
plum tree	ʃagaret bar'ū' (f)	شجرة برقوق
birch	batola (f)	بتولا
oak	ballūṭ (f)	بلّوط
linden tree	zayzafūn (f)	زيزفون
aspen	ḥūr rāgef	حور راجف
maple	qayqab (f)	قيقب
spruce	rateng (f)	راتينج
pine	ṣonober (f)	صنوبر
larch	arziya (f)	أرزية
fir tree	tanūb (f)	تنوب
cedar	el orz (f)	الأرز
poplar	ḥūr (f)	حور
rowan	ɣobayrā' (f)	غبيراء
willow	ṣefsāf (f)	صفصاف
alder	gār el mā' (m)	جار الماء
beech	el zān (f)	الزان
elm	derdar (f)	دردار
ash (tree)	marān (f)	مران
chestnut	kastanā' (f)	كستناء
magnolia	maɣnolia (f)	ماغنوليا
palm tree	naχla (f)	نخلة
cypress	el soro (f)	السرو
mangrove	mangrūf (f)	مانجروف
baobab	baobab (f)	باوباب
eucalyptus	eukalyptus (f)	أوكالبتوس
sequoia	sequoia (f)	سيكويا

228. Shrubs

bush	ʃogeyra (f)	شجيرة
shrub	ʃogayrāt (pl)	شجيرات

grapevine	karma (f)	كرمة
vineyard	karam (m)	كرم
raspberry bush	zar'et tūt el 'alī' el aḥmar (f)	زرعة توت العليق الأحمر
redcurrant bush	keʃmeʃ aḥmar (m)	كشمش أحمر
gooseberry bush	'enab el sa'lab (m)	عنب الثعلب
acacia	aqaqia (f)	أقاقيا
barberry	berbarīs (m)	برباريس
jasmine	yasmīn (m)	ياسمين
juniper	'ar'ar (m)	عرعر
rosebush	ʃogeyret ward (f)	شجيرة ورد
dog rose	ward el seyāg (pl)	ورد السياج

229. Mushrooms

mushroom	feṭr (f)	فطر
edible mushroom	feṭr ṣāleḥ lel akl (m)	فطر صالح للأكل
poisonous mushroom	feṭr sām (m)	فطر سام
cap	ṭarbūʃ el feṭr (m)	طربوش الفطر
stipe	sāq el feṭr (m)	ساق الفطر
cep, penny bun	feṭr boleṭe ma'kūl (m)	فطر بوليط مأكول
orange-cap boletus	feṭr aḥmar (m)	فطر أحمر
birch bolete	feṭr boleṭe (m)	فطر بوليط
chanterelle	feṭr el ʃanterel (m)	فطر الشانتريل
russula	feṭr russula (m)	فطر روسولا
morel	feṭr el ɣoʃna (m)	فطر الغوشنة
fly agaric	feṭr amanīt el ṭā'er (m)	فطر أمانيت الطائر
death cap	feṭr amanīt falusyāny el sām (m)	فطر أمانيت فالوسياني السام

230. Fruits. Berries

fruit	tamra (f)	تمرة
fruits	tamr (m)	تمر
apple	toffāḥa (f)	تفّاحة
pear	komettra (f)	كمّثرى
plum	bar'ū' (m)	برقوق
strawberry (garden ~)	farawla (f)	فراولة
cherry	karaz (m)	كرز
grape	'enab (m)	عنب
raspberry	tūt el 'alī' el aḥmar (m)	توت العليق الأحمر
blackcurrant	keʃmeʃ aswad (m)	كشمش أسود
redcurrant	keʃmeʃ aḥmar (m)	كشمش أحمر
gooseberry	'enab el sa'lab (m)	عنب الثعلب
cranberry	'enabiya ḥāda el χebā' (m)	عنبية حادة الخباء
orange	bortoqāl (m)	برتقال

tangerine	yosfy (m)	يوسفي
pineapple	ananās (m)	أناناس
banana	moze (m)	موز
date	tamr (m)	تمر
lemon	lymūn (m)	ليمون
apricot	meʃmeʃ (f)	مشمش
peach	χawχa (f)	خوخة
kiwi	kiwi (m)	كيوي
grapefruit	grabe frūt (m)	جريب فروت
berry	tūt (m)	توت
berries	tūt (pl)	توت
cowberry	ʻenab el sore (m)	عنب الثور
wild strawberry	farawla barriya (f)	فراولة برّيّة
bilberry	ʻenab al aḥrāg (m)	عنب الأحراج

231. Flowers. Plants

flower	zahra (f)	زهرة
bouquet (of flowers)	bokeyh (f)	بوكيه
rose (flower)	warda (f)	وردة
tulip	tolīb (f)	توليب
carnation	ʼoronfol (m)	قرنفل
gladiolus	el dalbūs (f)	الدَلْبُوث
cornflower	qanṭeryūn ʻanbary (m)	قنطريون عنبري
harebell	garīs mostadīr el awrāʼ (m)	جريس مستدير الأوراق
dandelion	handabāʼ (f)	هندباء
camomile	kamomile (f)	كاموميل
aloe	el alowa (m)	الألوّة
cactus	ṣabbār (m)	صبّار
rubber plant, ficus	faykas (m)	فيكس
lily	zanbaq (f)	زنبق
geranium	ɣarnūqy (f)	غرنوقي
hyacinth	el lavender (f)	اللافندر
mimosa	mimoza (f)	ميموزا
narcissus	nerges (f)	نرجس
nasturtium	abo χangar (f)	أبو خنجر
orchid	orkid (f)	أوركيد
peony	fawnia (f)	فاوانيا
violet	el banafseg (f)	البنفسج
pansy	bansy (f)	بانسي
forget-me-not	ʼāzān el faʼr (pl)	آذان الفأر
daisy	aqwaḥān (f)	أقحوان
poppy	el χoʃχāʃ (f)	الخشخاش
hemp	qanb (m)	قنب

mint	neʿnāʿ (m)	نعناع
lily of the valley	zanbaq el wādy (f)	زنبق الوادي
snowdrop	zahrat el laban (f)	زهرة اللبن
nettle	ʾarrāṣ (m)	قرّاص
sorrel	ḥammāḍ bostāny (m)	حمّاض بستاني
water lily	niloferiya (f)	نيلوفرية
fern	sarҳas (m)	سرخس
lichen	aʃna (f)	أشنة
conservatory (greenhouse)	ṣoba (f)	صوبة
lawn	ʿoʃb aҳḍar (m)	عشب أخضر
flowerbed	geneynet zohūr (f)	جنينة زهور
plant	nabāt (m)	نبات
grass	ʿoʃb (m)	عشب
blade of grass	ʿoʃba (f)	عشبة
leaf	wara'a (f)	ورقة
petal	wara'et el zahra (f)	ورقة الزهرة
stem	sāq (f)	ساق
tuber	darna (f)	درنة
young plant (shoot)	nabta saɣīra (f)	نبتة صغيرة
thorn	ʃawka (f)	شوكة
to blossom (vi)	fattaḥet	فتّحت
to fade, to wither	debel	ذبل
smell (odour)	rīḥa (f)	ريحة
to cut (flowers)	ʾaṭaʿ	قطع
to pick (a flower)	ʾaṭaf	قطف

232. Cereals, grains

grain	ḥobūb (pl)	حبوب
cereal crops	maḥaṣīl el ḥubūb (pl)	محاصيل الحبوب
ear (of barley, etc.)	sonbola (f)	سنبلة
wheat	ʾamḥ (m)	قمح
rye	ʃelm mazrūʿ (m)	شيلم مزروع
oats	ʃofān (m)	شوفان
millet	el deҳn (m)	الدُخن
barley	ʃeʿīr (m)	شعير
maize	dora (f)	ذرة
rice	rozz (m)	رزّ
buckwheat	ḥanṭa soda' (f)	حنطة سوداء
pea plant	besella (f)	بسلّة
kidney bean	faṣolya (f)	فاصوليا
soya	fūl el ṣoya (m)	فول الصويا
lentil	ʿads (m)	عدس
beans (pulse crops)	fūl (m)	فول

233. Vegetables. Greens

vegetables	xoḍār (pl)	خضار
greens	xoḍrawāt waraqiya (pl)	خضروات ورقية
tomato	ṭamāṭem (f)	طماطم
cucumber	xeyār (m)	خيار
carrot	gazar (m)	جزر
potato	baṭāṭes (f)	بطاطس
onion	baṣal (m)	بصل
garlic	tūm (m)	ثوم
cabbage	koronb (m)	كرنب
cauliflower	'arnabīṭ (m)	قرنبيط
Brussels sprouts	koronb broksel (m)	كرنب بروكسل
broccoli	brūkuli (m)	بروكلي
beetroot	bangar (m)	بنجر
aubergine	bātengān (m)	باذنجان
marrow	kōsa (f)	كوسة
pumpkin	qarʿ ʿasaly (m)	قرع عسلي
turnip	left (m)	لفت
parsley	ba'dūnes (m)	بقدونس
dill	ʃabat (m)	شبت
lettuce	xass (m)	خسّ
celery	karfas (m)	كرفس
asparagus	helione (m)	هليون
spinach	sabānex (m)	سبانخ
pea	besella (f)	بسلّة
beans	fūl (m)	فول
maize	dora (f)	ذرة
kidney bean	faṣolya (f)	فاصوليا
pepper	felfel (m)	فلفل
radish	fegl (m)	فجل
artichoke	xarʃūf (m)	خرشوف

REGIONAL GEOGRAPHY

234. Western Europe

Europe	orobba (f)	أوروبّا
European Union	el etteḥād el orobby (m)	الإتّحاد الأوروبّي
European (n)	orobby (m)	أوروبّي
European (adj)	orobby	أوروبّي
Austria	el nemsa (f)	النمسا
Austrian (masc.)	nemsāwy (m)	نمساوي
Austrian (fem.)	nemsāwiya (f)	نمساويّة
Austrian (adj)	nemsāwy	نمساوي
Great Britain	briṭaniya el ʿozma (f)	بريطانيا العظمى
England	engeltera (f)	إنجلّترا
British (masc.)	briṭāny (m)	بريطاني
British (fem.)	briṭaniya (f)	بريطانيّة
English, British (adj)	englīzy	إنجليزي
Belgium	balʒīka (f)	بلجيكا
Belgian (masc.)	balʒīky (m)	بلجيكي
Belgian (fem.)	balʒīkiya (f)	بلجيكيّة
Belgian (adj)	balʒīky	بلجيكي
Germany	almānya (f)	ألمانيا
German (masc.)	almāny (m)	ألماني
German (fem.)	almaniya (f)	ألمانيّة
German (adj)	almāniya	ألمانية
Netherlands	holanda (f)	هولندا
Holland	holanda (f)	هولندا
Dutch (masc.)	holandy (m)	هولندي
Dutch (fem.)	holandiya (f)	هولنديّة
Dutch (adj)	holandy	هولندي
Greece	el yunān (f)	اليونان
Greek (masc.)	yunāny (m)	يوناني
Greek (fem.)	yunaniya (f)	يونانيّة
Greek (adj)	yunāny	يوناني
Denmark	el denmark (f)	الدنمارك
Dane (masc.)	denmarky (m)	دنماركي
Dane (fem.)	denmarkiya (f)	دانماركيّة
Danish (adj)	denemarky	دانماركي
Ireland	irelanda (f)	أيرلندا
Irish (masc.)	irelandy (m)	أيرلندي
Irish (fem.)	irelandiya (f)	أيرلنديّة
Irish (adj)	irelandy	أيرلندي

Iceland	'āyslanda (f)	آيسلندا
Icelander (masc.)	'āyslandy (m)	آيسلندي
Icelander (fem.)	'āyslandiya (f)	آيسلنديّة
Icelandic (adj)	'āyslandy	آيسلندي
Spain	asbānya (f)	إسبانيا
Spaniard (masc.)	asbāny (m)	إسباني
Spaniard (fem.)	asbaniya (f)	إسبانيّة
Spanish (adj)	asbāny	إسباني
Italy	eṭālia (f)	إيطاليا
Italian (masc.)	eṭāly (m)	إيطالي
Italian (fem.)	eṭaliya (f)	إيطاليّة
Italian (adj)	eṭāly	إيطالي
Cyprus	'obroṣ (f)	قبرص
Cypriot (masc.)	'obroṣy (m)	قبرصي
Cypriot (fem.)	'obroṣiya (f)	قبرصية
Cypriot (adj)	'obroṣy	قبرصي
Malta	malṭa (f)	مالطا
Maltese (masc.)	malṭy (m)	مالطي
Maltese (fem.)	malṭiya (f)	مالطيّة
Maltese (adj)	malṭy	مالطي
Norway	el nerwīg (f)	النرويج
Norwegian (masc.)	nerwīgy (m)	نرويجي
Norwegian (fem.)	nerwīgiya (f)	نرويجية
Norwegian (adj)	nerwīgy	نرويجي
Portugal	el bortoɣāl (f)	البرتغال
Portuguese (masc.)	bortoɣāly (m)	برتغالي
Portuguese (fem.)	bortoɣaliya (f)	برتغاليّة
Portuguese (adj)	bortoɣāly	برتغالي
Finland	finlanda (f)	فنّلندا
Finn (masc.)	finlandy (m)	فنّلندي
Finn (fem.)	finlandiya (f)	فنّلنديّة
Finnish (adj)	finlandy	فنّلندي
France	faransa (f)	فرنسا
French (masc.)	faransāwy (m)	فرنساوي
French (fem.)	faransawiya (f)	فرنساويّة
French (adj)	faransāwy	فرنساوي
Sweden	el sweyd (f)	السويد
Swede (masc.)	sweydy (m)	سويدي
Swede (fem.)	sweydiya (f)	سويديّة
Swedish (adj)	sweydy	سويدي
Switzerland	swesra (f)	سويسرا
Swiss (masc.)	swesry (m)	سويسري
Swiss (fem.)	swesriya (f)	سويسريّة
Swiss (adj)	swesry	سويسري
Scotland	oskotlanda (f)	اسكتّلندا
Scottish (masc.)	oskotlandy (m)	اسكتّلندي

Scottish (fem.)	oskotlandiya (f)	اسكتّلنديّة
Scottish (adj)	oskotlandy	اسكتلندي
Vatican City	el vatikān (m)	الفاتيكان
Liechtenstein	liʃtenʃtayn (m)	ليشتنشتاين
Luxembourg	luksemburg (f)	لوكسمبورج
Monaco	monako (f)	موناكو

235. Central and Eastern Europe

Albania	albānia (f)	ألبانيا
Albanian (masc.)	albāny (m)	ألباني
Albanian (fem.)	albaniya (f)	ألبانيّة
Albanian (adj)	albāny	ألباني
Bulgaria	bolɣāria (f)	بلغاريا
Bulgarian (masc.)	bolɣāry (m)	بلغاري
Bulgarian (fem.)	bolɣariya (f)	بلغاريّة
Bulgarian (adj)	bolɣāry	بلغاري
Hungary	el magar (f)	المجر
Hungarian (masc.)	magary (m)	مجري
Hungarian (fem.)	magariya (f)	مجريّة
Hungarian (adj)	magary	مجري
Latvia	latvia (f)	لاتفيا
Latvian (masc.)	latvy (m)	لاتفي
Latvian (fem.)	latviya (f)	لاتفية
Latvian (adj)	latvy	لاتفي
Lithuania	litwānia (f)	ليتوانيا
Lithuanian (masc.)	litwāny (m)	لتواني
Lithuanian (fem.)	litwaniya (f)	لتوانية
Lithuanian (adj)	litwāny	لتواني
Poland	bolanda (f)	بولّندا
Pole (masc.)	bolandy (m)	بولندي
Pole (fem.)	bolandiya (f)	بولّنديّة
Polish (adj)	bolanndy	بولّندي
Romania	romānia (f)	رومانيا
Romanian (masc.)	romāny (m)	روماني
Romanian (fem.)	romaniya (f)	رومانيّة
Romanian (adj)	romāny	روماني
Serbia	ṣerbia (f)	صربيا
Serbian (masc.)	ṣerby (m)	صربي
Serbian (fem.)	ṣerbiya (f)	صربية
Serbian (adj)	ṣarby	صربي
Slovakia	slovākia (f)	سلوفاكيا
Slovak (masc.)	slovāky (m)	سلوفاكي
Slovak (fem.)	slovakiya (f)	سلوفاكيّة
Slovak (adj)	slovāky	سلوفاكي

Croatia	kroãtya (f)	كرواتيا
Croatian (masc.)	kroãty (m)	كرواتي
Croatian (fem.)	kroatiya (f)	كرواتية
Croatian (adj)	kroãty	كرواتي
Czech Republic	gomhoriya el tʃīk (f)	جمهورية التشيك
Czech (masc.)	tʃīky (m)	تشيكي
Czech (fem.)	tʃīkiya (f)	تشيكية
Czech (adj)	tʃīky	تشيكي
Estonia	estũnia (f)	إستونيا
Estonian (masc.)	estũny (m)	إستوني
Estonian (fem.)	estuniya (f)	إستونية
Estonian (adj)	estũny	إستوني
Bosnia and Herzegovina	el bosna wel harsek (f)	البوسنة والهرسك
North Macedonia	maqdũnia (f)	مقدونيا
Slovenia	slovenia (f)	سلوفينيا
Montenegro	el gabal el aswad (m)	الجبل الأسوّد

236. Former USSR countries

Azerbaijan	azrabiʒãn (m)	أذربيجان
Azerbaijani (masc.)	azrabiʒãny (m)	أذربيجاني
Azerbaijani (fem.)	azrabiʒaniya (f)	أذربيجانية
Azerbaijani, Azeri (adj)	azrabiʒãny	أذربيجاني
Armenia	armĩnia (f)	أرمينيا
Armenian (masc.)	armĩny (m)	أرميني
Armenian (fem.)	arminiya (f)	أرمينية
Armenian (adj)	armĩny	أرميني
Belarus	belarũsia (f)	بيلاروسيا
Belarusian (masc.)	belarũsy (m)	بيلاروسي
Belarusian (fem.)	belarũsiya (f)	بيلاروسية
Belarusian (adj)	belarũsy	بيلاروسي
Georgia	ʒorʒia (f)	جورجيا
Georgian (masc.)	ʒorʒy (m)	جورجي
Georgian (fem.)	ʒorʒiya (f)	جورجية
Georgian (adj)	ʒorʒy	جورجي
Kazakhstan	kazaχistãn (f)	كازاخستّان
Kazakh (masc.)	kazaχistãny (m)	كازاخستّاني
Kazakh (fem.)	kazaχistaniya (f)	كازاخستّانية
Kazakh (adj)	kazaχistãny	كازاخستّاني
Kirghizia	qirɣizestãn (f)	قيرغيزستان
Kirghiz (masc.)	qirɣizestãny (m)	قيرغيزستاني
Kirghiz (fem.)	qirɣizestaniya (f)	قيرغيزستانية
Kirghiz (adj)	qirɣizestãny	قيرغيزستاني
Moldova, Moldavia	moldãvia (f)	مولدافيا
Moldavian (masc.)	moldãvy (m)	مولدافي

Moldavian (fem.)	moldaviya (f)	مولدافيّة
Moldavian (adj)	moldāvy	مولدافي
Russia	rūsya (f)	روسيا
Russian (masc.)	rūsy (m)	روسي
Russian (fem.)	rusiya (f)	روسيّة
Russian (adj)	rūsy	روسي
Tajikistan	ṭaʒīkistan (f)	طاجيكستان
Tajik (masc.)	ṭaʒīky (m)	طاجيكي
Tajik (fem.)	ṭaʒikiya (f)	طاجيكيّة
Tajik (adj)	ṭaʒīky	طاجيكي
Turkmenistan	turkmānistān (f)	تركمانستان
Turkmen (masc.)	turkmāny (m)	تركماني
Turkmen (fem.)	turkmaniya (f)	تركمانيّة
Turkmenian (adj)	turkmāny	تركماني
Uzbekistan	uzbakistān (f)	أوزبكستان
Uzbek (masc.)	uzbaky (m)	أوزبكي
Uzbek (fem.)	uzbakiya (f)	أوزبكيّة
Uzbek (adj)	uzbaky	أوزبكي
Ukraine	okrānia (f)	أوكرانيا
Ukrainian (masc.)	okrāny (m)	أوكراني
Ukrainian (fem.)	okraniya (f)	أوكرانيّة
Ukrainian (adj)	okrāny	أوكراني

237. Asia

Asia	asya (f)	آسيا
Asian (adj)	'āsyawy	آسيوي
Vietnam	vietnām (f)	فيتنام
Vietnamese (masc.)	vietnāmy (m)	فيتنامي
Vietnamese (fem.)	vietnāmiya (f)	فيتناميّة
Vietnamese (adj)	vietnāmy	فيتنامي
India	el hend (f)	الهند
Indian (masc.)	hendy (m)	هندي
Indian (fem.)	hendiya (f)	هنديّة
Indian (adj)	hendy	هندي
Israel	isra'īl (f)	إسرائيل
Israeli (masc.)	isra'īly (m)	إسرائيلي
Israeli (fem.)	isra'iliya (f)	إسرائيليّة
Israeli (adj)	israīly	إسرائيلي
Jew (n)	yahūdy (m)	يهودي
Jewess (n)	yahudiya (f)	يهوديّة
Jewish (adj)	yahūdy	يهودي
China	el ṣīn (f)	الصين
Chinese (masc.)	ṣīny (m)	صيني

Chinese (fem.)	ṣīniya (f)	صينيّة
Chinese (adj)	ṣīny	صيني
Korean (masc.)	kūry (m)	كوري
Korean (fem.)	kuriya (f)	كوريّة
Korean (adj)	kūry	كوري
Lebanon	lebnān (f)	لبنان
Lebanese (masc.)	lebnāny (m)	لبناني
Lebanese (fem.)	lebnāniya (f)	لبنانيّة
Lebanese (adj)	lebnāny	لبناني
Mongolia	manɣūlia (f)	منغوليا
Mongolian (masc.)	manɣūly (m)	منغولي
Mongolian (fem.)	manɣuliya (f)	منغوليّة
Mongolian (adj)	manɣūly	منغولي
Malaysia	malīzya (f)	ماليزيا
Malaysian (masc.)	malīzy (m)	ماليزي
Malaysian (fem.)	maliziya (f)	ماليزيّة
Malaysian (adj)	malīzy	ماليزي
Pakistan	bakistān (f)	باكستان
Pakistani (masc.)	bakistāny (m)	باكستاني
Pakistani (fem.)	bakistaniya (f)	باكستانيّة
Pakistani (adj)	bakistāny	باكستاني
Saudi Arabia	el soʿodiya (f)	السعوديّة
Arab (masc.)	ʿaraby (m)	عربي
Arab (fem.)	ʿarabiya (f)	عربيّة
Arabic, Arabian (adj)	ʿaraby	عربي
Thailand	tayland (f)	تايلاند
Thai (masc.)	taylandy (m)	تايلانّدي
Thai (fem.)	taylandiya (f)	تايلانّديّة
Thai (adj)	taylandy	تايلانّدي
Taiwan	taywān (f)	تايوان
Taiwanese (masc.)	taywāny (m)	تايواني
Taiwanese (fem.)	taywaniya (f)	تايوانيّة
Taiwanese (adj)	taywāny	تايواني
Turkey	turkia (f)	تركيا
Turk (masc.)	turky (m)	تركي
Turk (fem.)	turkiya (f)	تركيّة
Turkish (adj)	turky	تركي
Japan	el yabān (f)	اليابان
Japanese (masc.)	yabāny (m)	ياباني
Japanese (fem.)	yabaniya (f)	يابانيّة
Japanese (adj)	yabāny	ياباني
Afghanistan	afɣanistan (f)	أفغانستان
Bangladesh	bangladeʃ (f)	بنجلاديش
Indonesia	indonisya (f)	إندونيسيا
Jordan	el ordon (m)	الأردن

Iraq	el ʻerāq (m)	العراق
Iran	iran (f)	إيران
Cambodia	kambodya (f)	كمبوديا
Kuwait	el kuweyt (f)	الكويت
Laos	laos (f)	لاوس
Myanmar	myanmar (f)	ميانمار
Nepal	nebāl (f)	نيبال
United Arab Emirates	el emārāt el ʻarabiya el mottaḥeda (pl)	الإمارات العربية المتّحدة
Syria	soria (f)	سوريا
Palestine	felesṭīn (f)	فلسطين
South Korea	korea el ganūbiya (f)	كوريا الجنوبيّة
North Korea	korea el ʃamāliya (f)	كوريا الشماليّة

238. North America

United States of America	el welayāt el mottaḥda el amrīkiya (pl)	الولايات المتّحدة الأمريكيّة
American (masc.)	amrīky (m)	أمريكي
American (fem.)	amrīkiya (f)	أمريكيّة
American (adj)	amrīky	أمريكي
Canada	kanada (f)	كندا
Canadian (masc.)	kanady (m)	كندي
Canadian (fem.)	kanadiya (f)	كنديّة
Canadian (adj)	kanady	كندي
Mexico	el maksīk (f)	المكسيك
Mexican (masc.)	maksīky (m)	مكسيكي
Mexican (fem.)	maksīkiya (f)	مكسيكيّة
Mexican (adj)	maksīky	مكسيكي

239. Central and South America

Argentina	arʒantīn (f)	الأرجنتين
Argentinian (masc.)	arʒantīny (m)	أرجنتيني
Argentinian (fem.)	arʒantiniya (f)	أرجنتينية
Argentinian (adj)	arʒantīny	أرجنتيني
Brazil	el barazīl (f)	البرازيل
Brazilian (masc.)	barazīly (m)	برازيلي
Brazilian (fem.)	baraziliya (f)	برازيليّة
Brazilian (adj)	barazīly	برازيلي
Colombia	kolombia (f)	كولومبيا
Colombian (masc.)	kolomby (m)	كولومبي
Colombian (fem.)	kolombiya (f)	كولومبية
Colombian (adj)	kolomby	كولومبي
Cuba	kūba (f)	كوبا
Cuban (masc.)	kūby (m)	كوبي

Cuban (fem.)	kūbiya (f)	كوبيّة
Cuban (adj)	kūby	كوبي
Chile	tʃīly (f)	تشيلي
Chilean (masc.)	tʃīly (m)	تشيلي
Chilean (fem.)	tʃīliya (f)	تشيلية
Chilean (adj)	tʃīly	تشيلي
Bolivia	bolivia (f)	بوليفيا
Venezuela	venzweyla (f)	فنزويلا
Paraguay	baraguay (f)	باراجواي
Peru	beru (f)	بيرو
Suriname	surinam (f)	سورينام
Uruguay	uruguay (f)	أوروجواي
Ecuador	el equador (f)	الإكوادور
The Bahamas	gozor el bahāmas (pl)	جزر البهاماس
Haiti	haīti (f)	هايتي
Dominican Republic	gomhoriya el dominikan (f)	جمهوريّة الدومينيكان
Panama	banama (f)	بنما
Jamaica	ʒamayka (f)	جامايكا

240. Africa

Egypt	maṣr (f)	مصر
Egyptian (masc.)	maṣry (m)	مصري
Egyptian (fem.)	maṣriya (f)	مصريّة
Egyptian (adj)	maṣry	مصري
Morocco	el maɣreb (m)	المغرب
Moroccan (masc.)	maɣreby (m)	مغربي
Moroccan (fem.)	maɣrebiya (f)	مغربية
Moroccan (adj)	maɣreby	مغربي
Tunisia	tunis (f)	تونس
Tunisian (masc.)	tunsy (m)	تونسي
Tunisian (fem.)	tunesiya (f)	تونسية
Tunisian (adj)	tunsy	تونسي
Ghana	ɣana (f)	غانا
Zanzibar	zanʒibār (f)	زنجبار
Kenya	kenya (f)	كينيا
Libya	libya (f)	ليبيا
Madagascar	madaɣaʃkar (f)	مدغشقر
Namibia	namibia (f)	ناميبيا
Senegal	el senɣāl (f)	السنغال
Tanzania	tanznia (f)	تنزانيا
South Africa	afreqia el ganūbiya (f)	أفريقيا الجنوبيّة
African (masc.)	afrīqy (m)	أفريقي
African (fem.)	afriqiya (f)	أفريقية
African (adj)	afrīqy	أفريقي

241. Australia. Oceania

Australia	ostorālya (f)	أستراليا
Australian (masc.)	ostorāly (m)	أسترالي
Australian (fem.)	ostoraleya (f)	أستراليّة
Australian (adj)	ostorāly	أسترالي
New Zealand	nyu zelanda (f)	نيوزيلنّدا
New Zealander (masc.)	nyu zelandy (m)	نيوزيلنّدي
New Zealander (fem.)	nyu zelandiya (f)	نيوزيلنّديّة
New Zealand (as adj)	nyu zelandy	نيوزيلنّدي
Tasmania	tasmania (f)	تاسمانيا
French Polynesia	bolenezia el faransiya (f)	بولينزيا الفرنسيّة

242. Cities

Amsterdam	amesterdam (f)	امستردام
Ankara	ankara (f)	أنقرة
Athens	atīna (f)	أثينا
Baghdad	baɣdād (f)	بغداد
Bangkok	bangkok (f)	بانكوك
Barcelona	barʃelona (f)	برشلونة
Beijing	bekīn (f)	بيكين
Beirut	beyrut (f)	بيروت
Berlin	berlin (f)	برلين
Mumbai (Bombay)	bombay (f)	بومباى
Bonn	bonn (f)	بون
Bordeaux	bordu (f)	بوردو
Bratislava	bratislava (f)	براتيسلافا
Brussels	broksel (f)	بروكسل
Bucharest	buχarest (f)	بوخارست
Budapest	budabest (f)	بودابست
Cairo	el qahera (f)	القاهرة
Kolkata (Calcutta)	kalkutta (f)	كلكتا
Chicago	ʃikāgo (f)	شيكاجو
Copenhagen	kobenhāgen (f)	كوبنهاجن
Dar-es-Salaam	dar el salām (f)	دار السلام
Delhi	delhi (f)	دلهي
Dubai	dubaī (f)	دبي
Dublin	dablin (f)	دبلن
Düsseldorf	dusseldorf (f)	دوسلدورف
Florence	florensa (f)	فلورنسا
Frankfurt	frankfurt (f)	فرانكفورت
Geneva	ʒenive (f)	جنيف
The Hague	lahāy (f)	لاهاى
Hamburg	hamburg (m)	هامبورج

Hanoi	hanoy (f)	هانوى
Havana	havana (f)	هافانا
Helsinki	helsinki (f)	هلسنكي
Hiroshima	hiroʃima (f)	هيروشيما
Hong Kong	hong kong (f)	هونج كونج
Istanbul	isṭanbul (f)	إسطنبول
Jerusalem	el qods (f)	القدس
Kyiv	kyiv (f)	كييف
Kuala Lumpur	kuala lumpur (f)	كوالالمبور
Lisbon	laʃbūna (f)	لشبونة
London	london (f)	لندن
Los Angeles	los anʒeles (f)	لوس أنجلوس
Lyons	lyon (f)	ليون
Madrid	madrīd (f)	مدريد
Marseille	marsilia (f)	مرسيليا
Mexico City	madīnet meksiko (f)	مدينة مكسيكو
Miami	mayami (f)	ميامي
Montreal	montreal (f)	مونتريال
Moscow	moskū (f)	موسكو
Munich	munix (f)	ميونخ
Nairobi	nayrobi (f)	نيروبي
Naples	naboli (f)	نابولي
New York	nyu york (f)	نيويورك
Nice	nīs (f)	نيس
Oslo	oslo (f)	أوسلو
Ottawa	ottawa (f)	أوتاوا
Paris	baris (f)	باريس
Prague	braɣ (f)	براغ
Rio de Janeiro	rio de ʒaneyro (f)	ريو دي جانيرو
Rome	roma (f)	روما
Saint Petersburg	sant betersburɣ (f)	سانت بطرسبرغ
Seoul	seūl (f)	سيول
Shanghai	ʃanghay (f)	شنجهاي
Singapore	sinɣafūra (f)	سنغافورة
Stockholm	stokxolm (f)	ستوكهولم
Sydney	sydney (f)	سيدني
Taipei	taybey (f)	تايبيه
Tokyo	ṭokyo (f)	طوكيو
Toronto	toronto (f)	تورونتو
Venice	venesya (f)	فينيسيا
Vienna	vienna (f)	فيينا
Warsaw	warsaw (f)	وارسو
Washington	waʃinṭon (f)	واشنطن

243. Politics. Government. Part 1

politics	seyāsa (f)	سياسة
political (adj)	seyāsy	سياسي

politician	seyāsy (m)	سياسي
state (country)	dawla (f)	دولة
citizen	mowāṭen (m)	مواطن
citizenship	mewaṭna (f)	مواطنة
national emblem	ʃe'ār waṭany (m)	شعار وطني
national anthem	naʃīd waṭany (m)	نشيد وطني
government	ḥokūma (f)	حكومة
head of state	ra's el dawla (m)	رأس الدولة
parliament	barlamān (m)	برلمان
party	ḥezb (m)	حزب
capitalism	ra'smaliya (f)	رأسماليّة
capitalist (adj)	ra'smāly	رأسمالي
socialism	eʃterakiya (f)	إشتراكيّة
socialist (adj)	eʃterāky	إشتراكي
communism	ʃeyū'iya (f)	شيوعيّة
communist (adj)	ʃeyū'y	شيوعي
communist (n)	ʃeyū'y (m)	شيوعي
democracy	dīmoqraṭiya (f)	ديموقراطيّة
democrat	demoqrāṭy (m)	ديموقراطي
democratic (adj)	demoqrāṭy	ديموقراطي
Democratic party	el ḥezb el demokrāṭy (m)	الحزب الديموقراطي
liberal (n)	librāly (m)	ليبيرالي
Liberal (adj)	librāly	ليبيرالي
conservative (n)	moḥāfeẓ (m)	محافظ
conservative (adj)	moḥāfeẓ	محافظ
republic (n)	gomhoriya (f)	جمهورية
republican (n)	gomhūry (m)	جمهوري
Republican party	el ḥezb el gomhūry (m)	الحزب الجمهوري
elections	entaχabāt (pl)	إنتخابات
to elect (vt)	entaχab	إنتخب
elector, voter	nāχeb (m)	ناخب
election campaign	ḥamla enteχabiya (f)	حملة إنتخابيّة
voting (n)	taṣwīt (m)	تصويت
to vote (vi)	ṣawwat	صوّت
suffrage, right to vote	ḥa' el enteχāb (m)	حق الإنتخاب
candidate	morasʃaḥ (m)	مرشّح
to run for (~ President)	rasʃaḥ nafsoh	رشّح نفسه
campaign	ḥamla (f)	حملة
opposition (as adj)	mo'āreḍ	معارض
opposition (n)	mo'arḍa (f)	معارضة
visit	zeyāra (f)	زيارة
official visit	zeyāra rasmiya (f)	زيارة رسميّة
international (adj)	dawly	دولي

negotiations	mofawḍāt (pl)	مفاوضات
to negotiate (vi)	tafāwaḍ	تفاوض

244. Politics. Government. Part 2

society	mogtama' (m)	مجتمع
constitution	dostūr (m)	دستور
power (political control)	solṭa (f)	سلطة
corruption	fasād (m)	فساد
law (justice)	qanūn (m)	قانون
legal (legitimate)	qanūny	قانوني
justice (fairness)	'adāla (f)	عدالة
just (fair)	'ādel	عادل
committee	lagna (f)	لجنة
bill (draft law)	maʃrū' qanūn (m)	مشروع قانون
budget	mowazna (f)	موازنة
policy	seyāsa (f)	سياسة
reform	eṣlāḥ (m)	إصلاح
radical (adj)	oṣūly	أصولي
power (strength, force)	'owwa (f)	قوّة
powerful (adj)	'awy	قوي
supporter	mo'ayed (m)	مؤيد
influence	ta'sīr (m)	تأثير
regime (e.g. military ~)	nezām ḥokm (m)	نظام حكم
conflict	χelāf (m)	خلاف
conspiracy (plot)	mo'amra (f)	مؤامرة
provocation	estefzāz (m)	إستفزاز
to overthrow (regime, etc.)	asqaṭ	أسقط
overthrow (of a government)	esqāṭ (m)	إسقاط
revolution	sawra (f)	ثوّرة
coup d'état	enqelāb (m)	إنقلاب
military coup	enqelāb 'askary (m)	إنقلاب عسكري
crisis	azma (f)	أزمة
economic recession	rokūd eqteṣādy (m)	ركود إقتصادي
demonstrator (protester)	motaẓāher (m)	متظاهر
demonstration	mozahra (f)	مظاهرة
martial law	ḥokm 'orfy (m)	حكم عرفي
military base	qa'eda 'askariya (f)	قاعدة عسكريّة
stability	esteqrār (m)	إستقرار
stable (adj)	mostaqerr	مستقرّ
exploitation	esteɣlāl (m)	إستغلال
to exploit (workers)	estaɣall	إستغلّ
racism	'onṣoriya (f)	عنصريّة
racist	'onṣory (m)	عنصري

fascism	faʃiya (f)	فاشيّة
fascist	fāʃy (m)	فاشي

245. Countries. Miscellaneous

foreigner	agnaby (m)	أجنبي
foreign (adj)	agnaby	أجنبي
abroad (in a foreign country)	fel ɣāreg	في الخارج
emigrant	mohāger (m)	مهاجر
emigration	hegra (f)	هجرة
to emigrate (vi)	hāgar	هاجر
the West	el ɣarb (m)	الغرب
the East	el ʃar' (m)	الشرق
the Far East	el ʃar' el aqṣa (m)	الشرق الأقصى
civilization	ḥaḍāra (f)	حضارة
humanity (mankind)	el baʃariya (f)	البشريّة
the world (earth)	el 'ālam (m)	العالم
peace	salām (m)	سلام
worldwide (adj)	'ālamy	عالمي
homeland	waṭan (m)	وطن
people (population)	ʃa'b (m)	شعب
population	sokkān (pl)	سكّان
people (a lot of ~)	nās (pl)	ناس
nation (people)	omma (f)	أمّة
generation	gīl (m)	جيل
territory (area)	arḍ (f)	أرض
region	mante'a (f)	منطقة
state (part of a country)	welāya (f)	ولاية
tradition	ta'līd (m)	تقليد
custom (tradition)	'āda (f)	عادة
ecology	'elm el bī'a (m)	علم البيئة
Indian (Native American)	hendy aḥmar (m)	هندي أحمر
Gypsy (masc.)	ɣagary (m)	غجري
Gypsy (fem.)	ɣagariya (f)	غجريّة
Gypsy (adj)	ɣagary	غجري
empire	embraṭoriya (f)	إمبراطورية
colony	mosta'mara (f)	مستعمرة
slavery	'obūdiya (f)	عبودية
invasion	ɣazw (m)	غزو
famine	magā'a (f)	مجاعة

246. Major religious groups. Confessions

religion	dīn (m)	دين
religious (adj)	dīny	ديني

faith, belief	emān (m)	إيمان
to believe (in God)	aman	أمن
believer	mo'men (m)	مؤمن
atheism	el elḥād (m)	الإلحاد
atheist	molḥed (m)	ملحد
Christianity	el masīḥiya (f)	المسيحيّة
Christian (n)	mesīḥy (m)	مسيحي
Christian (adj)	mesīḥy	مسيحي
Catholicism	el kasolekiya (f)	الكاثوليكيّة
Catholic (n)	kasolīky (m)	كاثوليكي
Catholic (adj)	kasolīky	كاثوليكي
Protestantism	brotestantiya (f)	بروتستانتية
Protestant Church	el kenīsa el brotestantiya (f)	الكنيسة البروتستانتية
Protestant (n)	brotestanty (m)	بروتستانتي
Orthodoxy	orsozeksiya (f)	الأرثوذكسيّة
Orthodox Church	el kenīsa el orsozeksiya (f)	الكنيسة الأرثوذكسيّة
Orthodox (n)	arsazoksy (m)	أرثوذكسي
Presbyterianism	maʃīχiya (f)	مشيخية
Presbyterian Church	el kenīsa el maʃīχiya (f)	الكنيسة المشيخية
Presbyterian (n)	maʃīχiya (f)	مشيخية
Lutheranism	el luseriya (f)	اللوثرية
Lutheran (n)	luterriya (m)	لوثرية
Baptist Church	el kenīsa el meʿmedaniya (f)	الكنيسة المعمدانية
Baptist (n)	meʿmedāny (m)	معمداني
Anglican Church	el kenīsa el anʒlekaniya (f)	الكنيسة الإنجليكانية
Anglican (n)	enʒelikāny (m)	أنجليكاني
Mormonism	el moromoniya (f)	المورمونية
Mormon (n)	mesīḥy mormōn (m)	مسيحي مرمون
Judaism	el yahūdiya (f)	اليهودية
Jew (n)	yahūdy (m)	يهودي
Buddhism	el būziya (f)	البوذية
Buddhist (n)	būzy (m)	بوذي
Hinduism	el hindūsiya (f)	الهندوسية
Hindu (n)	hendūsy (m)	هندوسي
Islam	el islām (m)	الإسلام
Muslim (n)	muslim (m)	مسلم
Muslim (adj)	islāmy	إسلامي
Shiah Islam	el mazhab el ʃeeʿy (m)	المذهب الشيعي
Shiite (n)	ʃeeʿy (m)	شيعي
Sunni Islam	el mazhab el sunny (m)	المذهب السنّي
Sunnite (n)	sunni (m)	سنّي

247. Religions. Priests

priest	kāhen (m)	كاهن
the Pope	el bāba (m)	البابا
monk, friar	rāheb (m)	راهب
nun	rāheba (f)	راهبة
pastor	'essīs (m)	قسّيس
abbot	ra'īs el deyr (m)	رئيس الدير
vicar (parish priest)	viqār (m)	فيقار
bishop	asqof (m)	أسقف
cardinal	kardinal (m)	كاردينال
preacher	mobaſſer (m)	مبشّر
preaching	tabſīr (f)	تبشير
parishioners	ra'yet el abraſiya (f)	رعية الأبرشية
believer	mo'men (m)	مؤمن
atheist	molḥed (m)	ملحد

248. Faith. Christianity. Islam

Adam	'ādam (m)	آدم
Eve	ḥawwā' (f)	حوّاء
God	allah (m)	الله
the Lord	el rabb (m)	الربّ
the Almighty	el qadīr (m)	القدير
sin	zanb (m)	ذنب
to sin (vi)	aznab	أذنب
sinner (masc.)	mozneb (m)	مذنب
sinner (fem.)	mozneba (f)	مذنبة
hell	el gaḥīm (f)	الجحيم
paradise	el ganna (f)	الجنّة
Jesus	yasū' (m)	يسوع
Jesus Christ	yasū' el masīḥ (m)	يسوع المسيح
the Holy Spirit	el rūḥ el qods (m)	الروح القدس
the Saviour	el masīḥ (m)	المسيح
the Virgin Mary	maryem el 'azrā' (f)	مريم العذراء
the Devil	el ſayṭān (m)	الشيطان
devil's (adj)	ſeyṭāny	شيطاني
Satan	el ſayṭān (m)	الشيطان
satanic (adj)	ſeyṭāny	شيطاني
angel	malāk (m)	ملاك
guardian angel	malāk ḥāres (m)	ملاك حارس
angelic (adj)	malā'eky	ملائكي

apostle	rasūl (m)	رسول
archangel	el malāk el ra'īsy (m)	الملاك الرئيسي
the Antichrist	el masīḥ el daggāl (m)	المسيح الدجّال
Church	el kenīsa (f)	الكنيسة
Bible	el ketāb el moqaddas (m)	الكتاب المقدّس
biblical (adj)	tawrāty	توراتي
Old Testament	el 'aḥd el 'adīm (m)	العهد القديم
New Testament	el 'aḥd el gedīd (m)	العهد الجديد
Gospel	engīl (m)	إنجيل
Holy Scripture	el ketāb el moqaddas (m)	الكتاب المقدّس
Heaven	el ganna (f)	الجنّة
Commandment	waṣiya (f)	وصيّة
prophet	naby (m)	نبي
prophecy	nobū'a (f)	نبوءة
Allah	allah (m)	الله
Mohammed	moḥammed (m)	محمّد
the Koran	el qor'ān (m)	القرآن
mosque	masged (m)	مسجد
mullah	mullah (m)	ملا
prayer	ṣalāh (f)	صلاة
to pray (vi, vt)	ṣalla	صلّى
pilgrimage	ḥagg (m)	حج
pilgrim	ḥagg (m)	حاج
Mecca	makka el mokarrama (f)	مكة المكرّمة
church	kenīsa (f)	كنيسة
temple	ma'bad (m)	معبد
cathedral	katedra'iya (f)	كاتدرائية
Gothic (adj)	qūṭy	قوطي
synagogue	kenīs (m)	كنيس
mosque	masged (m)	مسجد
chapel	kenīsa saɣīra (f)	كنيسة صغيرة
abbey	deyr (m)	دير
convent	deyr (m)	دير
monastery	deyr (m)	دير
bell (church ~s)	garas (m)	جرس
bell tower	borg el garas (m)	برج الجرس
to ring (ab. bells)	da''	دق
cross	ṣalīb (m)	صليب
cupola (roof)	'obba (f)	قبّة
icon	ramz (m)	رمز
soul	nafs (f)	نفس
fate (destiny)	maṣīr (m)	مصير
evil (n)	ʃarr (m)	شرّ
good (n)	χeyr (m)	خير
vampire	maṣṣāṣ demā' (m)	مصّاص دماء

witch (evil ~)	sāḥera (f)	ساحرة
demon	ʃeṭān (m)	شيطان
spirit	roḥe (m)	روح
redemption (giving us ~)	takfīr (m)	تكفير
to redeem (vt)	kaffar ʿan	كفّر عن
church service	qedās (m)	قداس
to say mass	ʾām be χedma dīniya	قام بخدمة دينية
confession	eʿterāf (m)	إعتراف
to confess (vi)	eʿtaraf	إعترف
saint (n)	qeddīs (m)	قدّيس
sacred (holy)	moqaddas (m)	مقدّس
holy water	maya moqaddesa (f)	ماية مقدّسة
ritual (n)	ʃaʿāʾer (pl)	شعائر
ritual (adj)	ʃaʿāʾery	شعائري
sacrifice	zabīḥa (f)	ذبيحة
superstition	χorāfa (f)	خرافة
superstitious (adj)	moʾmen bel χorafāt (m)	مؤمن بالخرافات
afterlife	aχra (f)	الآخرة
eternal life	ḥayat el abadiya (f)	حياة الأبدية

MISCELLANEOUS

249. Various useful words

background (green ~)	χalefiya (f)	خلفية
balance (of the situation)	tawāzon (m)	توازن
barrier (obstacle)	ḥāgez (m)	حاجز
base (basis)	asās (m)	أساس
beginning	bedāya (f)	بداية
category	fe'a (f)	فئة
cause (reason)	sabab (m)	سبب
choice	eχteyār (m)	إختيار
coincidence	ṣodfa (f)	صدّفة
comfortable (~ chair)	morīḥ	مريح
comparison	moqarna (f)	مقارنة
compensation	ta'wīḍ (m)	تعويض
degree (extent, amount)	daraga (f)	درجة
development	tanmeya (f)	تنمية
difference	far' (m)	فرق
effect (e.g. of drugs)	ta'sīr (m)	تأثير
effort (exertion)	mag-hūd (m)	مجهود
element	'onṣor (m)	عنصر
end (finish)	nehāya (f)	نهاية
example (illustration)	mesāl (m)	مثال
fact	ḥaī'a (f)	حقيقة
frequent (adj)	motakarrer (m)	متكرّر
growth (development)	nomoww (m)	نموّ
help	mosa'da (f)	مساعدة
ideal	mesāl (m)	مثال
kind (sort, type)	nū' (m)	نوع
labyrinth	matāha (f)	متاهة
mistake, error	χaṭa' (m)	خطأ
moment	laḥza (f)	لحظة
object (thing)	mawḍū' (m)	موضوع
obstacle	'aqaba (f)	عقبة
original (original copy)	aṣl (m)	أصل
part (~ of sth)	goz' (m)	جزء
particle, small part	goz' (m)	جزء
pause (break)	estrāḥa (f)	إستراحة
position	mawqef (m)	موّقف
principle	mabda' (m)	مبدأ
problem	moʃkela (f)	مشكلة
process	'amaliya (f)	عمليّة

progress	ta'addom (m)	تقدّم
property (quality)	xaṣṣa (f)	خاصّة
reaction	radd fe'l (m)	ردّ فعل
risk	moxaṭra (f)	مخاطرة
secret	serr (m)	سرّ
series	selsela (f)	سلسلة
shape (outer form)	ʃakl (m)	شكل
situation	ḥāla (f), waḍ' (m)	حالة, وضع
solution	ḥall (m)	حلّ
standard (adj)	'ādy -qeyāsy	عادي, قياسي
standard (level of quality)	'eyās (m)	قياس
stop (pause)	estrāḥa (f)	إستراحة
style	oslūb (m)	أسلوب
system	nezām (m)	نظام
table (chart)	gadwal (m)	جدول
tempo, rate	eqā' (m)	إيقاع
term (word, expression)	moṣṭalaḥ (m)	مصطلح
thing (object, item)	ḥāga (f)	حاجة
truth (e.g. moment of ~)	ḥa'ī'a (f)	حقيقة
turn (please wait your ~)	dore (m)	دور
type (sort, kind)	nū' (m)	نوع
urgent (adj)	mesta'gel	مستعجل
urgently	be ʃakl 'āgel	بشكل عاجل
utility (usefulness)	manf'a (f)	منفعة
variant (alternative)	ʃakl moxtalef (m)	شكل مختلف
way (means, method)	ṭarī'a (f)	طريقة
zone	mante'a (f)	منطقة

250. Modifiers. Adjectives. Part 1

additional (adj)	eḍāfy	إضافي
ancient (~ civilization)	'adīm	قديم
artificial (adj)	ṣenā'y	صناعي
back, rear (adj)	xalfy	خلفي
bad (adj)	weḥeʃ	وحش
beautiful (~ palace)	gamīl	جميل
beautiful (person)	gamīl	جميل
big (in size)	kebīr	كبير
bitter (taste)	morr	مرّ
blind (sightless)	a'ma	أعمى
calm, quiet (adj)	hady	هادئ
careless (negligent)	mohmel	مهمل
caring (~ father)	mohtamm	مهتمّ
central (adj)	markazy	مركزي
cheap (low-priced)	rexīṣ	رخيص
cheerful (adj)	farḥān	فرحان

children's (adj)	lel aṭfāl	للأطفال
civil (~ law)	madany	مدني
clandestine (secret)	serry	سرّي
clean (free from dirt)	neḍīf	نظيف
clear (explanation, etc.)	wāḍeḥ	واضح
clever (intelligent)	zaky	ذكي
close (near in space)	ʾarīb	قريب
closed (adj)	maʾfūl	مقفول
cloudless (sky)	ṣāfy	صافي
cold (drink, weather)	bāred	بارد
compatible (adj)	motawāfaq	متوافق
contented (satisfied)	rāḍy	راضي
continuous (uninterrupted)	motawāṣal	متواصل
cool (weather)	monʿeʃ	منعش
dangerous (adj)	χaṭīr	خطير
dark (room)	ḍalma	ظلمة
dead (not alive)	mayet	ميّت
dense (fog, smoke)	kasīf	كثيف
destitute (extremely poor)	moʿdam	معدم
different (not the same)	moχtalef	مختلف
difficult (decision)	ṣaʿb	صعب
difficult (problem, task)	ṣaʿb	صعب
dim, faint (light)	bāhet	باهت
dirty (not clean)	weseχ	وسخ
distant (in space)	beʿīd	بعيد
dry (clothes, etc.)	nāʃef	ناشف
easy (not difficult)	sahl	سهل
empty (glass, room)	χāly	خالي
even (e.g. ~ surface)	mosaṭṭaḥ	مسطّح
exact (amount)	maẓbūṭ	مظبوط
excellent (adj)	momtāz	ممتاز
excessive (adj)	mofreṭ	مفرط
expensive (adj)	ɣāly	غالي
exterior (adj)	χāregy	خارجي
far (the ~ East)	beʿīd	بعيد
fast (quick)	sareeʿ	سريع
fatty (food)	dasem	دسم
fertile (land, soil)	χeṣb	خصب
flat (~ panel display)	mosaṭṭaḥ	مسطّح
foreign (adj)	agnaby	أجنبي
fragile (china, glass)	qābel lel kasr	قابل للكسر
free (at no cost)	be balāʃ	ببلاش
free (unrestricted)	ḥorr	حر
fresh (~ water)	ʿazb	عذب
fresh (e.g. ~ bread)	ṭāza	طازة
frozen (food)	mogammad	مجمّد
full (completely filled)	malyān	مليان

gloomy (house, forecast)	mozlem	مظلم
good (book, etc.)	kewayes	كويّس
good, kind (kindhearted)	ṭayeb	طيّب
grateful (adj)	ʃāker	شاكر
happy (adj)	saʿīd	سعيد
hard (not soft)	gāmed	جامد
heavy (in weight)	teʾīl	ثقيل
hostile (adj)	meʃ weddy	مش ودّي
hot (adj)	soχn	سخن
huge (adj)	ḍaχm	ضخم
humid (adj)	roṭob	رطب
hungry (adj)	geʿān	جعان
ill (sick, unwell)	ʿayān	عيّان
immobile (adj)	sābet	ثابت
important (adj)	mohemm	مهمّ
impossible (adj)	mostaḥīl	مستحيل
incomprehensible	meʃ wāḍeḥ	مش واضح
indispensable (adj)	ḍarūry	ضروري
inexperienced (adj)	ʾalīl el χebra	قليل الخبرة
insignificant (adj)	meʃ mohemm	مش مهمّ
interior (adj)	dāχely	داخلي
joint (~ decision)	moʃtarak	مشترك
last (e.g. ~ week)	māḍy	ماضي
last (final)	ʾāχer	آخر
left (e.g. ~ side)	el ʃemāl	الشمال
legal (legitimate)	qanūny	قانوني
light (in weight)	χafīf	خفيف
light (pale color)	fāteḥ	فاتح
limited (adj)	maḥdūd	محدود
liquid (fluid)	sāʾel	سائل
long (e.g. ~ hair)	ṭawīl	طويل
loud (voice, etc.)	ʿāly	عالي
low (voice)	wāṭy	واطي

251. Modifiers. Adjectives. Part 2

main (principal)	raʾīsy	رئيسي
matt, matte	maṭfy	مطفي
meticulous (job)	motqan	متقن
mysterious (adj)	γāmeḍ	غامض
narrow (street, etc.)	ḍayeʾ	ضيّق
native (~ country)	aṣly	أصلي
nearby (adj)	ʾarīb	قريب
needed (necessary)	lāzem	لازم
negative (~ response)	salby	سلبي
neighbouring (adj)	mogāwer	مجاور
nervous (adj)	ʿaṣaby	عصبي

new (adj)	gedīd	جديد
next (e.g. ~ week)	elly gayī	اللي جاي
nice (agreeable)	laṭīf	لطيف
pleasant (voice)	laṭīf	لطيف
normal (adj)	ʿādy	عادي
not big (adj)	meʃ kebīr	مش كبير
not difficult (adj)	meʃ ṣaʿb	مش صعب
obligatory (adj)	ḍarūry	ضروري
old (house)	ʾadīm	قديم
open (adj)	maftūḥ	مفتوح
opposite (adj)	moqābel	مقابل
ordinary (usual)	ʿādy	عادي
original (unusual)	aṣly	أصلي
past (recent)	elly fāt	اللي فات
permanent (adj)	dāʾem	دائم
personal (adj)	ʃaχṣy	شخصي
polite (adj)	moʾaddab	مؤدّب
poor (not rich)	faʾīr	فقير
possible (adj)	momken	ممكن
present (current)	ḥāḍer	حاضر
previous (adj)	elly fāt	اللي فات
principal (main)	asāsy	أساسي
private (~ jet)	χāṣṣa	خاصّة
probable (adj)	moḥtamal	محتمل
prolonged (e.g. ~ applause)	momtad	ممتد
public (open to all)	ʿām	عام
punctual (person)	daqīq	دقيق
quiet (tranquil)	hady	هادئ
rare (adj)	nāder	نادر
raw (uncooked)	nayī	نيّ
right (not left)	el yemīn	اليمين
right, correct (adj)	ṣaḥīḥ	صحيح
ripe (fruit)	mestewy	مستوّي
risky (adj)	mogāzef	مجازف
sad (~ look)	zaʿlān	زعلان
sad (depressing)	zaʿlān	زعلان
safe (not dangerous)	ʾāmen	آمن
salty (food)	māleḥ	مالح
satisfied (customer)	rāḍy	راضي
second hand (adj)	mostaʿmal	مستعمل
shallow (water)	ḍaḥl	ضحل
sharp (blade, etc.)	ḥād	حاد
short (in length)	ʾaṣīr	قصير
short, short-lived (adj)	ʾaṣīr	قصير
short-sighted (adj)	ʾaṣīr el naẓar	قصير النظر
significant (notable)	mohemm	مهم

similar (adj)	ʃabīh	شبيه
simple (easy)	basīṭ	بسيط
skinny	rofayaʿ	رفيّع
small (in size)	ṣoɣeyyir	صغيّر
smooth (surface)	amlas	أملس
soft (~ toys)	nāʿem	ناعم
solid (~ wall)	matīn	متين
sour (flavour, taste)	ḥāmeḍ	حامض
spacious (house, etc.)	wāseʿ	واسع
special (adj)	χāṣṣ	خاصّ
straight (line, road)	mostaqīm	مستقيم
strong (person)	ʾawy	قويّ
stupid (foolish)	ɣaby	غبي
suitable (e.g. ~ for drinking)	monāseb	مناسب
sunny (day)	moʃmes	مشمس
superb, perfect (adj)	momtāz	ممتاز
swarthy (dark-skinned)	asmar	أسمر
sweet (sugary)	mesakkar	مسكّر
tanned (adj)	asmar	أسمر
tasty (delicious)	ṭaʿmo ḥelw	طعمه حلو
tender (affectionate)	ḥanūn	حنون
the highest (adj)	aʿla	أعلى
the most important	ahamm	أهمّ
the nearest	aʾʾrab	أقرب
the same, equal (adj)	momāsel	مماثل
thick (e.g. ~ fog)	kasīf	كثيف
thick (wall, slice)	teχīn	تخين
thin (person)	rofayaʿ	رفيّع
tight (~ shoes)	ḍayeʾ	ضيّق
tired (exhausted)	taʿbān	تعبان
tiring (adj)	motʿeb	متعب
transparent (adj)	ʃaffāf	شفّاف
unclear (adj)	meʃ wāḍeḥ	مش واضح
unique (exceptional)	farīd	فريد
various (adj)	moχtalef	مختلف
warm (moderately hot)	dāfeʾ	دافئ
wet (e.g. ~ clothes)	mablūl	مبلول
whole (entire, complete)	koll el nās	كلّ
wide (e.g. ~ road)	wāseʿ	واسع
young (adj)	ʃāb	شاب

MAIN 500 VERBS

252. Verbs A-C

to accompany (vt)	rāfaq	رافق
to accuse (vt)	ettaham	إتّهم
to acknowledge (admit)	e'taraf	إعترف
to act (take action)	'amal	عمل
to add (supplement)	aḍāf	أضاف
to address (speak to)	χāṭab	خاطب
to admire (vi)	o'gab be	أعجب بـ
to advertise (vt)	a'lan	أعلن
to advise (vt)	naṣaḥ	نصح
to affirm (assert)	aṣarr	أصرّ
to agree (say yes)	ettafa'	إتّفق
to aim (to point a weapon)	ṣawwab 'ala …	صوّب على …
to allow (sb to do sth)	samaḥ	سمح
to amputate (vt)	batr	بتر
to answer (vi, vt)	gāwab	جاوب
to apologize (vi)	e'tazar	إعتذر
to appear (come into view)	ẓahar	ظهر
to applaud (vi, vt)	ṣaffa'	صفّق
to appoint (assign)	'ayen	عيّن
to approach (come closer)	'arrab	قرّب
to arrive (ab. train)	weṣel	وصل
to ask (~ sb to do sth)	ṭalab	طلب
to aspire to …	sa'a	سعى
to assist (help)	sā'ed	ساعد
to attack (mil.)	hagam	هجم
to attain (objectives)	balaɣ	بلغ
to avenge (get revenge)	entaqam	إنتقم
to avoid (danger, task)	tagannab	تجنّب
to award (give a medal to)	manaḥ	منح
to battle (vi)	qātal	قاتل
to be (vi)	kān	كان
to be a cause of …	sabbeb	سبّب
to be afraid	χāf	خاف
to be angry (with …)	ettḍāye'	إتّضايق
to be at war	ḥārab	حارب
to be based (on …)	estanad 'ala	إستند على
to be bored	zehe'	زهق

to be convinced	eqtanaʿ	إقتنع
to be enough	kaffa	كفّى
to be envious	ḥasad	حسد
to be indignant	estāʾ	إستاء
to be interested in ...	ehtamm be	إهتمّ بـ
to be lost in thought	saraḥ	سرح
to be lying (~ on the table)	kān mawgūd	كان موّجود
to be needed	maṭlūb	مطلوب
to be perplexed (puzzled)	eḥtār	إحتار
to be preserved	ḥafaẓ	حفظ
to be required	maṭlūb	مطلوب
to be surprised	etfāgeʾ	إتفاجئ
to be worried	ʾeleʾ	قلق
to beat (to hit)	ḍarab	ضرب
to become (e.g. ~ old)	baʾa	بقي
to behave (vi)	taṣarraf	تصرّف
to believe (think)	eʿtaqad	إعتقد
to belong to ...	χaṣṣ	خصّ
to berth (moor)	rasa	رسا
to blind (other drivers)	ʿama	عمي
to blow (wind)	habb	هبّ
to blush (vi)	eḥmarr	إحمرّ
to boast (vi)	tabāha	تباهى
to borrow (money)	estalaf	إستلف
to break (branch, toy, etc.)	kasar	كسر
to breathe (vi)	ettnaffes	إتّنفّس
to bring (sth)	gāb	جاب
to burn (paper, logs)	ḥaraʾ	حرق
to buy (purchase)	eʃtara	إشترى
to call (~ for help)	estaɣās	إستغاث
to call (yell for sb)	nāda	نادى
to calm down (vt)	ṭamʾan	طمأن
can (v aux)	ʾeder	قدر
to cancel (call off)	alɣa	ألغى
to cast off (of a boat or ship)	aqlaʿ	أقلع
to catch (e.g. ~ a ball)	mesek	مسك
to change (~ one's opinion)	ɣayar	غيّر
to change (exchange)	ṣarraff	صرّف
to charm (vt)	fatan	فتن
to choose (select)	eχtār	إختار
to chop off (with an axe)	ʾaṭṭaʿ	قطّع
to clean (e.g. kettle from scale)	naḍḍaf	نظّف
to clean (shoes, etc.)	naḍḍaf	نظّف
to clean up (tidy)	ratteb	رتّب
to close (vt)	ʾafal	قفل

to comb one's hair	masʃaṭ	مشّط
to come down (the stairs)	nezel	نزل
to come out (book)	ṣadar	صدر
to compare (vt)	qāran	قارن
to compensate (vt)	ʿawwaḍ	عوّض
to compete (vi)	nāfes	نافس
to compile (~ a list)	gammaʿ	جمّع
to complain (vi, vt)	ʃaka	شكا
to complicate (vt)	ʿaʾʾad	عقّد
to compose (music, etc.)	laḥḥan	لحّن
to compromise (reputation)	sawwaʾ somʿetoh	سوّء سمعته
to concentrate (vi)	rakkez	ركّز
to confess (criminal)	eʿtaraf	إعترف
to confuse (mix up)	etlaχbaṭ	إتلخبط
to congratulate (vt)	hanna	هنّأ
to consult (doctor, expert)	estaʃār ...	إستشار...
to continue (~ to do sth)	estamar	إستمر
to control (vt)	et-ḥakkem	إتحكّم
to convince (vt)	aqnaʿ	أقنع
to cooperate (vi)	taʿāwan	تعاون
to coordinate (vt)	nassaq	نسّق
to correct (an error)	ṣaḥḥaḥ	صحّح
to cost (vt)	kallef	كلّف
to count (money, etc.)	ʿadd	عدّ
to count on ...	eʿtamad ʿala ...	إعتمد على...
to crack (ceiling, wall)	etʃaʾʾeʾ	إتشقّق
to create (vt)	ʿamal	عمل
to crush, to squash (~ a bug)	faʿʿaṣ	فعّص
to cry (weep)	baka	بكي
to cut off (with a knife)	ʾaṭṭaʿ	قطّع

253. Verbs D-G

to dare (~ to do sth)	etthadda	إتّحدّى
to date from ...	tarīχo	تاريخه
to deceive (vi, vt)	χadaʿ	خدع
to decide (~ to do sth)	ʾarrar	قرّر
to decorate (tree, street)	zayen	زيّن
to dedicate (book, etc.)	karras	كرّس
to defend (a country, etc.)	dāfaʿ	دافع
to defend oneself	dāfaʿ ʿan nafsoh	دافع عن نفسه
to demand (request firmly)	ṭāleb	طالب
to denounce (vt)	estankar	إستنكر
to deny (vt)	ankar	أنكر
to depend on ...	eʿtamad ʿala ...	إعتمد على...
to deprive (vt)	ḥaram men	حرم من

to deserve (vt)	estaḥaqq	إستحقّ
to design (machine, etc.)	ṣammam	صمّم
to desire (want, wish)	kān ʿāyez	كان عايز
to despise (vt)	eḥtaqar	إحتقر
to destroy (documents, etc.)	atlaf	أتلف
to differ (from sth)	eχtalaf	إختلف
to dig (tunnel, etc.)	ḥafar	حفر
to direct (point the way)	waggeh	وجّه
to disappear (vi)	eχtafa	إختفى
to discover (new land, etc.)	ektaʃaf	إكتشف
to discuss (vt)	nāʾeʃ	ناقش
to distribute (leaflets, etc.)	wazzaʿ	وزّع
to disturb (vt)	azʿag	أزعج
to dive (vi)	ɣāṣ	غاص
to divide (math)	ʾasam	قسم
to do (vt)	ʿamal	عمل
to do the laundry	ɣasal el malābes	غسل الملابس
to double (increase)	ḍāʿaf	ضاعف
to doubt (have doubts)	ʃakk fe	شكّ في
to draw a conclusion	estantag	إستنتج
to dream (daydream)	ḥelem	حلم
to dream (in sleep)	ḥelem	حلم
to drink (vi, vt)	ʃereb	شرب
to drive a car	sāʾ ʿarabiya	ساق عربية
to drive away (scare away)	χawwef	خوّف
to drop (let fall)	waʾʾaʿ	وقّع
to drown (ab. person)	ɣereʾ	غرق
to dry (clothes, hair)	gaffaf	جفّف
to eat (vi, vt)	akal	أكل
to eavesdrop (vi)	tanaṣṣat	تنصّت
to emit (diffuse - odor, etc.)	fāḥ	فاح
to enjoy oneself	estamtaʿ	إستمتع
to enter (on the list)	saggel	سجّل
to enter (room, house, etc.)	daχal	دخل
to entertain (amuse)	salla	سلّى
to equip (fit out)	gahhez	جهّز
to examine (proposal)	baḥs fi	بحث في
to exchange (sth)	tabādal	تبادل
to excuse (forgive)	ʿazar	عذر
to exist (vi)	kān mawgūd	كان موجود
to expect (anticipate)	tawaqqaʿ	توقّع
to expect (foresee)	tanabbaʾ	تنبّأ
to expel (from school, etc.)	faṣal	فصل
to explain (vt)	ʃaraḥ	شرح
to express (vt)	ʿabbar	عبّر
to extinguish (a fire)	ṭaffa	طفّى

to fall in love (with …)	ḥabb	حبّ
to fancy (vt)	ʿagab	عجب
to feed (provide food)	akkel	أكّل
to fight (against the enemy)	qātal	قاتل
to fight (vi)	etχāneʾ	إتخانق
to fill (glass, bottle)	mala	ملأ
to find (~ lost items)	laʾa	لقى
to finish (vt)	χallaṣ	خلّص
to fish (angle)	eṣṭād samak	إصطاد سمك
to fit (ab. dress, etc.)	nāseb	ناسب
to flatter (vt)	gāmal	جامل
to fly (bird, plane)	ṭār	طار
to follow … (come after)	tatabbaʿ	تتبّع
to forbid (vt)	manaʿ	منع
to force (compel)	agbar	أجبر
to forget (vi, vt)	nesy	نسي
to forgive (pardon)	ʿafa	عفا
to form (constitute)	ʃakkal	شكّل
to get dirty (vi)	ettwassaχ	إتّوسّخ
to get infected (with …)	etʿada	إتعدى
to get irritated	enzaʿag	إنزعج
to get married	ettgawwez	إتّجوز
to get rid of …	ettχallaṣ min …	إتّخلّص من...
to get tired	teʿeb	تعب
to get up (arise from bed)	ʾām	قام
to give (vt)	edda	أدّى
to give a bath (to bath)	ḥammem	حمّم
to give a hug, to hug (vt)	ḥaḍan	حضن
to give in (yield to)	estaslam	إستسلم
to glimpse (vt)	lamaḥ	لمح
to go (by car, etc.)	rāḥ	راح
to go (on foot)	meʃy	مشى
to go for a swim	sebeḥ	سبح
to go out (for dinner, etc.)	χarag	خرج
to go to bed (go to sleep)	nām	نام
to greet (vt)	sallem ʿala	سلّم على
to grow (plants)	anbat	أنبت
to guarantee (vt)	ḍaman	ضمن
to guess (the answer)	χammen	خمّن

254. Verbs H-M

to hand out (distribute)	wazzaʿ ʿala	وزّع على
to hang (curtains, etc.)	ʿallaʾ	علّق
to have (vt)	malak	ملك

to have a bath	estaḥamma	إستحمّى
to have a try	ḥāwel	حاول
to have breakfast	feṭer	فطر
to have dinner	etʿasʃa	إتعشّى
to have lunch	etɣadda	إتغدّى
to head (group, etc.)	raʾs	رأس
to hear (vt)	semeʿ	سمع
to heat (vt)	sakχan	سخّن
to help (vt)	sāʿed	ساعد
to hide (vt)	χabba	خبّأ
to hire (e.g. ~ a boat)	aggar	أجّر
to hire (staff)	waẓẓaf	وظّف
to hope (vi, vt)	tamanna	تمنّى
to hunt (for food, sport)	eṣṭād	إصطاد
to hurry (vi)	estaʿgel	إستعجل
to imagine (to picture)	taṣawwar	تصوّر
to imitate (vt)	ʾalled	قلّد
to implore (vt)	etwassel	إتوسّل
to import (vt)	estawrad	إستورد
to increase (vi)	ezdād	إزداد
to increase (vt)	zawwed	زوّد
to infect (vt)	ʿada	عدى
to influence (vt)	assar fi	أثّر في
to inform (e.g. ~ the police about …)	ʾāl le	قال لـ
to inform (vt)	ʾāl ly	قال لي
to inherit (vt)	waras	ورث
to inquire (about …)	estafsar	إستفسر
to insert (put in)	dakχal	دخّل
to insinuate (imply)	lammaḥ	لمّح
to insist (vi, vt)	aṣarr	أصرّ
to inspire (vt)	alham	ألهم
to instruct (teach)	ʿallem	علّم
to insult (offend)	ahān	أهان
to interest (vt)	hamm	همّ
to intervene (vi)	etdakχal	إتدخّل
to introduce (sb to sb)	ʿarraf	عرّف
to invent (machine, etc.)	eχtaraʿ	إخترع
to invite (vt)	ʿazam	عزم
to iron (clothes)	kawa	كوى
to irritate (annoy)	estafazz	إستفزّ
to isolate (vt)	ʿazal	عزل
to join (political party, etc.)	enḍamm le	إنضمّ لـ
to joke (be kidding)	hazzar	هزّر
to keep (old letters, etc.)	eḥtafaẓ	إحتفظ
to keep silent, to hush	seket	سكت
to kill (vt)	ʾatal	قتل

to knock (on the door)	da''	دقّ
to know (sb)	ʿeref	عرف
to know (sth)	ʿeref	عرف
to laugh (vi)	ḍeḥek	ضحك
to launch (start up)	aṭlaq	أطلق
to leave (~ for Mexico)	sāb	ساب
to leave (forget sth)	sāb	ساب
to leave (spouse)	sāb	ساب
to liberate (city, etc.)	ḥarrar	حرّر
to lie (~ on the floor)	ra'ad	رقد
to lie (tell untruth)	kedeb	كذب
to light (campfire, etc.)	wallaʿ	ولّع
to light up (illuminate)	nawwar	نوّر
to limit (vt)	ḥadded	حدّد
to listen (vi)	semeʿ	سمع
to live (~ in France)	seken	سكن
to live (exist)	ʿāʃ	عاش
to load (gun)	ʿammar	عمّر
to load (vehicle, etc.)	ʃaḥn	شحن
to look (I'm just ~ing)	baṣṣ	بصّ
to look for ... (search)	dawwar ʿala	دوّر على
to look like (resemble)	kān yeʃbeh	كان يشبه
to lose (umbrella, etc.)	ḍayaʿ	ضيّع
to love (e.g. ~ dancing)	ḥabb	حبّ
to love (sb)	ḥabb	حبّ
to lower (blind, head)	nazzel	نزّل
to make (~ dinner)	ḥaḍḍar	حضّر
to make a mistake	ɣeleṭ	غلط
to make angry	narfez	نرفز
to make easier	sahhal	سهّل
to make multiple copies	ṣawwar	صوّر
to make the acquaintance	taʿarraf	تعرّف
to make use (of ...)	estanfaʿ	إستنفع
to manage, to run	adār	أدار
to mark (make a mark)	ʿallem	علّم
to mean (signify)	'aṣad	قصد
to memorize (vt)	ḥafaẓ	حفظ
to mention (talk about)	zakar	ذكر
to miss (school, etc.)	ɣāb	غاب
to mix (combine, blend)	χalaṭ	خلط
to mock (make fun of)	saχar	سخر
to move (to shift)	ḥarrak	حرّك
to multiply (math)	ḍarab	ضرب
must (v aux)	kān lāzem	كان لازم

255. Verbs N-R

to name, to call (vt)	samma	سمّى
to negotiate (vi)	tafāwaḍ	تفاوض
to note (write down)	katab molaḥẓa	كتب ملاحظة
to notice (see)	lāḥaẓ	لاحظ
to obey (vi, vt)	ṭāʿ	طاع
to object (vi, vt)	eʿtaraḍ	إعترض
to observe (see)	rāqab	راقب
to offend (vt)	ahān	أهان
to omit (word, phrase)	ḥazaf	حذف
to open (vt)	fataḥ	فتح
to order (in restaurant)	ṭalab	طلب
to order (mil.)	amar	أمر
to organize (concert, party)	nazzam	نظّم
to overestimate (vt)	bāleɣ fel taʾdīr	بالغ في التقدير
to own (possess)	malak	ملك
to participate (vi)	ʃārek	شارك
to pass through (by car, etc.)	marr be	مرّ بـ
to pay (vi, vt)	dafaʿ	دفع
to peep, to spy on	etgasses ʿala	إتجسس على
to penetrate (vt)	dakχal	دخّل
to permit (vt)	samaḥ	سمح
to pick (flowers)	ʾaṭaf	قطف
to place (put, set)	ḥaṭṭ	حطّ
to plan (~ to do sth)	χaṭṭeṭ	خطّط
to play (actor)	massel	مثّل
to play (children)	leʿeb	لعب
to point (~ the way)	ʃāwer	شاور
to pour (liquid)	ṣabb	صبّ
to pray (vi, vt)	ṣalla	صلّى
to prefer (vt)	faḍḍal	فضّل
to prepare (~ a plan)	ḥaḍḍar	حضّر
to present (sb to sb)	ʾaddem	قدّم
to preserve (peace, life)	ḥafaẓ	حفظ
to prevail (vt)	ɣalab	غلب
to progress (move forward)	taʾaddam	تقدّم
to promise (vt)	waʿad	وعد
to pronounce (vt)	naṭaʾ	نطق
to propose (vt)	ʿaraḍ	عرض
to protect (e.g. ~ nature)	ḥama	حمى
to protest (vi)	eḥtagg	إحتجّ
to prove (vt)	asbat	أثبت
to provoke (vt)	estafazz	إستفزّ
to pull (~ the rope)	ʃadd	شدّ
to punish (vt)	ʿāqab	عاقب

to push (~ the door)	za''	زقّ
to put away (vt)	ʃāl	شال
to put in order	nazzam	نظّم
to put, to place	ḥaṭṭ	حطّ
to quote (cite)	estaʃ-hed	إستشهد
to reach (arrive at)	weṣel	وصل
to read (vi, vt)	'ara	قرأ
to realize (a dream)	ḥa''a'	حقّق
to recognize (identify sb)	mayez	ميّز
to recommend (vt)	naṣaḥ	نصح
to recover (~ from flu)	ʃefy	شفي
to redo (do again)	ʿād	عاد
to reduce (speed, etc.)	'allel	قلّل
to refuse (~ sb)	rafaḍ	رفض
to regret (be sorry)	nedem	ندم
to reinforce (vt)	ʿazzez	عزّز
to remember (Do you ~ me?)	eftakar	إفتكر
to remember (I can't ~ her name)	eftakar	إفتكر
to remind of ...	fakkar be ...	فكّر بـ....
to remove (~ a stain)	ʃāl	شال
to remove (~ an obstacle)	ʃāl, azāl	شال, أزال
to rent (sth from sb)	est'gar	إستأجر
to repair (mend)	ṣallaḥ	صلّح
to repeat (say again)	karrar	كرّر
to report (make a report)	'addem taqrīr	قدّم تقرير
to reproach (vt)	lām	لام
to reserve, to book	ḥagaz	حجز
to restrain (hold back)	manaʿ nafso	منع نفسه
to return (come back)	regeʿ	رجع
to risk, to take a risk	χāṭar	خاطر
to rub out (erase)	masaḥ	مسح
to run (move fast)	gery	جري
to rush (hurry sb)	estaʿgel	إستعجل

256. Verbs S-W

to satisfy (please)	rāḍa	راضى
to save (rescue)	anqaz	أنقذ
to say (~ thank you)	'āl	قال
to scold (vt)	wabbeχ	وبّخ
to scratch (with claws)	χarbeʃ	خربش
to select (to pick)	eχtār	إختار
to sell (goods)	bāʿ	باع
to send (a letter)	arsal	أرسل
to send back (vt)	aʿād	أعاد

to sense (~ danger)	ḥass be	حسّ بـ
to sentence (vt)	ḥakam	حكم
to serve (in restaurant)	χaddem	خدّم
to settle (a conflict)	sawwa	سوّى
to shake (vt)	ragg	رجّ
to shave (vi)	ḥala'	حلق
to shine (gleam)	lem'	لمع
to shiver (with cold)	erta'aʃ	إرتعش
to shoot (vi)	ḍarab bel nār	ضرب بالنار
to shout (vi)	ṣarraχ	صرّخ
to show (to display)	'araḍ	عرض
to shudder (vi)	erta'aʃ	ارتعش
to sigh (vi)	tanahhad	تنهّد
to sign (document)	waqqa'	وقّع
to signify (mean)	dallel	دلّل
to simplify (vt)	bassaṭ	بسّط
to sin (vi)	aznab	أذنب
to sit (be sitting)	'a'ad	قعد
to sit down (vi)	'a'ad	قعد
to smell (emit an odor)	fāḥ	فاح
to smell (inhale the odor)	ʃamm	شمّ
to smile (vi)	ebtasam	إبتسم
to snap (vi, ab. rope)	et'aṭa'	إتقطع
to solve (problem)	ḥall	حلّ
to sow (seed, crop)	bezr	بذر
to spill (liquid)	dala'	دلق
to spill out, scatter (flour, etc.)	sa'aṭ	سقط
to spit (vi)	taff	تفّ
to stand (toothache, cold)	etthammel	إتّحمّل
to start (begin)	bada'	بدأ
to steal (money, etc.)	sara'	سرق
to stop (for pause, etc.)	wa''af	وقّف
to stop (please ~ calling me)	baṭṭal	بطّل
to stop talking	seket	سكت
to stroke (caress)	masaḥ 'ala	مسح على
to study (vt)	daras	درس
to suffer (feel pain)	'āna	عانى
to support (cause, idea)	ayed	أيّد
to suppose (assume)	eftaraḍ	إفترض
to surface (ab. submarine)	ertafa' le saṭ-ḥ el maya	إرتفع لسطح الميّة
to surprise (amaze)	fāga'	فاجئ
to suspect (vt)	eʃtabah fi	إشتبه في
to swim (vi)	'ām, sabaḥ	عام، سبح
to take (get hold of)	aχad	أخذ
to take a rest	ertāḥ	إرتاح

to take away (e.g. about waiter)	rāḥ be	راح بـ
to take off (aeroplane)	aqla'	أقلع
to take off (painting, curtains, etc.)	ʃāl	شال
to take pictures	ṣawwar	صوّر
to talk to …	kallem …	كلّم…
to teach (give lessons)	darres	درّس
to tear off, to rip off (vt)	'aṭa'	قطع
to tell (story, joke)	ḥaka	حكى
to thank (vt)	ʃakar	شكر
to think (believe)	e'taqad	إعتقد
to think (vi, vt)	fakkar	فكّر
to threaten (vt)	hadded	هدّد
to throw (stone, etc.)	rama	رمى
to tie to …	rabaṭ be …	ربط بـ…
to tie up (prisoner)	rabaṭ	ربط
to tire (make tired)	ta'ab	تعّب
to touch (one's arm, etc.)	lamas	لمس
to tower (over …)	ertafa'	إرتفع
to train (animals)	darrab	درّب
to train (sb)	darrab	درّب
to train (vi)	etdarrab	إتدرّب
to transform (vt)	ḥawwel	حوّل
to translate (vt)	targem	ترجم
to treat (illness)	'ālag	عالج
to trust (vt)	wasaq	وثق
to try (attempt)	ḥāwel	حاول
to turn (e.g., ~ left)	ḥād	حاد
to turn away (vi)	a'raḍ 'an	أعرض عن
to turn off (the light)	ṭaffa	طفّى
to turn on (computer, etc.)	fataḥ, ʃagɣal	فتح, شغّل
to turn over (stone, etc.)	'alab	قلب
to underestimate (vt)	estaχaff	إستخفّ
to underline (vt)	ḥaṭṭ χaṭṭ taḥt	حطّ خطّ تحت
to understand (vt)	fehem	فهم
to undertake (vt)	'ām be	قام بـ
to unite (vt)	waḥḥed	وحّد
to untie (vt)	fakk	فكّ
to use (phrase, word)	estaχdam	إستخدم
to vaccinate (vt)	laqqaḥ	لقّح
to vote (vi)	ṣawwat	صوّت
to wait (vt)	estanna	إستنّى
to wake (sb)	ṣaḥḥa	صحّى
to want (wish, desire)	'āyez	عايز
to warn (of a danger)	ḥazzar	حذّر

to wash (clean)	ɣasal	غسل
to water (plants)	sa'a	سقى
to wave (the hand)	ʃāwer	شاور
to weigh (have weight)	wazan	وزن
to work (vi)	eʃtaɣal	إشتغل
to worry (make anxious)	a'la'	أقلق
to worry (vi)	'ala'	قلق
to wrap (parcel, etc.)	laff	لفّ
to wrestle (sport)	ṣāra'	صارع
to write (vt)	katab	كتب
to write down	katab	كتب

www.ingramcontent.com/pod-product-compliance
Lightning Source LLC
Chambersburg PA
CBHW071331090426
42738CB00012B/2850
* 9 7 8 1 7 8 7 1 6 7 0 8 7 *